SEMEIA 36

Early Christian Apocalypticism: Genre and Social Setting

Guest Editor:
Adela Yarbro Collins

Published by
SCHOLARS PRESS
P.O. Box 1608
Decatur, GA 30031–1608

Printed in the United States of America
on acid-free paper

CONTENTS

CONTRIBUTORS TO THIS ISSUE

David E. Aune
St. Xavier College
3700 West 103rd Street
Chicago, IL 60655

Adela Yarbro Collins
Department of Theology
University of Notre Dame
Notre Dame, IN 46556

Elisabeth Schüssler Fiorenza
Episcopal Divinity School
Cambridge, MA 02138

David Hellholm
Department of Religion
University of Bergen
Sydnesplass 9
N-5000 Bergen
Norway

Martha Himmelfarb
Department of Religion
Princeton University
613 Seventy-Nine Hall
Princeton, NJ 08544

Carolyn Osiek
Catholic Theological Union
5401 South Cornell Avenue
Chicago, IL 60637

Leonard Thompson
Department of Religion
Lawrence University
P.O. Box 599
Appleton, WI 54912

INTRODUCTION

Adela Yarbro Collins
University of Notre Dame

This volume of essays is intended to continue the work begun by the Apocalypse Group of the Society of Biblical Literature's Genres Project. That group consisted of Harold W. Attridge, Francis T. Fallon, Anthony J. Saldarini, Adela Yarbro Collins, and John J. Collins (Chair). It was active from about 1975 to 1978. The results of its collaborative work were published in volume 14 of *Semeia* (1979). These results included a definition of the genre "apocalypse," a master paradigm of the significant features of representatives of the genre from the points of view of form and content, and a typology of the genre (delineation of types and subtypes).

Shortly after *Semeia* 14 appeared, an International Colloquium on Apocalypticism was held at Uppsala, sponsored by the Royal Academy of Letters, History and Antiquities and the Faculty of Theology at the University of Uppsala (August, 1979). Professor Geo Widengren chaired the Organizing Committee. Dr. David Hellholm served as Secretary to the Committee and edited the volume in which the papers were later published, *Apocalypticism in the Mediterranean World and the Near East* (1983). The Colloquium provided an opportunity for an initial assessment of the proposals made by the Apocalypse Group.

One strength of the definition proposed in *Semeia* 14 is that it distinguishes the apocalypses from the prophetic texts of the Hebrew Bible on the one hand and from other types of revelatory literature in the Greco-Roman world on the other. At the Colloquium in Uppsala and in various publications from about that time, a number of scholars have proposed alternative definitions. E. P. Sanders has attempted to define the essence of Jewish apocalypses as variations on the themes of revelation and reversal of fortunes. A major problem with this definition is that it does not distinguish the apocalypses in any clear and precise way from the prophetic literature. At the other extreme, J. Carmignac, H. Stegemann, and C. Rowland have proposed definitions in which eschatology is not included as an essential element. The problem here is that the distinctiveness of the apocalypses vis-à-vis other forms of revelatory literature in the Greco-Roman world is not taken into account.

In 1981 a Consultation on Early Christian Apocalypticism was held at the Annual Meeting of the SBL in San Francisco. The Steering Committee for the Consultation consisted of David Aune, Carolyn Osiek, Leonard Thompson, and Adela Yarbro Collins (Chair). David Hellholm has been an active member since the beginning. The purpose of the Consultation was to confer about ways to pursue the study of the genre apocalypse with special reference to early Christianity. After a second session as a Consultation (1982), the program unit was designated a Seminar, with the same Steering Committee, to hold sessions at the Annual Meetings from 1983–87. The major foci of the seminar have been the pursuit of the question of genre and the study of the social settings and functions of particular apocalypses. This volume represents some results of the seminar's work.

The Question of Genre

There has been virtually no criticism of the attempt to define the genre apocalypse as such. Most scholars have recognized the need for greater conceptual clarity in this regard. W. Vorster has argued that the term genre should be reserved for a higher level of abstraction from that proposed in *Semeia* 14. David Hellholm, however, has confirmed the appropriateness of using the concept "genre" for a middle level of abstraction (1982: 169; in this volume: 28–30).

The definition proposed by the Apocalypse Group is the following: *"Apocalypse" is a genre of revelatory literature with a narrative framework, in which a revelation is mediated by an otherworldly being to a human recipient, disclosing a transcendent reality which is both temporal, insofar as it envisages eschatological salvation, and spatial insofar as it involves another, supernatural world* (Collins, 1979: 9). As noted above, this definition deliberately focuses on matters of form and content. Although these aspects are intimately related, they may be distinguished for purposes of discussion.

1. Matters of Form
David Hellholm is willing to accept the definition of an apocalypse quoted above, as far as it goes (1982: 168; in this volume: 27). David Aune, in his reformulation of the definition (below: 86–87), omits one formal element and adds two. He omits the mediation of the revelation by an otherworldly, usually heavenly, being. The omission of this element would broaden the range of texts which could be considered apocalypses. For example, accounts of the consultation of a human representative of a

.ine being at an oracle could qualify as apocalypses; similarly, almost
٬ vision account could also be so defined, especially if eschatology is
،ken to be a frequent, but not essential characteristic, as Aune suggests
٬7). It would seem that the mediated quality of the revelation in
apocalypses is one of the essential characteristics which distinguishes
them as a group from other genres of revelatory literature.

Aune's positive proposals with regard to form are worthy of serious
consideration. He adds the characteristic "in autobiographical form" (86);
in other words, the report of the revelatory experience is in the first
person. Among the Jewish works classified as apocalypses in *Semeia* 14,
most are largely first person accounts. Two early Jewish apocalypses,
however, are associated with narratives of considerable length in the third
person. The apocalypse proper of the book of Daniel (chaps. 7–12) is
prefaced by tales about Daniel (chaps. 1–6). A prose narrative in the third
person based on Gen 6:1–4 has been incorporated into the Book of the
Watchers (*1 Enoch* 6–11). *Jubilees* 23 and *Test. Abraham* 10–15 are entirely
in the third person. Among the Christian works classified as apocalypses
in *Semeia* 14, the apocalyptic portions in the *Test. Isaac* and *Test. Jacob*
(except for a small portion in the Bohairic version) are in the third
person. The narrative frameworks of the *Questions of Bartholomew* and
of the *Book of the Resurrection of Jesus Christ by Bartholomew the
Apostle* are also in the third person. The *Apocalypse of Esdras* (= Greek
Apocalypse of Ezra) begins in the first but shifts to the third person.
Most strikingly, the *Apocalypse of Sedrach*, a heavenly journey, is entirely in the third person. Some Gnostic works classified as apocalypses
in *Semeia* 14 are in the third person: *Sophia of Jesus Christ*, the first
Apocalypse of James, and the *Letter of Peter to Philip*. Among the Greco-
Roman examples, the account of Er's heavenly journey is related in the
third person by Socrates (Plato, *Republic* 614B–621B). A Persian apocalypse, the *Zand-i Vohuman Yasn*, is also in the third person. Since these
works are so similar in other formal aspects and in content to the first
person accounts, it seems that the characteristic "in autobiographical
form" should be regarded as a frequent, but not essential characteristic.
It is thus analogous to the formal characteristic of pseudonymity.

Aune's inclusion of the characteristic "in autobiographical form" in
the definition seems to be related to his emphasis on the authorization of
the message as an aspect of the function of apocalypses (87). This point
will be taken up below.

The other proposed addition to the definition with regard to form is
"revelatory visions . . . so structured that the central revelatory message
constitutes a literary climax . . ." (86–87). The inclusion of this element
reflects Aune's positive assessment of Hellholm's text-linguistic analysis of
The Shepherd of Hermas and the book of Revelation (Aune: 70–74). He is
impressed by Hellholm's argument that the most profoundly embedded

texts in these two apocalypses (i.e., the texts on the highest communication level) coincide with the texts which are at the highest grade of the textsequential structure (71). There are several reasons for concluding that the inclusion of this element in the definition is premature. First of all, Hellholm's text-linguistic analyses of *Hermas* and Revelation have not yet received the close scrutiny which they deserve. His analysis of the book of Revelation especially is abbreviated and preliminary. Before it can be taken as definitive, he must show that it is actually based on scientific linguistic criteria and not, at crucial points, on intuitive criteria similar to those used in previous analyses of the composition and structure of Revelation. A number of questions must be answered in the process; for example, are there text-linguistic grounds for including Rev 12:1–22:5 as part of the revelation of the "Heavenly Scroll" of chap. 5? Or is the judgment that it is based on the more traditional (and questionable) literary arguments of G. Bornkamm whom he cites on this point (1982: 189, n. 154; in this volume: 53)? If these chapters are *not* part of the revelation of the "Heavenly Scroll," then the speech of God in Rev 21:5–8 may not be both on the highest communication level and on the highest text-sequential grade. Similar questions can be raised about the conclusion that Rev 12:1–14:20 constitutes an intercalation (1982: 186; in this volume: 50). It seems prudent to wait for detailed assessment of Hellholm's work before incorporating the results in a definition of "apocalypse."

Another reason for caution in this regard is the pitfalls involved in isolating "the central revelatory message" of an apocalypse. Such language calls to mind A. Juelicher's procedure in interpreting the parables. He argued that each parable has a single point which can be expressed as a general moral principle (Perrin: 93–97). Similarly, J. Jeremias contended that each parable can be fitted under one of nine rubrics which together make up "the message of the parables" (Perrin: 105). C. H. Dodd before Jeremias and the most influential interpreters of the parables after him have argued persuasively that the parables, individually or as a group, cannot be reduced to a principle or a message. As metaphorical narrative, they make their impact on the audience through the concreteness of the story itself and by evoking participation (Perrin: 98–100, 106). In his discussion of the function of apocalypses, Aune makes the helpful suggestion that they have a literary function similar to that of parables. Like parables, apocalypses both reveal and conceal divine truth. Like parables, apocalypses maximize participation of the audience in the revelatory experience (84–86). If this insight is valid, it is hard to understand how the speech of God in Rev 21:5–8 or the quotations from the little book and the Book of Eldad and Modat in *Herm. Vis.* 2.2.5 and 2.3.4 can be said to express the central revelatory messages of these two apocalypses. The quotation from the little book in *Herm. Vis.* 2.2.5

concerns a second repentance. That this text expresses the central message of the book is called into question also by Carolyn Osiek's contention that the promulgation of a second repentance is not the comprehensive or even primary function of *Hermas* as a whole (117).

2. *Matters of Content*

As indicated above, David Hellholm does not propose any modifications of the definition of the genre apocalypse proposed in *Semeia* 14 with regard to content. David Aune agrees with the emphasis in that definition on transcendence. He demotes, however, the characteristic "eschatological" from an essential to a frequent element (87). This modification seems to be due to an appreciation of the arguments of those who have faulted much scholarship on apocalypticism for its overemphasis on history, politics and cosmic eschatology. Similarly, Martha Himmelfarb claims that *Semeia* 14 reacts against such an overemphasis, but is not entirely free of its influence (106).

As implied near the beginning of this introduction, one of the challenges in defining the genre apocalypses is to recognize the continuity of these texts with prophetic literature in the Hebrew Bible, while showing how they are distinguished from it. Likewise, the phenomenological similarities between apocalypses and other genres of revelatory literature must be taken into account, but the distinctive characteristics of each revelatory genre should also be delineated. It seems that eschatological content is the primary distinguishing mark of apocalypses over against other revelatory texts which are very similar in form, such as ritual prescriptions for creating revelatory experience and texts dealing with revelatory magic. Such texts are important for the study of apocalypses, but should probably be distinguished from them generically.

As Aune notes, eschatology was defined broadly in *Semeia* 14, to include personal afterlife. A significant number of the texts designated apocalypses have no cosmic eschatology, but look only to individual rewards and punishments after death. The major typological distinction among the apocalypses is formal: those in which otherworldly revelation is received in a thisworldly context, and those in which it is received through an otherworldly journey. These two main types were then divided into subtypes on the basis of content: (a) those with a review of history, an eschatological crisis, and cosmic or political eschatology; (b) those with public (cosmic or political) eschatology; and (c) those with only personal eschatology (types a and b have personal eschatology as well of course). It is difficult to see how "the centrality of cosmic and/or political eschatology for the *Semeia* volume shows the continued influence of the traditional scholarly view of such eschatology as the most important aspect of apocalyptic literature" (Himmelfarb, 97). Such eschatology is certainly a major element in some apocalypses. Perhaps the problem lies

with those works in which such eschatology is present, but not emphasized, such as the Apocalypse of Paul. The question arises whether they
should be classified under subtype (b) or (c), but it is not clear how such
works show the weakness of the typology itself. The reasons for choosing
eschatology as a significant criterion of content are both its prominence in
apocalypses and its absence in other genres. Himmelfarb is correct that
relatively little attention was paid to "otherworldly elements" (109). Her
book *Tours of Hell* and her essay in this volume contribute to the
supplying of that lack.

3. *Matters of Function*

David Hellholm has proposed that the definition in *Semeia* 14 be
expanded to include function: *"intended for a group in crisis with the
purpose of exhortation and/or consolation by means of divine authority"*
(1982: 168; in this volume: 27). His intention is to provide a definition of
function which is on the same level of abstraction as the definition of form
and content. He is quite right that the definition of genre should include
the aspect of function. This generalized function need not be based on a
study of the actual functions of all apocalypses in their original and
subsequent social settings, but may be based on the implied function (in
the text itself), i.e., on the illocutionary/perlocutionary aspect of the text
(1982: 160; in this volume: 18).

Some questions arise, however, about Hellholm's proposed addition.
First of all, his language seems to take the perspective of the implied
author as an accurate representation of reality. What is a crisis from the
perspective of the implied author may not be a crisis from the perspective
of every hearer or reader of the text. In other words, the proposed
definition does not take seriously enough the degree to which an apocalypse may interpret reality, even to the point of creating a "world" or
symbolic system. The terms "console" and "exhort" fit some apocalypses,
but they are perhaps too strong for the indirect way in which most
apocalypses work. The use of the word "group" seems rooted in the older
scholarly notion that apocalypses were produced by and for conventicles,
small sect-like groups. It is now recognized that such a notion needs to be
tested rather than assumed.

David Aune agrees that matters of function ought to be included in
the definition and offers an alternative formulation: "(a) to legitimate the
transcendent authorization of the message, (b) by mediating a new actualization of the original revelatory experience through literary devices,
structures and imagery, which function to 'conceal' the message which
the text 'reveals,' so that (c) the recipients of the message will be
encouraged to modify their cognitive and behavioral stance in conformity
with transcendent perspectives" (87). Important strengths of Aune's
proposal are its appropriate level of abstraction and its attempt to infer

function from the text rather than from hypothetical notions about the setting. Weaknesses include its wordiness, its implication that authorization is an end in itself, and the wide scope of "transcendent perspectives."

Aune's emphasis on authorization of "the message" (the question of reduction arises again) seems to be related to his emphasis on the autobiographical form of (some) apocalypses. It would seem that the supernatural origin of the revelation communicated authorizes it whether the account is in the first or the third person. The first person is crucial only when the implied author and the actual author are the same and when the authorization of the actual author's person is an important factor (such is probably the case with the book of Revelation; see also Alexander: 239).

In light of the suggestions made by Hellholm and Aune, the following addition to the definition of "apocalypse" in *Semeia* 14 may be made: *intended to interpret present, earthly circumstances in light of the supernatural world and of the future, and to influence both the understanding and the behavior of the audience by means of divine authority.*

4. The Extension of the Genre

In his article in this volume, David Aune raises the question whether the *Martyrdom of Perpetua and Felicitas* is an apocalypse (74 and n. 4). This question is related to his discussion of the whole and the part in ancient Mediterranean literature, in which he speaks of host genres which can include a variety of literary forms. He concludes that apocalypses can exist as independent texts or as a constituent part of a host genre (80). This conclusion is compatible with the results of the work of the Apocalypse Group which classified some independent texts and some texts within larger units as apocalypses.

In the case of the *Martyrdom of Perpetua and Felicitas*, it would seem that the work as a whole is a martyrdom, since in its present form it is primarily an account of the behavior of a group of martyrs during their imprisonment, interrogation and execution. This martyrdom, however, functions as a host genre for five vision accounts. These visions are emphasized in the introduction to the work (chap. 1) as signs of the activity of the Spirit in the last days. One of these visions (11:1–13:8) can be classified as an apocalypse and should be added to the list of early Christian apocalypses. It is a vision which Saturus experienced in prison in the form of a heavenly journey. Four angels conducted Saturus and Perpetua to paradise and to the heavenly throne room. In Paradise they saw four who had been martyred before them. If only this portion of the *Martyrdom* is an apocalypse, the question of communication levels (embedment) and textual grades needs to be reexamined.

The essays in Part One of this volume make important contributions

to the discussion about the genre apocalypse. A major contribution of
David Hellholm's essay is its demonstration of the validity and usefulness
of both paradigmatic and syntagmatic studies of the genre and its initial
attempt to relate the two. David Aune offers thoughtful observations on a
number of points, perhaps most helpfully on the literary function of
apocalypses and its hermeneutical implications. He rightly calls attention
to an important essay by H. D. Betz (1983), who has been a consistent
participant in the seminar. Betz argued that certain apocalyptic texts in
Greco-Roman literature, such as the *Myth of Er,* generated an experience of fear by depicting the punishment of the wicked and motivated
the readers to live good lives. This function is surely implicitly present
also in the early Christian apocalypses which contain visions or tours of
places of punishment.

Martha Himmelfarb's essay is a study of the experience of the visionary with reference to two early Christian apocalypses, the Ascension of
Isaiah and the Apocalypse of Paul. She is interested in the nature of such
experience, e.g., whether the visionary is transformed or not, and what
implications such factors may have for creating a typology of early Christian apocalypses. Carolyn Osiek's essay has been included in Part Two,
because it treats the social setting of the *Shepherd of Hermas.* She also
discusses the question of its genre and concludes that it is an apocalypse.

Social Settings and Function

The question of social function was deliberately left aside in the
survey of apocalypses in *Semeia* 14. At the Colloquium in Uppsala, a
segment of the program was devoted to "The Sociology of Apocalypticism
and the 'Sitz-im-Leben' of Apocalypses." Papers in this section were
given by George Nickelsburg on Palestinian Jewish Apocalypticism,
Martin Hengel on the Jewish revolt in the Diaspora under Trajan, Wayne
Meeks on Pauline Christianity, Luise Schottroff on the "Synoptic Apocalypse," Adela Yarbro Collins on the book of Revelation, and Hans
Kippenberg on a comparison of Jewish, Christian and Gnostic Apocalypticism.

In this volume Carolyn Osiek analyzes the paraenesis in *Hermas* and
draws inferences from it about the author's perception of a crisis within
the Christian congregations of Rome (and perhaps Campania) with regard
to the disposition of individual Christians and the quality of their relationships with one another. Elisabeth Schüssler Fiorenza argues that
Revelation must be understood as a poetic-rhetorical construction of an
alternative symbolic universe that "fits" its historical rhetorical situation.
She illustrates this understanding by means of an exegesis of Rev 14:1–5,
the vision of the Lamb and the 144,000 on Mount Zion, which she
understands as an "anti-image" to the vision of the beast and its followers

(chap. 13) as well as to the glory of Babylon (chap. 17). The juxtaposition of image and anti-image underlines the fundamental decision that the audience faces: to worship the anti-divine powers embodied by Rome or to worship God.

Fiorenza then raises the question whether the rhetorical response of Revelation to the social-political and religious situation of the congregations in western Asia Minor was a "fitting" response. She replies in the affirmative, since she assumes that Pliny's letter to Trajan about the Christians of Bithynia (X.96) written in the early second century represents the same circumstances as those to which Revelation is responding (135). The delineation of the social setting of Revelation which follows her quotation of Pliny seems to exaggerate the hardships faced by the audience (see Yarbro Collins, 1984 and L. Thompson in this volume). In any case, Fiorenza has illustrated a useful theoretical framework for the analysis of an apocalyptic text in terms of its social setting.

In his article Leonard Thompson articulates an interpretation of Revelation which seeks to relate text and social setting in a more complex and adequate way than has been done heretofore. In the process he offers critical assessments of theories of crisis, deprivation and compensation. He criticizes them for granting a higher degree of reality to social, institutional entities than to literary symbolic ones and for seeing the flow of causality primarily from institution to symbol. As alternatives, he points to theories of replication or reiteration, of homologues and proportions. Such theories seem very promising for the task of articulating the meaning of Revelation in its present form as text and inferring the social function of its symbolic universe. It is not clear, however, that they have much potential for explaining the genesis of Revelation and its symbolic universe. The crucial question is whether the apparent explanatory power of crisis and related theories is illusory and therefore to be abandoned, or whether such theories need to be reformulated in order to meet the criticisms which have been made.

This volume is being published in the hope that it will stimulate further discussion and research on early Christian apocalypticism and related matters.

WORKS CONSULTED

Alexander, P.
    1983   "3 (Hebrew Apocalypse of) Enoch. Pp. 223–315 in *The Old Testament Pseudepigrapha*, vol. 1. Ed. James H. Charlesworth. Garden City: Doubleday.

Betz, H. D.
    1983   "The Problem of Apocalyptic Genre in Greek and Hellenistic

Literature: The Case of the Oracle of Trophonius." Pp. 577–97 in
Hellholm (ed.), 1983.

Carmignac, J.
1979   "Qu'est-ce que l'Apocalyptique? Son emploi à Qumran," *RQ* 10:
3–33.

Collins, A. Y.
1979   "The Early Christian Apocalypses." *Semeia* 14: 61–121.
1983   "Persecution and Vengeance in the Book of Revelation." Pp.
729–49 in Hellholm, ed.
1984   *Crisis and Catharsis: The Power of the Apocalypse.* Philadelphia: Westminster.

Collins, J. J.
1979   "Introduction: Towards the Morphology of a Genre." *Semeia* 14:
1–20.

de Villiers, P. G. R.
1983   "Solving the Riddle? Recent Trends in Apocalyptic Research."
Pp. 39–58 in *Die Ou-testamentiese Werkgemeenskap in Suid-
Afrika* 25 and 26. Ed. W. C. van Wyk. Pretoria, 1982–83.

Hellholm, D.
1982   "The Problem of Apocalyptic Genre and the Apocalypse of John"
in *Society of Biblical Literature Seminar Papers*. Ed. Kent H.
Richards. Chico, CA: Scholars Press.

Hellholm, D., ed.
1983   *Apocalypticism in the Mediterranean World and the Near East.*
Proceedings of the International Colloquium on Apocalypticism.
Uppsala, August 12–17, 1979. Tuebingen: J. C. B. Mohr (Paul
Siebeck).

Hengel, M.
1983   "Messianische Hoffnung und politischen 'Radikalismus' in der
'juedish-hellenistischen Diaspora.'" Pp. 655–86 in Hellholm,
ed.

Himmelfarb, M.
1983   *Tours of Hell: An Apocalyptic Form in Jewish and Christian
Literature.* Philadelphia: University of Pennsylvania Press.

Kippenberg, H. G.
1983   "Ein Vergleich juedischer, christlicher und gnostiker Apokalyptik." Pp. 751–68 in Hellholm, ed.

Meeks, W. A.
1983   "Social Functions of Apocalyptic Language in Pauline Christianity." Pp. 687–705 in Hellholm, ed.

Musurillo, H.
1972   *The Acts of the Christian Martyrs.* Oxford Early Christian Texts.
Oxford: Clarendon Press.

Nickelsburg, G. W. E.
  1983   "Social Aspects of Palestinian Jewish Apocalypticism." Pp. 641–54 in Hellholm, ed.

Perrin, N.
  1976   *Jesus and the Language of the Kingdom: Symbol and Metaphor in New Testament Interpretation*. Philadelphia: Fortress Press.

Rowland, C.
  1982   *The Open Heaven: A Study of Apocalyptic in Judaism and Early Christianity*. New York: Crossroad.

Sanders, E. P.
  1983   "The Genre of Palestinian Jewish Apocalypses." Pp. 447–59 in Hellholm, ed.

Schottroff, L.
  1983   "Die Gegenwart in der Apokalyptik der synoptischen Evangelien." Pp. 707–728 in Hellholm, ed.

Stegemann, H.
  1983   "Die Bedeutung der Qumranfunde für die Erforschung der Apokalyptik." Pp. 495–530 in Hellholm, ed.

Vorster, W. S.
  1983   "1 Enoch and the Jewish Literary Setting of the New Testament: A Study in Text Types." *Neotestamentica* 17: 1–14.

THE PROBLEM OF APOCALYPTIC GENRE AND THE APOCALYPSE OF JOHN*

David Hellholm
University of Bergen, Norway

ABSTRACT

In analyzing generic concepts from a paradigmatic point of view, Hellholm notes that genres participate in three separate, though related, aspects: form, content, and function. This is true for all levels of abstraction, called (in linguistic analysis) *sub-sememe, sememe, archisememe, superarchisememe*, etc. Applying this to apocalypses, the author suggests 31 *semes-noemes;* no apocalypse has all characteristics but all have some from each aspect. In spite of the necessary hierarchization of these characteristics, Hellholm maintains that even this is unsatisfactory. We need to complement it with text-linguistic analysis. This approach can take into account not only content, form, and function, but also the syntagmatic aspects (micro- as well as macro-syntagmatic structures). This latter analysis requires hierarchically-arranged communication levels of different ranks. The final result is a three-dimensional analysis of texts. Using a previous text analysis he did with *The Shepherd of Hermas* as a model, the author concludes by performing this procedure on the Apocalypse of John, noting both significant similarities and differences.

For Geo Widengren
on his 75th birthday

1. Models and Reality[1]

1.1 "Texts are abbreviations; they abridge, they simplify what is to be designated—and they do so by omitting" (Raible, 1979a: 2; Husserl: 354–

---

*Public lecture delivered on February 18, 1982, at the Divinity School, The University of Chicago.

[1]Regarding concepts defined by extension I am—as far as textlinguistic analyses are concerned—in total agreement with Kurt Baldinger (269), when he writes that these "have no ontological implications concerning, for instance, the distinction between 'real' and 'fictitious'

55; Gulich/Raible, 1977: 14ff). This statement by Wolfgang Raible with reference to Edmund Husserl regarding such complex signs as texts can be illustrated by using a simple sign like "chair." The word or to be more exact: the concept "chair" contains only a small number of semantically distinctive characteristics (linguistically stated: *semes*) in comparison to what is common for existing chairs. Thus the concept "chair" is more abstract than the original! This is true as can be seen when we with Kurt Baldinger list the characteristics of the concept (linguistically speaking: *sememe*) "chair": 1) with solid material; 2) raised above the ground; 3) with a back; 4) for one person; 5) to sit on (62ff, esp. 67 with table 4). This is to say that we usually work with models and not with reality. A number of characteristics of an original chair are left out when in language we use the concept "chair": whether it is small or large, blue or red, of metal or wood is of no concern to the concept "chair." If specified, we, in fact, introduce a concept on a lower level of abstraction. This becomes immediately evident, if we add two further characteristics of "chair" to those pointed out earlier: 6) with arms and 7) with upholstery, thus producing the concept of "armchair." This is of great importance for the problem of genres, not least that of genres and subgenres, as I will try to show later (see 2.2.3.2., 2.2.3.3., and 3.3.4.). The use of concepts is the very reason why language can function at all, that is, why we can communicate with one another and with generations past.

1.2   As I just tried to show, models or signs can be more or less abstract and consequently we erect a hierarchy of models. If the concept "chair" is constituted of the five mentioned characteristics, we find that by selecting three of these—let us say #1 (with solid material)[2], #2 (raised above the ground), and #5 (to sit on)—we arrive at the even more

---

referents" (cf. 25–61; also Hellholm, 1980: 34, 88; Heger, 1976: 35). This statement is correct, but none the less somewhat too rigid and has to be qualified by means of differentiations: a) the statement is true insofar as it is not the linguist's or the exegete's primary task to ask ontological questions *per se;* b) however, in cases of specifications *in the texts themselves* pertaining to "possible worlds" (cf. 4.2.1.3.2. and Kubczak, 1978:47, 79), the question of function of this specification has to be taken into consideration. This is of great importance in connection with the role of "Substitution on the meta-level" and its function discussed in sec. 4.2.1.3.1. (esp. #[2] b] and note 46).

Concerning the differences between *logical semantics and linguistic semantics*, see Hellholm, 1980: 37, fig. 7, and Kamlah/Lorenzen, 91–92. Heger's suggestion to translate the truth-values in logical semantics into positive and negative notations in linguistic semantics is a good example of the affinity of the two types of semantics and yet their differences (1976: 192–94; Kubczak, 1975: 124).

[2] Baldinger (62ff) includes only *semes* #2 and #5 in the *archisememe* "seat" (see note 3) which thus are said to be the intersection of the *sememes* "armchair," "chair," "stool," and "sofa." This is a fallacy in Baldinger's theory, since it is hardly conceivable to have a *seme* of function without a *seme* of content. The reasons for this fallacy are, first, Baldinger's neglect of grouping the *semes*, and second, his neglect of a hierarchical ranking of the *semes* themselves, in spite of his statement that "a *seme* can be very specific or very general" (81). *Seme* #1 (with solid material)

abstract concept "seat." In linguistic terminology the concept at this abstraction level would be called *"archisememe."* We could easily generalize even further and say that "seats" themselves can be classified under still more comprehensive *archisememes* such as "furniture," thus constituting a *"superarchisememe"* and so on.[3]

Thus with regard to single signs it is possible to establish a hierarchy: "armchair," "chair," "seat," "furniture"; a hierarchy which is characterized by the rules: the larger the *intension*, the smaller the *extension* and vice versa (Menne: 23, 75; Allwood et al.: 125ff; Wunderlich: 205ff; Heger, 1979a: 59; Raible, 1979a: 22; esp. Kubczak, 1975). In the words of Wolfgang Raible: "Signs with few characteristics have the character of 'supreme-concepts,' they can designate a number of things in an unspecified manner, while signs with many characteristics are typical subconcepts, i.e., specified designations" (1979a: 23; cf. Baldinger: 72; Coseriu, 1964: 139–86).

1.3 If, instead of subordinating the *subsememe* "armchair" under the *sememe* "chair" and thus erecting a hierarchy of concepts, we take these two concepts as a true *"sememe*-opposition," we encounter another problem, viz. that of mixed concepts, which is also highly significant for genre analysis. Klaus Heger has pointed to this problem in connection with the above mentioned *sememe* #6 (with arms) and #7 (with upholstery). He writes:

> As long as the person using the two *signemes*,[4] "chair" and "armchair," from among the seating furniture for the use of one person, encounters only furniture without upholstery and without arms or only furniture with upholstery and with arms, the multifarious definition in these two alternatives makes no difference to him. However, as soon as there appears in his perspective corresponding seating furniture without upholstery but with arms and/or with upholstery and without arms, he is no better off than the analytical linguist and he finds himself encountering an insoluble task, that of having to decide in favor of one or other of the alternative *seme*-pairs (1979a: 34).[5]

---

can mean different things, depending on the abstraction level; it can mean "solid" in opposition to "liquid" or "gas," but it can also mean "solid" in opposition to the less abstract concept "soft"; this is in fact the meaning presupposed by Baldinger, since he excludes the *sememe* "pouffe" when establishing the *semes* of the intersection. See note 7 and 3.3.4.

[3] Baldinger distinguishes between *sememe* and *archisememe* and still further concepts of abstraction without, however, introducing proper terminology, thus either using an "empty position" (104ff) or using the same lexeme on different conceptual levels. In order to avoid confusion, I introduce the term *"superarchisememe"* for the next higher rank of conceptual abstraction.

[4] Italics mine. See note 9. The term *sign* in this paper is used for the most part in the sense *signeme*.

[5] Italics mine. See also Baldinger's reference to a "border zone or zone of transition" (27).

Heger continues by giving two possible solutions: a) by postulating a double polysemy or b) by stressing a primary conceptual point *(begriffliche Schwerpunktsetzung)* (34–35). Another possibility, which in my opinion is preferable, is the above suggested conceptual hierarchization, in which an "armchair" is reckoned as a *subsememe* of the *sememe* "chair," and the acknowledgement of "empty positions," i.e., concepts without lexicalization, for the two "mixed *sememes.*" This solution is of theoretical significance for the question of mixed literary genres in two ways: a) with regard to conceptual hierarchization and b) with regard to historical development of genres and subgenres, both of these having to do with the relationship between synchrony and diachrony in genre analysis (see 3.3.4.).

1.4   Before turning to the next section, I need to make two more—as I see it—important observations with regard to the distinctive characteristics of a concept.

1.4.1.   First, then, it is easy to see that the five characteristics constituting the concept "chair" are to be found in other concepts as well, e.g., #1 (with solid material) is also a constitutive element of, e.g., a "car" and a "house"; #2 (raised above the ground) is also characteristic of a "table" or a "desk"; #3 (with a back) is characteristic of a "sofa" and a "book" as well; #4 (for one person): taken in itself this characteristic is also a constitutive element of a "watch," a "ring," "glasses," etc.; #5 (to sit on) is certainly characteristic also of a "sofa," a "seat," a "bench," a "pew," and so forth. This observation makes it clear that it is by no means enough just to list a *number of characteristics* in order to arrive at a concept, but that we rather have to ask for the type, the sequence, and above all the interdependence and relationship of these *semes* to each other in constituting a *sememe* or on one abstraction level higher the grouping of the intersection of several *sememes* in constituting an *archisememe* and so on (see notes 2 and 7). The concept then can be defined as an "abstraction from many realities which are related to each other" (Baldinger: 62; see also 3.3.2 [b]).

1.4.2   The second observation is perhaps not so evident but none the less of equal importance. When making use of Baldinger's characteristics of the concept "chair," I rearranged the sequential order of them to arrive at a grouping to which he has paid no attention.[6] By so doing, I am able to show that these characteristics can be divided into three groups:
    a)   the first group is constituted by *seme* #1 (with solid material) and refers to *content;*

---

[6] Raible is the only one to my knowledge who, in structural semantics, has paid special attention to at least the third group (function) (1981: 33–34).

b) the second group is made of *semes* #2 (raised above the ground) and #3 (with a back) and refers to *form;*

c) the third group is made up by *semes* #4 (for one person) and #5 (to sit on) and refers to *function* in a twofold way: aa) for whom it functions and bb) in what way or how it functions.

The importance of this threefold grouping becomes apparent, when we consider the *archisememe* "seat": Also on this level of abstraction we find the same grouping as on the lower abstraction level, viz., content, form, and function. This means that the grouping itself is not accidental or variable but rather constitutive and invariable: a) the first group: *content* is constituted by *seme* #1 (with solid material); b) the second group: *form* is in this case made up by only one *seme* on this level, viz., #2 (raised above the ground); here *seme* #3 is left out; c) the third group: *function* is made up partly by a more general *seme* #4 (for persons) and *seme* #5 (to sit on).[7]

That the *grouping of the semes,* not the *semes* themselves, is indeed invariable becomes evident when we move to yet a higher level of abstraction, the *superarchisememe* as I called it:

a) the first group is also here made up of the same *seme* #1 (with solid material) (see notes 2 and 7);

b) the second is also made up of the same *seme* on the previous level, viz., #2 (raised above the ground);

c) the third group, however, is in this case constituted by a seemingly[8] new and more general *seme,* viz, to furnish. Here we also observe how on this abstraction level the concept has obtained its lexeme from its function.

This observation points to the obvious fact that the constituents of a *sememe* (i.e., concept), and *archisememe* or even a *superarchisememe* are made up of *semes* belonging to the three groups: content, form and function, and that none of these groups is variable but indeed constitutive and will all have to be taken into account when establishing or analyzing concepts. This circumstance is of far-reaching consequences, in particular, when we leave the single concept and move up to more complex signs or models such as texts and even genres.

2. Genres and Reality

2.1   As the initial quotation from Raible/Husserl indicated, the simplification of reality is not restricted to simple signs but applies also to more complex signs as sentences and texts. This has been elaborated in

---

[7] This is precisely the intersection of the *sememes* "chair," "armchair," "stool," "sofa," and "pouffe." The last can be included or excluded, depending upon the abstraction level of *seme* #1 (with solid material; see note 2 and 3.3.4.). Unfortunately, Baldinger has paid no attention to the necessity of abstract ranking of the *semes* as can be seen on p. 62 and in table 4 of p. 67.

[8] Here the need for a ranking of *semes* in abstraction levels becomes particularly apparent; see notes 2, 7 and 3.3.4.

great detail by Klaus Heger in his work *Monem, Wort, Satz und Text,*
published in the 2nd edition in 1976. Time and space does not permit a
development from the single sign *"monem"* all the way up to the complex
sign *"text"* (= *signeme*[9]) on this occasion. Let me only briefly indicate
how I see the relationship between the groupings established earlier with
regard to the single concept "chair" and the more complex sign of a
"sentence" (Hellholm, 1980:52ff, esp. 56 with fig. 8; also Beck and
Sökeland):

  a) the *propositional* aspect corresponds to content;
  b) the *utterance* aspect—oral or written—corresponds to form;
  c) the *illocutionary/perlocutionary* aspect corresponds to the func-
      tion aspect as I have called it.

Thus, even with regard to *"sentences"* the grouping remains intact and
enables communication and understanding, since also here all three
groups function in an interrelationship with one another (Hellholm, 1980:
57–58).

2.2   The even more complex sign *"text"* can have three different meanings that, from a methodological point of view, have to be kept apart
(Heger, 1976: 26–28; Raible, 1979b: 63; Bach/Harnisch).

2.2.1.   First, in ordinary language "text" usually refers to the realization
of a certain entity *hic et nunc* or with regard to ancient texts *illic et tunc*.
Used in this way text is understood as an individual work by itself, e.g.,
The Red Room by August Strindberg or *Anna Karenina* by Leo Tolstoy
or, linguistically stated, as a manifestation on the level of *parole;* and yet
we must not forget that such texts in comparison with reality itself are
abbreviated models, since, as has been pointed out so neatly by Prof.

---

[9]In his system Heger has replaced *"moneme"* with *"signeme,"* since "it is obvious that the
model should be usable not only for the analysis of minimal meaningful units *(monemes)* but also
for the analysis of meaningful units of higher hierarchical ranks" (1976: 40, with note 47; cf.
Baldinger: 262). This fact means, as Heger states, that the extended trapezium model referring
to the level of *langue* "allows for being used there for *paradigmatic* as well as for *syntagmatic*
analyses of *signemes*" (1976: 59; Baldinger: 271; italics mine). For the sake of clarification, I give
the present form of the trapezium as found in Heger: 58 and Baldinger: 260:

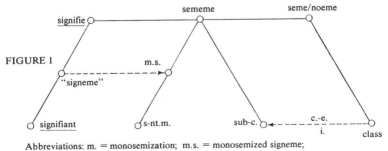

Abbreviations: m. = monosemization; m.s. = monosemized signeme;
  s-nt.m = signifiant of the monosemized signeme;
  c.-e. = relation of class to elements; i. = inclusion;
  sub.-c. = subclass.

Raible, "total information is almost equivalent to no information at all; only by means of reduction of the complexity, only by erecting simplified models will sense and coherence along with structure be recognizable" (Raible, 1979a: 4).

2.2.2.   Second, in ordinary language text can be used as referring to a *group* or *class* of texts being held together by *one* specific invariant (Hempfer, 1973: 27–28; 106–7, 224; Raible, 1979a: 20; Heger, 1976: 24–30, 60).[10] This is the case when we, e.g., ask the question in which way a certain text is similar to other texts. The possibility of grouping is abundant: we can talk about biblical texts or on a lower level of abstraction about New Testament texts or on a still lower level of abstraction about Pauline or Johannine texts. In doing so, however, we do not really enter the question of generic structures, since in all these instances we are concerned with only one specific invariant or isolated similarity in each case, viz., that it is a part of the Bible, or the New Testament, or the Pauline, or the Johannine corpus. I will illustrate this by going back to where I began, viz., with simple signs. If we take into account only one or if we expand it to even two *semes* #1 (of solid material) and #2 (raised above the ground), we could come up with such a bundle of things as "house," "table," "rock," "chair," "car," etc. These two *semes* were taken, one from the group of contents, the other from the group of forms. If we, however, add one *seme* more from the group of function —#4(for one person)—we reduce the possibilities considerably and by adding #5 (to sit on) we arrive at the concept "chair."

From these examples we can draw three conclusions:
   a) this type of taxonomical grouping or classification has little or no bearing at all on the question of generic structures;
   b) there is a need to go beyond taxonomic-classifying procedures in order to arrive at a process of relating elements or characteristics to each other by investigating their interrelationship and function (Ullmann: vii; Seiler: 46; cf. note 20).[11]
   c) there is a necessity for all three groups of characteristics to be represented; the question of function cannot be left out!

2.2.3.   Third, by "text" we can refer to a whole *hierarchy* of *concepts of generic nature*. In this connection we have to ask the question in which ways certain texts are structurally similar to each other and characteristically different from others. In dealing with simple signs such as predicates, I tried to show the importance of establishing a hierarchy of abstraction levels such as "armchair," "chair," "seat," "furniture." In

[10]The relevance of this type of groupings (S—Parole) for genre analysis is furthermore distinctly limited due to the fact that frequency classes cannot stand in syntagmatic contexts as pointed out by Heger, 1976: 29–30, 60; see sec. 4 below.

[11]That interrelationship between the elements is important in the analysis of apocalyptic texts has been recognized by Biblical scholars as well; cf. Smith: 132 and MacRae: 317.

dealing with such complex signs as "genres," we have to proceed analogously, if genre-analysis is to be successful at all. To my satisfaction there seems to be an increasing agreement among linguists, literary critics, and even form-critics that such a hierarchization is an absolute necessity. This is true, even if the terminology may differ and the theoretical reflection may have reached various levels of awareness.

2.2.3.1. In *linguistics,* ever since de Saussure, one distinguishes between *parole* as the level of actualization in speech and writing; *langue* as the level of a single-language structure and *language* as the level of language competence in general, i.e., language as system (Baldinger: 150–51; Heger, 1976: 15–19).

2.2.3.2. In *literary criticism* a similar although more detailed abstraction hierarchy is being used in comparing the following genre concepts (see Hempfer, 1973: 26–29; Hellholm, 1980: 62–64; Raible, 1979a: 28).[12]

  a) The *"communication situation";* i.e., the factors characterizing the relationship between a sender and a receiver in which a speech-act is carried out;

  b) The *"mode of writing"* and *"type of writing";* i.e., *ahistoric* generic invariants such as the narrative, the epic, the dramatic, or the satiric modes of writing.[13] That the generic concept on this abstraction level is of an *ahistoric* nature and none the less fully legitimate becomes obvious, when we turn to such a sign-model as "mammal." Nobody using the concept "mammal" is actually looking for the incarnation or the pure form of the mammal,—at least I hope so!

  c) The *"genre"* is the *historic* and concrete realizations of the potential generic invariant structures of the "modes" and/or "types of writing" on the *ahistoric* level of abstraction. *Historic* realizations of the *ahistoric* concept narrative, for instance, are a novel, a biography, a tale, etc, just as historic realizations of the *ahistoric* concept "mammal" can be a "dog" or a "human being."

  d) The *"subgenres":* on an even lower abstraction level we find such realization of the genre "novel" as "love-story," "detective-story," and so on. With regard to the concept "human being" it can be subdivided into the obvious subconcepts "female" and "male" by adding one *seme* more.

___

[12] Heger emphasizes rightly, however, that it is true also of System-Linguistics: "dass der Uebergang von der Parole zur Langue nicht aus einem einzigen, sondern aus mehreren Abstraktionsschritten besteht" (1976: 16; also see Hellholm, 1984).

[13] Concerning the question for a theoretical necessity of introducing the "type of writing" as a level between "mode of writing" and "genre," see Hempfer, 1973: 233–34, note 102. Cf. in connection with the problem of genre "Apocalypse," 3.3.4. and note 31.

2.2.3.3.   In *form-criticism* we also encounter a similar hierarchy of abstraction levels, a fact which I can only briefly hint at on this occasion:

a) *"Sitz im Leben"* is by and large the equivalence in biblical scholarship to the "communication situation" in linguistics and literary criticism, although with considerably more attention paid to the situation of the sender than that of the receiver, to the origin rather than to the use.

b) *"Mode of writing"* as a "name" for *ahistoric* generic structures is to my knowledge in biblical scholarship left with an *"empty position,"* i.e., a concept without lexicalization, in spite of the fact that the concept itself is there; after all we do talk about "Narrative Texts" or "Argumentative Texts" in connection with *genres* and about "Narrative Forms," "Sayings of Jesus," and "Middle Forms" in connection with *forms*.[14]

c) *"Genres"* as a designation for historic generic structure has been employed since the formation of the form-critical school *("Gattung"/"Form")* and has like "Sitz im Leben" become to such a degree a part of biblical scholarship that even those scholars opposing new linguistic methods or theories today make use of them as an inherent part of their vocabulary and their conceptual understanding. We analyze the genre of "Gospels," "Letters" (although problematic; cf. Ermert), and "Apocalypses" in connection with *genres,* and "Miracle stories," "Similitudes," or "Prophetic and Apocalyptic Sayings" in connection with *forms* (see note 14).

d) This also applies to *"subgenres"* as can easily be demonstrated by pointing to the concept of "Synoptic Gospels."

2.3   The hierarchic structures of the complex models of "single texts, subgenres, genres, modes of writing and communication situations" adhere to the same rule as the hierarchy of simple signs, viz. that the larger the *intension* the smaller the *extension* and vice versa. In variation of my quotation from Raible above, we can say that generic structures with few characteristics have the character of "supreme-concepts," while generic structures with many characteristics are typical "sub-concepts." Applied to my topic today, this means that there are fewer common characteristics

---

[14] Concerning the differentiation between "form" and "genre" (= *Gattung*), see my reference to Rudolf Bultmann's programmatic statement in RGG[2]II (1928), 418, and the discussion in Hellholm, 1980: 68. The distinction between "form" and "Gattung" on the one hand and "genre" on the other by E. P. Sanders (449 and 453) is not very illuminating in view of the quotation from Gunkel (see note 23) and the fact that form-critics like Hans Conzelmann and Günther Bornkamm make a distinction precisely between *"Gattung* (= genre)" and *"Form."* Cf. also Robinson (72, note 3).

of a "Narrative" than of an "Apocalypse," thus allowing more texts to be classified as "Narratives" than as "Apocalypses."

3. Genres and Paradigms
3.1   So far I have deliberated on the hierarchical structures to be applied in genre analysis.

When I now turn to the problem of genres and paradigms, I will inevitably have to restrict myself to one generic concept, viz., that of an "Apocalypse." When entering upon a specific concept like "Apocalypse," we must not forget that genre designations function as *names* for texts (Raible, 1972: 204ff; 1979a: 21ff; Heger, 1979: 49–50). This means first of all that genre designations are simple signs for more complex signs that are themselves complex signs for a far more complex reality. However, this also means that, when analyzing texts as generic concepts, we have constantly to be conscious of the level on which we are posing our analyses. This does not *per se* favor any particular level of investigation; on the contrary, it should explicitly be stated that text-linguistic and form-critical studies can legitimately be carried out on any of these levels, "subgenre," "genre," "mode of writing," etc., but that we can only move from one to any other if we are aware of what we are doing.

3.2.   What are the characteristics, the *semes/noemes*,[15] of the macro-sign "Apocalypse"? That the answer to this question is by no means an easy one ought to be self-evident from our discussion so far and is indeed confirmed by the various suggestions put forward by such scholars as Philipp Vielhauer (1965: 583–94; 1975:487–92), Klaus Koch (1970: 24–33), and John J. Collins (1979b: 28). In order to avoid doing too much injustice to any one of these scholars I will list the following *semes/noemes* which include most characteristics mentioned in connection with attempts at defining the literary group "Apocalypse."

A. Content—Propositions and Themes (text-semantic aspect)
s1   Eschatology as history in future form
s2   Cosmic history divided into periods ("Weltalterlehre")
s3   Description of the other-world
s4   Combat between dualistic macro-cosmic powers
s5   Combat between dualistic micro-cosmic powers and/or groups
s6   Other worldly mediators or revealers
s7   This-worldly recipients

---

[15] While "*seme* is defined as the minimal distinctive unit (of the content substance) with reference to the *sememe*, which is *bound to the structure of a given language*," noeme is "a concept intensionally defined, which *does not depend on the structure of a given language*" (Heger, 1976: 338–39; Baldinger: 267). In order not to predetermine at this point the status of the genre concept "Apocalypse," I give *seme/noeme* alternatively.

s8   Addressees of recipient's revelation
s9   Paraenesis
s10   Command to recipient to reveal and/or to write by other-worldly mediator
s11   Systematization of numbers, etc.

B. Form—Style (text-syntactic aspect)
s12   Narrative framework
s13   Epistolary prescript and/or postscript
s14   Removal to a this-worldly place of revelation
s15   Heavenly journey to an other-worldly place of revelation
s16   Account of vision(s)
s17   Account of audition(s)
s18   Interpretation of vision(s)
s19   Interpretation of audition(s)
s20   Discourse of mediators
s21   Dialogues between mediator(s) and receiver
s22   Heavenly writings (letters and/or books from Heaven)
s23   Quotations of the Supreme Divinity
s24   Communication embedment
s25   Pictorial language
s26   Pseudonymity
s27   Combination of smaller forms

C. Function—Communication function (text-pragmatic aspect)
s28   Intended for a group in crisis
s29   Exhortation to steadfastness and/or repentance
s30   Promise of vindication and redemption or more generally stated: consolation
s31   Authorization of message

3.3.   Is this listing of a substantial number of characteristics of Apocalypses pointed out by biblical scholars sufficient to enable us to arrive at the concept "Apocalypse" in a *semasiological* approach[16] or are they all contained in the concept "Apocalypse" in an onomasiological approach?[17]

3.3.1.   The *first observation* to be made is that practically no *semes/noemes* can be tied exclusively to the concept of Apocalypse, as is the case with *semes/noemes* of simple concepts (cf. 1.4.1; Hanson: 33; Car-

[16] That is, starting from the sign *(signeme)* "Apocalypse" in order to arrive at a monosemized concept *(sememe)*; see Baldinger: 110–57; Heger, 1979: 59–61. For the distinction between semasiology and onomasiology, see 3.3.5.
[17] That is, starting from the concept *(sememe)* "Apocalypse" in order to arrive at a proper lexicalization *(signeme)*; see Baldinger: 110–57; Heger, 1979: 59–61; note 15 above.

mignac, 1979: 17; 1982: par. 1; Stone: 440; Sanders: 449–50). Time and space do not allow for a scrutiny of all 31 *semes/noemes*, but let me only point to a few constituents that normally are regarded as typical apocalyptic characteristics:

    a) *Eschatology:* not even this *seme/noeme* can be claimed to be an exclusive characteristic of an Apocalypse as its appearance in Pauline letters or in the Gospels demonstrates;

    b) *Visions:* neither are these nor are heavenly journeys reserved for Apocalypses as their appearance in Pauline, Hermetic, and Gnostic literature indicates;

    c) *Consolation* and *authorization:* even these two functional *semes/noemes* are typical not only for apocalypses, e.g., authorization can be achieved by pseudepigraphal letters also.

3.3.2.   The *second observation* tells us that all these 31 *semes/noemes* in fact are not present in any single writing designated as an Apocalypse. Where does this take us? What conclusions need to be drawn from this obvious state of affairs? In my opinion *two,* to begin with:

    a) First, we must recall that the designation "Apocalypse" is a model abridging the model "text," which means that *per definitionem* we cannot expect all characteristics pertaining to single texts on the *parole* level to be included in a generic concept on various levels of abstraction.[18]

       This takes us one step further: depending on where we locate the generic concept "Apocalypse," we can expect fewer or more characteristics to make up the concept; as a *supreme-concept* on the *ahistoric* level of "mode of writing," the *semes/noemes* will inevitably have to be fewer; as a *sub-concept* on the historic levels of genre or subgenre, the *semes/noemes* will have to be many more. And as stated twice already: the more *semes/noemes* the fewer Apocalypses, the fewer *semes/noemes* the more Apocalypses![19]

    b) Second, in my opinion this state of affairs leads to the same conclusion I drew earlier with regard to the simple predicate "chair" (1.4.1): it is by no means enough just to list a number of 31 characteristic *semes* or *noemes* in order to arrive at the generic

[18] As Heger, 1979: 52 and 60 points out, only the determinative characteristics on the levels of *langue* or *langage* constitute *semes/noemes*, not, however, the specific characteristics of single texts. Cf. with regard to simple signs, 1.1.

[19] These deliberations show how essential it is to approach the question of genre not by utilizing merely inductive but rather by combining inductive and deductive methods. See Hellholm, 1980: 64–67; Gülich/Raible, 1977: 18ff; Ermert: 29–30; also 1.4.2.; 3.3.3 and 4.2.1.3.4. #(b).

concept "Apocalypse," but rather we have to ask for the type, the sequential order and the interrelationship of these characteristics to each other in constituting a possible genre "Apocalypse"; or on one abstraction level higher, the grouping of the intersection of several types of texts on the same level in constituting a narrative (Hempfer, 1973: 138ff, 190; Hellholm, 1980: 67; Hartman, 1983: 333–34; see also note 11).[20]

3.3.3. The *third observation* I have already revealed by grouping the above listed 31 elements in order to avoid repetition (cf. similar grouping in Hartman, 1983: 332–36). The problem of such groupings becomes apparent as soon as one discovers that not a small number of characteristics could show up in one or even two more groups as well, depending on the perspective; e.g., from one point of view the account of a vision is a stylistic or formal characteristic, while from another perspective it certainly belongs to the group of contents. This was particularly striking in the classification of the *seme/noeme* 15, "Heavenly writing": from a literary or *text-syntactical* point of view it is a specific form of revelation; from a *text-semantic* point of view it is filled with content; and from the perspective of *text-pragmatics* it has a specific function in the macro-structure of the apocalyptic writing as such and, what is much more important for our argument, of the generic structure of Apocalypses.[21]

From a semiotically and linguistically defined "communication-specific model of definition," this circumstance is in no way surprising, since pragmatics includes semantics and syntactics, and semantics includes syntactics as well:[22]

[20] Such an arrangement of *semes/noemes* can preclude the "naturalistic fallacy" described by Olsson: 22.

[21] The same is true also of s9 (Paraenesis); an indication of this particular problem in the grouping of the *semes* is the fact that Collins and the SBL-group include paraenesis neither in the "Manner of Revelation" nor in the "Content: Temporal or Spatial Axis" but set it apart as an entity by itself. The question of the grouping of the *semes/noemes* as well as the whole question of definition becomes exceptionally problematic, when Hartmut Stegemann writes (527, note 107): "In any event one can speak of a literary 'genre' if one does not understand this concept in the sense of a 'Gattung' but orientates oneself exclusively to the criteria of content (so e.g., J. J. Collins 1979)." The reference to Collins here is in my opinion misleading, since Collins' "master-paradigm" contains both criteria of form and of content. Furthermore, Stegemann himself has convincingly pointed to the *seme* "authorization," a criterion of function, as a determinative characateristic of the genre "Apocalypse" (504–8; Raible, 1979a: 27).

[22] For further details and references to relevant literature, see Hellholm (1980, 22ff). For the importance of distinguishing between pragmatics (function of symptom and function of signal) and semantics (function of symbol) with regard to synonymy, see Baldinger: 212–253, especially 230–40. For the function of symbol, sympton, and signal in the trapezium, see Baldinger: 254–59; Heger, 1976: 45–46; Karl Bühler: 28ff.

Pragmatics: Relation between Signs, Designata, and Users =
    R(S,D,U,);
Semantics: Relation between Signs and Designata = R(S,D);
Syntactics: Relation between Signs and other Signs = R(S,S').

When grouping the *semes* of the *sememe* "chair," I came to the
conclusion that *semes* had to be derived from all of the three groups
(content, form, and function), in order to establish the concept "chair." In
apocalyptic research, up until the project of the SBL-group directed by
Collins, that has been the starting point also in analyzing such complex
models as generic concepts.[23] Now, Collins and the SBL-group give the
following definition of the genre "Apocalypse":

> "Apocalypse" is a genre of revelatory literature with a narrative
> framework, in which a revelation is mediated by an otherworldy
> being to a human recipient, disclosing a transcendent reality
> which is both temporal, insofar as it envisages eschatological
> salvation and spatial insofar as it involves another, supernatural
> world. (Collins, 1979a: 9; in this definition the groups "form" and
> "content" are represented).

This definition, operating on a fairly high abstraction level, brings to
one's mind the question: why were Apocalypses ever written? From what
Collins has noted elsewhere, I believe he would answer something like
this: each Apocalypse has its specific function but one cannot arrive at an
invariant function.[24] This, however, does not resolve the problem at
stake, since such an answer would only transfer the question from the
level of *langue*, on which generic investigations operate, to the level of
parole, dealing with single texts.[25] I believe that one reason for the

[23] That all three dimensions have to be taken into account was stressed by Hermann Gunkel
(1924: 182–83; Eng. trans. in Hayes: 127–28; also 1925: 283–84) when in a letter to Adolf Jülicher
he writes: "Particularly displeasing to me is the word 'form*geschichtlich*' or even '*stil*kritisch'; I
rather talk of '*Literaturgeschichte*' that organizes the material according to 'genres.' Genres I
establish a) according to the common store of thoughts and moods, b) according to the similar
Sitz im Leben, c) according to the constant forms of expression" (see also Rollmann: 283, note
16; Sanders: 448–49). The acknowledgment of the necessity of an interrelationship of all three
dimensions in establishing genres is explicitly stressed in Gunkel (1924: 183): "Only where we
have all three criteria preserved together . . . have we the right to speak of a genre." What
Gunkel, however, does not discuss is the nature of the interrelationship or the possibility of a
hierarchization of the criteria.

[24] J. Collins (1982: 94): "Rather than assuming that there is a common setting and function . . .
we need to examine the individual texts bearing in mind the differentiation of levels demanded
by Knierim (1973)." Cf., however, note 18 and Hellholm, 1980: 13, 61, 64).

[25] For this distinction that plays such an eminent role in linguistics today and has done so
since de Saussure (1916), see the decisive remarks for form criticism by Bultmann from 1913:
"Aber die methodisch zuerst zu beantwortende Frage ist die nach der literarischen Art des

reluctance toward functional aspects as generic *semes/noemes* must be seen in connection with the lack of hierarchization of *semes/noemes* in the discussion of function, a problem I will return to in the next section. Another reason probably is the concentration on the "Sitz im Leben" aspect for genre definitions among form-critics instead of the integration of the three dimensions.[26] Personally I am inclined to think that such characteristics as s28 (intended for a group in crisis); s29 (exhortation to steadfastness or repentance); s30 (promise of vindication and redemption); or s31 (authorization of the message) are general enough to serve on the level of *langue* or even *language*. This implies the conviction that these are indeed appropriate *semes/noemes* derived from the texts themselves. Thus, the grouping and hierarchization are derived *deductively* from the methodology applied, while the specific *semes/noemes* within the group are derived *inductively* from the texts themselves (see 4.2.1.3.4.#[b]).

For a paradigmatically established definition of the genre "Apocalypse" I would be willing to accept the definition quoted above, provided the following addition on the same level of abstraction: "*intended for a group in crisis with the purpose of exhortation and/or consolation by means of divine authority.*"[27]

Streitgesprächs und seinem Ursprung als literarischer Grösse. Das ist die Frage nach dem 'Sitz im Leben'; denn diese fragt *nicht nach dem Ursprung eines einzelnen Berichtes in einer einzelnen geschichtlichen Begebenheit,* sondern nach dem Ursprung und Zugehörigkeit *einer bestimmten Gattung in und zu typischen Situationem* und Verhaltungen einer Gemeinschaft. Natürlich hat in solchen Gattungen und in ihrem einzelnen Exemplaren das wirkliche Leben seinen Niederschlag gefunden; aber das einzelne uns vorliegende literarische Produkt kan von uns zunächst nur auf dem Wege über die Gattung verstanden werden (1964: 40–41, italics mine; see also Hellholm, 1984).

[26] As Gunkel was right in rejecting genre definitions using only *formal* criteria (see note 23), so are Collins and the SBL-group right in rejecting *function* as *the* decisive criterion. There is no equality between form, content, and function: ". . . . as with all linguistic signs form has to be distinguished from function" (Raible: 1979b: 68). Cf. also Kubczak: 1984: 16–17; Brinker: 128.

[27] Here I am in agreement with such scholars as Hartman (1983: 334–35, 337–39), Sanders (455–59) and Olsson (30–31). See, however, already Gunkel (1928: 62): "Who is speaking? Who are the listeners? What is the *mise en scène* at the time? What effect is aimed at?" Cf. also the *elementa narrationis* (Lausberg: 182–83): *quis, quid, ubi, quibus auxillis, cur, quomodo, quando* (or in the words of the English rhetorician Thomas Wilson [16th century]: "Who, what, and where, by what help, and by whose: Why, how, and when, do many things disclose" quoted in Plett: 12). Cf. also John Collins, 1982: 110. Further Adela Yarbro Collins (1983: 729), who, however, limits her functional analysis to a single text, the Book of Revelation, when she states: "Since consensus has not yet been reached on the definition of the literary genre apocalypse or the function of apocalypticism, generalizations about the function of apocalypticism would be premature at this stage of the discussion. The most appropriate approach for the present seems to be the investigation of the function of particular apocalyptic writings in their historical settings." Nonetheless she goes on to an abstraction beyond the historical phenemenon when she writes: "In the course of this study, a common generalization about apocalypticism will be tested, namely, that it arises in social settings of crisis and alienation." This test holds for

3.3.4.   The *fourth* observation has to do with the hierarchization of the
semes/noemes themselves. In John Collins' *master-paradigm* in *Semeia* 14
(1979): 6–8, he has paid due attention to this very important methodological approach. I can only emphasize my agreement at this point.
When one turns, however, to the chart on p. 28 it becomes obvious that
he has not carried his methodological insight over into practical use so
that the characteristics listed there vary in abstraction, a feature which
also returns in all the other contributions to that *Semeia* volume (A.
Collins, 1979: 104–5; Fallon: 148; Attridge: 161–74). Now, we should be
grateful to Collins for the hierarchization of the *semes/noemes* in his
master-paradigm, especially since I have found no attempts at such a
ranking in any other paradigm of apocalyptic *semes/noemes* available;[28]
and yet I have to point to the fact that there remain serious problems with
that master-paradigm as one striking inaccuracy demonstrates. In divid-
ing existent Apocalypses into types Collins states that "the most obvious
and fundamental distinction is between apocalypses which do not have an
otherworldly journey (Type I) and those that do (Type II)" (13).

   If we take a closer look at the paradigm, however, this "fundamental
distinction" is not accounted for in the paradigm itself, since the *seme/
noeme* #1.3 ("other-worldly journey") has no equivalence in, e.g., a
seme/noeme #1.2 ("other-worldly revelation in this world") on the same
level. On the contrary, *semes/noemes* #1.1 ("visual revelation") and #1.2
("auditory revelation") are said to be the corresponding *semes/noemes* to
#1.3 ("other-worldly journey"). This is obviously incorrect, since both
Apocalypses with or without other-worldly journeys have visual and
auditory revelations. In the case of the Revelation of John we have both
types represented in one and the same Apocalypse. Thus the hierarchical
arrangement, which is so commendable, must still be judged as imper-
fect and in need of improvement.

   The need for a hierarchization of *semes/noemes* constituting generic
concepts has to do with the hierarchic levels of abstraction made manifest

---

Revelation even though it does so on the level of imagination. Thus A. Collins can conclude by
stating: "a major function of apocalyptic language is to resolve a social crisis on the level of
imagination." Cf. now, A. Collins, 1984. Similar results came from Tord Olsson in his opening
address in Uppsala: "We can observe that revelatory world-views are regularly actualized in
situations of conflict or crisis, real or imagined, or in the context of fear of such situations" (30–
31). Contrary to A. Collins, Olsson in his analysis generalizes the crisis situation to be a typical
phenomenon for apocalyptic movements in various settings in the ancient as well as in the
modern world (45–46).

[28] Theoretically, however, demands for such rankings have been advocated by others, e.g.,
Knierim (465), Hellholm (1980: 43–44, 52, 70–71), Hempfer (1977: 14–21); Plett (1977a: 142–43):
"In order to realize these [sc. rhetorical situations], a cultural typology of the rhetorical
situations is needed." Raible (1979a: 29): "In the range of the communication situation an
establishment of types pertaining to the intentions of authors is important." See further
Hartman (335–36) and now J. Collins (1982: 92–94).

in the *super-archisememe* like "mode of writing," and *archisememe* like "type of text,"[29] a *sememe* like "genre," a *subsememe* like "sub-genre" or the text itself like "The Apocalypse of John." This means: the more abstract the generic structure, the more abstract, and the fewer, the *semes* (cf. notes 2 and 7; sec. 3.3.3.).

The simplified diagram on the following page may serve as an example of such a hierarchy of generic concepts *(sememes)* for which a hierarchy of *semes/noemes* is required.[30]

One advantageous result of such a generic stemma of hierarchically arranged abstraction levels is the obvious fact that it provides the theoretical possibility for an author to generate and for recipients to recognize new and/or mixed genres and subgenres (cf. sec. 1.3). This is a possibility in those cases when *semes/noemes* from various *superarchi-* or *archisememes* in the process of ahistoric transformations are combined in historic *sememes* or *subsememes* or when *semes/noemes* from various *sememes* by means of historic transformation are combined in *subsememes* of various kinds (Hempfer, 1973: 27, 139–50; and cf. sec. 3.3.5.). Thus, the historic development of new and/or mixed genres/subgenres can be accounted for and instead of a merely synchronic-static analysis we can also allow a diachronic-dynamic investigation of genres (Hempfer, 1973: 122ff, 131–32, 140, 192–220; Coseriu, 1974; 1980: 134, 137–38, 143; Raible, 1979a, 8–9, 23; Baldinger: 277–309; Hellholm, 1980: 64; Kubczak, 1978: 124ff).

3.3.5.   The *fifth observation* has to do with "language in its fundamental function, in its *communicative function*" between sender and receiver (Baldinger: 132; cf. Hellholm, 1980: 14–22; Hartman, 1983: 334–35). This observation may simultaneously serve as a transition to the next section dealing with "Genres and Structures."

When designing the diagram above, I did not indicate by means of arrows in which direction it should be read. The reason for this is that it ought to function both ways as the following deliberations will try to show. The bipolarity between sender and receiver

> correspond(s) exactly to the opposition between *semasiology* and *onomasiology* (italics mine). The hearer receives from his interlocutor forms, the meaning of which he must determine in order to understand them. Thus, the hearer's task is semasiological. The speaker, on the other hand, has to communicate mental objects

[29] "Type" here is understood as an ahistoric constancy and not as a subgrouping of a genre; cf. Hempfer (1973: 23–24).

[30] In the diagram below the following abbreviations are being used: Discourses = Discourses between the Risen Lord and His disciples; o.w. = other-worldly; Icar. = Icaromenippus.

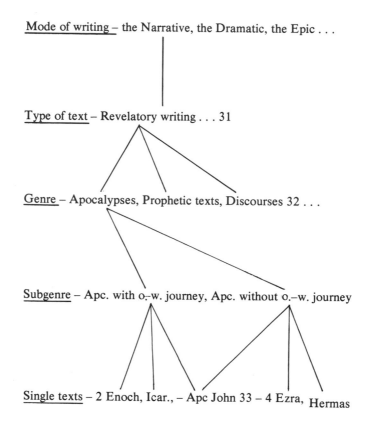

Mode of writing – the Narrative, the Dramatic, the Epic . . .

Type of text – Revelatory writing . . . 31

Genre – Apocalypses, Prophetic texts, Discourses 32 . . .

Subgenre – Apc. with o.-w. journey, Apc. without o.-w. journey

Single texts – 2 Enoch, Icar., – Apc John 33 – 4 Ezra, Hermas

---

31 See Olsson (30): "I would prefer then to speak of a *revelatory world-view* which is embraced by apocalyptists but also by others." See also Berger: 207.

32 Concerning this genre, see Vielhauer, 1975: 680–92, esp. 690ff; Koester (1971: 210ff).

33 If in inductive investigations more texts of the mixed genre type group appear, these would form another subgenre: "Apocalypses with *and* without other-worldly journey."

(concepts). He must select designations[34] from the vocabulary placed at his disposal by his memory; he must link concepts to acoustic images, so converging them into *significants;* that is, his task is onomasiological. (Baldinger: 132; cf. 110, 157–59, 211, and 306–8)

Now this differentiation between semasiology and onomasiology with regard to simple signs or concepts applies also to more complex signs and concepts, e.g., genres.

3.3.5.1.   When writing an Apocalypse, the author has at his disposal the structure of such a genre, i.e., the *sememe* or concept of Apocalypse, and has to find the appropriate way of expressing his conceptual structure of this particular genre. This process of encoding, at least partly internalized (Hempfer, 1973: 126), occurs as transformation from various levels of abstractions or, in different terminology, from various deep structure levels[35] all the way to the single Apocalypse, or in other words, to the surface structure of an Apocalypse. This theory of transformation[36] provides a concept of structure that is dynamic in so far as it allows diachrony in the development of generic structures, as well as superimposition of more than one generic structure at one level of abstraction upon a lower level in the hierarchy of conceptual abstraction as stated above (sec. 3.3.4.; Hempfer, 1973: 140–42).

3.3.5.2.   When reading or listening to a text the receiver, who perceives forms already selected by the author, has to determine the structure of that text—in our case, not primarily of that particular text but rather its generic structure.[37] As will be shown in the next section, a paradigmatic approach is hereby not sufficient; instead, a syntagmatic approach or a combination of both is necessary.

The process of decoding occurs through observations of the text as it stands, i.e., the generic surface structure, which is determined by a macro-structure of functional textsequences of various ranks (see note 39; Gülich/Raible, 1977: 56–57). This macro-structure must be recognizable on the surface level, since the receiver "obtains from the author neither a macro-structure nor a text deep structure but a text *tel quel.* Conse-

[34] "Signification proceeds from a *signifiant* (form) to a concept (mental object), and designation proceeds from a concept towards a *signifiant*" (Baldinger: 110).

[35] Cf. Hempfer (1973: 141): "relative or absolue constancy of deep structures"; Grosse (1979: 595): "On closer examination, text as a totality almost always displays *several macro-structural dimensions* superimposing upon each other. . . ." Gülich/Raible, ed. (1977: 56ff).

[36] Cf. Jean Piaget, and Noam Chomsky: "Notice that in this view one major function of the transformational rules is to convert an abstract deep structure that expresses the content of a sentence into a fairly concrete surface structure that indicates the form" (136).

[37] This is the reason why we here must talk of *determining* the structure of texts.

quently there must exist signals—called delimitation markers—by means
of which the reader or listener can arrive at such a macro-structure"
(Gülich/Raible, 1977a: 163; 1977: 54; van Dijk, 1977: 149ff and 1979:
519).[38] This is the *semasiological* approach, since it poses the problem
from the viewpoint of the receiver and his decoding of a given macro-
sign.

3.3.5.3.   When analyzing or interpreting a text, the scholar has to do
justice to both aspects, the *onomasiological* as well as the *semasiological*.
The role of the scholarly interpreter is thus different from that of the
ordinary receiver (see Hempfer's critique of Hirsch in 1973: 251, n. 387;
also Schenk: 27–28).

As indicated above, "macro-structures always display an abstraction
of the concrete text-form and are in all generative models established in
the deep structure" (Kallmeyer/Meyer-Hermann, 1980: 254). This is how
a text is being analyzed from the point of view of the sender and the
message he wants to communicate. "Notwithstanding, the existence of
macro-structure must be recognizable on the text surface level" (254), as
we indicated above. This is how a text is being analyzed from the point of
view of the receiver in order for him to disclose the message communicated by the sender. Recognizing the appropriateness of these two approaches on the part of the interpreter, we must, however, not forget that
in his analytical work the scholar is at first always put in the same position
as the receiver: he has to work with the form that was given the text by
the sender; he does not have immediate access to the deep structure of
either a single text or a text representing a generic structure.

Therefore, the central phenomenon in recognizing the macro-structure is the delimitation of texts into *functional text-sequences* of different
ranks.[39] The delimitation is pursued by means of hierarchically ranked
delimitation markers on the surface level (see sec. 4.2.1.3.).

3.3.5.4.   In conclusion it should be stated that there is a close connection between textual macro-structure and text-delimitation (see sec.
4.2.). This connection reflects the two aspects of semasiology and
onomasiology as described above:

---

[38] See also W. Hendricks: "Present day analysts . . . have not advanced beyond the work of
Propp in that they continue to bypass what may be termed the 'textual surface' of narratives,
i.e., the constituent sentences of the narratives as it is presented to the reader (hearer)" (175).

[39] "Functional textsequences" denote a) *text delimitation* into textsequences of different ranks
(syntactical macro-structure); b) *semantic macro-structures* disclosing thematic text-sequences;
c) *pragmatic macro-structures*, i.e., *macro-speech acts* accomplishing a certain sequence of
speech acts; (cf. Hellholm, 1980: 36, 60–61; van Dijk, 1979: 518ff; Rosengren: 278 and 280;
Brinker: 145; also notes 22 and 49 in this article).

> Text-delimitation as a phenomenon on the surface level is on the one hand an *important way* to recognize macro-structures in the *process of reception and analysis;* on the other hand it is a *necessary result in realizing macro-structures* as well as in using principles of textuality in the process of production. (Kallmeyer/ Meyer-Hermann, 1980: 251 (italics mine))

In this statement the three aspects or approaches of functional communication dealt with above have been taken into due consideration and it must be the starting point for an adequate approach to the whole question of genres and structures.

4. Genres and Structures

4.1.   So far I have mainly discussed the problem of generic concepts from a paradigmatic point of view. In this lecture I have concentrated on paradigms,[40] since in genre analysis up until now this has been the prevailing method. It was my intent to present the paradigmatic approach, which works so well on simple models, to complex models in order to help us recognize its advantages, but at the same time reveal its weaknesses. Its obvious strength is its simplicity, even if developed so as to try to take the relationship between the characteristic features and the grouping of these features and even the hierarchization of these characteristic *semes/noemes* into account. Its disadvantages are equally obvious: a paradigm has the tendency to remain taxonomic and static in spite of hierarchization, grouping into dimensions, and establishment of relationships between elements. In other words, it has a tendency to be static instead of dynamic. I do not believe that we can do without paradigmatic analyses in genre investigations, but I also believe that a text-linguistic approach in its true meaning, i.e., as a syntagmatic ap-

---

[40] So far this paper is a complement to my doctoral dissertation, in which I concentrated on syntagmatic aspects. When J. Collins (1981: 96, note 11) maintains that the approach in Hellholm 1980 "suffers from his failure to analyze the pattern of contents," he has not observed a) that my approach was essentially syntagmatic and not paradigmatic, and b) that in the analysis of the text of *Hermas* on pp. 140–89, the designation of content is in fact dealt with quite extensively and also utilized in the chart on pp. 136–39. The "content *pattern*" can, of course, only be dealt with after other Apocalypses have been analyzed syntagmatically too. This is the goal set for the first part of my second volume. My reasons for concentrating on a syntagmatic analysis was not—as Collins seems to believe—due to a dismissal of "any genre analysis which does not employ an explicit linguistic model," but to the very fact a) that no syntagmatic analyses existed at the time (cf. now, however, even if only for a section of Daniel: Koch, 1983; for 4 Ezra: Harnisch; and for sections of the Apocalypse of John, Hartman, 1980), and b) that such analyses are *necessary* complements to the predominantly paradigmatic approaches in the field of scholarly research. The linguistic justification for syntagmatic analyses of various ranks is given in note 9. Indirectly Tord Olsson also justifies the syntagmatic approach by demonstrating the "naturalistic fallacy" in the "theoretical discussion on Apocalypticism" (21–22), which is mainly paradigmatic.

proach on the level of macro-structures, is, if not an alternative, at least a necessary complement.[41]

4.1.1.   When switching from the paradigmatic to the syntagmatic analysis, I will begin by listing six dimensions, noted by Raible and further developed by me, from which genre designations ought to derive their characteristics (Raible: 1979a: 23–28; also Hellholm, 1980; Hartman, 1980; Lambrecht, 1980; Harnisch, 1983; Koch, 1982, for syntagmatic investigation of apocalyptic texts).

1) *The communication situation between sender and receiver (text-pragmatic aspect)*
   Here we have to distinguish between two levels of communication (see Hellholm, 1980: 43–44, 77–78, 83–84; also Ermert: 25, 27–28, 32–41):
   a) *first,* the text*external* level between sender and receiver, between author and readers.
      Within this level of communication we encounter
      aa)   the purpose of the author in writing his work, e.g., to persuade, to inform, to admonish, etc. (Hellholm, 1980: 52–61; Raible, 1979a: 24; see note 39);
      bb)   the description of the sender and his situation;
      cc)   the description of the intended audience and its situation;
   b) *second,* the text*internal* level between *dramatis personae* within the text itself.
      Within this level of communication we encounter
      aa)   further textinternal levels of communication and their internal functions;
      bb)   all levels which have as their purpose to serve the course of the author in his communication with the readers on the external level (Hellholm, 1980: 191).
2) *The scope of objects (text-semantic aspect)*
   Under this dimension we can subsume (see Lewis; Hellholm, 1980: 88, note 67)
   a)   subject matters such as propositions, themes, motifs, etc.;
   b)   persons: individuals as well as types, e.g., this-worldly and other-worldly;
   c)   temporal and local constituents.
3) *The relationship to reality,* i.e., various possible worlds *(text-semantic aspect)*
   Distinctions have to be made (see van Dijk, 1977: 29–30; Hellholm, 1980: 87–91; Olsson, 30)

---

[41]Cf. Lausberg (244): "Die *dispositio* ist die notwendige Ergänzung zur *inventio*, die ohne *dispositio* ein beziehungsloser Vorgang wäre," where the *dispositio* corresponds to the *syntagma* and the *inventio* to the *paradigma*.

   a) between this world and a fictive world of a novel, for instance, and

   b) between this-world and the other-world in religious literature

      aa) with regard to the present as well as

      bb) with regard to the future situation (cf. Collins temporal and spatial axis; 1979a: 62–63);

   c) between various this-worldly relations as under b) above.

4) *Macro-syntagmatic structures of order (text-grammatical aspect* encompassing text-pragmatics, -semantics, and -syntactics)

Together with #1, #5, and #6 this is the eminently text-linguistic dimension,[42] since it encompasses

   a) the macro-structures of the text, usually in combination with characteristics from other dimensions;

   b) the relationship between macro-structures and micro-structures (Raible, 1979b: 69, 72; Hellholm, 1980: 60–61, 76 and 3.3.5. above; Gülich/Raible, 1977: 53–54; van Dijk, 1979: 519–20 and 4.1.2. below);

   c) the combination and/or overlapping of structures from other abstraction levels in the process of transformation (see 3.3.4. and 3.3.5.).

5) *The medium (text-grammatical aspect* encompassing text-pragmatics, -semantics, -syntactics)

Here we can distinguish between

   a) the medium language in *combination with other media,* e.g., music, meter, rhythm, etc.,

   b) the *carrier media* allowing the direct act of communication to be transferred into an indirect act, e.g., heavenly letters! (Hellholm, 1980: 43–44, 77–78, 83–84; Ermert, 25, 27–28, 32–41)

   c) the *form media* allowing an act of communication to be transmitted in "forms," e.g., dialogues!

6) *The literary modes of presentation (text-grammatical aspect* encompassing text-pragmatics, -semantics, -syntactics)

In this dimension we have to distinguish between

   a) various literary modes of representation such as narrative, dramatic, descriptive, instructive, and argumentative modes of presentation (Raible, 1979a: 27; Hempfer, 1973: 128–36; Hellholm, 1980: 64–66);

   b) the opposition between long and short ways of presentation, e.g., between "Gattung" and "Form" (see note 14).

---

[42] It should explicitly be noted that textlinguistics has been defined as a *"transphrastic approach"* on the one hand and as a *"communication oriented approach"* on the other (so Kallmeyer/Meyer-Hermann, 1973: 221ff.), thus taking *syntagmatic* and *functional* aspects into account (see Hellholm, 1980: 46ff; Hartman, 1980: 132; Coseriu, 1981: 51ff and 154ff).

4.1.2. The advantage of this paradigm of syntagmatic dimensions, in spite of its more complex differentiation, is that it takes into account 1) the three major *paradigmatic* groups I mentioned earlier (see 3.3.3.), viz., content, form, and function and 2) the *syntagmatic* aspects, in forms of micro- as well as macro-syntagmatic structures.

Literally, *textus/textura* means web and as such is two-dimensional. The first dimension of the web is made up by the warp; the second dimension is constituted by the woof (Harweg, 1979: 21, 148; 1973: 69–70; Gülich/Raible, 1977: 51–55; Hellholm, 1980: 75–76). Transferred into *textus/textura* in the meaning of text, this also provides us at first with a two-dimensional aspect of texts:

   a) the *first* dimension, the warp, constitutes the "chain-work" or linguistically stated, the *micro-syntagmatic* structure by means of syntagmataic substitution (Harweg, 1979: 21, 148; 1978; Hellholm, 1980: 30 and note 68). As in the woof this dimension is a necessary although not a sufficient condition for establishing texts;

   b) the *second dimension*, the woof, is a necessary and in combination with the former, a sufficient condition for establishing texts. This second dimension in its two different aspects allows specific patterns to stand out. This is the *macro-syntagmatic* structure of texts and genres, operating not on the level of sentences but on the level of texts and textsequences.

The two aspects of the second dimension are (see Gülich/Raible: 1975 and 1977a; Hellholm, 1980: 77–78 and 78–149; also see below, 4.2.1.2. on Hermas and 4.2.2.1., 4.2.2.2. on Apocalypse of John):

   1) hierarchically arranged communication levels;

   2) hierarchically arranged textsequences of different ranks.

Thus, we arrive in fact at a three-dimensional analysis of texts. These three dimensions will have to be used in a *macro-syntagmatic* approach to the analysis of generic structures:

The *first* step in the text analysis will be to divide the text into various functional communication levels, a possibility which is restricted to certain generic structures, primarily, but not exclusively, to narrative texts.

The *second* step will be to delimit the text into hierarchical and functional textsequences constituting—together with step one—the generic structures (Gülich/Raible, 1977: 53; Hellholm, 1980: 75–76; see footnote 39 above). Underlying these two *macro-structural* syntagmatic dimensions is the *micro-structural* syntagmatic dimension in the form of syntagamatic substitution.[43]

---

[43] Cf. Hempfer's distinction between *micro-structures* on the sentence level and *macro-structures* on the textlevel (1973: 144 and 179–80; also Gülich/Raible, 1977: 126–27; van Dijk, 1977: 143; von Kutschera: 140; Hellholm, 1980: 60–61; 84–85; Grosse, 1979: 609).

As emphasized above more than once regarding paradigmatic analyses, now, regarding syntagmatic analysis, we likewise have to emphasize the importance of determining "interdependences and relationships between constituents of different dimensions," as the ones discussed above in paragraph 3.3.5. (Raible, 1979a: 27). This becomes particularly important when we enter the field of *macro-syntagmatic* analyses, since neither sentences nor textsequences of various degrees "have *per se* any function but only obtain their function from a superior totality, e.g., (with regard to tones) within a melody or, as far as texts are concerned, within a superior unity of meaning" (Raible, 1979b: 69; von Humboldt: 205; Baldinger, 1980: XVII; Grosse, 1976: 26; Gülich/Raible, 1977: 53; Raible, 1979a: 12–13; Hempfer, 1973: 140; von Kutschera: 130; Kallmeyer/Meyer-Hermann, 1980: 242ff; Stegemann: 498–500); also Heger, 1976: 1; Rosengren: 1980; K. Zimmermann: 1978).

4.2. The syntagmatic analysis of the functional macro-structures of genres (see note 39) has to be carried out by means of textdelimitations of generic texts as they are available to the scholarly interpreter.[44] Thus, as indicated above, the analyst has to take the surface structure of the text as his starting point in pursuing syntagmatic analyses in order to arrive at the deep structure as conceived by the author (see 3.3.5.3.).

4.2.1. In my work on the *Shepherd of Hermas*, I have utilized the syntagmatic method *in extenso*, with special attention paid to the surface structure.

4.2.1.1. With regard to *communication levels* I arrived at a hierarachy of six levels of communication (Hellholm, 1980: 98):
1) Level *one:* between author and addressees;
2) Level *two:* between other-worldly mediators and the author as the human recipient;
2a) Level *two-a:* between other-worldly mediators and the addressees;
3) Level *three:* between a "Heavenly book" quoted in the text itself and the author;
3a) Level *three-a:* between the "Heavenly book" and the addressees;
4) Level *four:* between a quotation of an oath of the Supreme Divinity within the "Heavenly book" and the addressees.
This deep text-*pragmatic* embedment of the message from the other-

---

[44] See above 3.3.5.2.; Gülich/Raible, 1977: 54: "one can furthermore assume that these textsequences which designate the macro-structure of a text, must be recognizable directly on the surface of the text."

world to this-world recipients is the first most striking set of syntagmatic *semes/noemes* of the generic concept "Apocalypse." All (sets of) syntagmatic *semes/noemes* constituting an Apocalypse are ranked in an abstraction hierarachy.

4.2.1.2.   Regarding the *macro-structure* of the text as it emerges from the *text-pragmatic-semantic-syntactic* delimitation of textsequences of different ranks, two methodologically important observations are appropriate:

a) the ranking of textsequences *per definitionem* leads not only to a sequential order but also, and more importantly, to the establishment of hierarchically and functionally well-defined interrelationships between various textsequences, that is to say, how textsequences on higher levels function within the next lower level in rank all the way down to level 0 (see note 39);

b) there is a necessity for establishing hierarachically defined delimitation markers of a pragmatic, semantic, and syntactic nature, since in order to arrive at a delimitation of texts into hierarchichal textsequences there is a need for hierarchically defined delimitation markers (Gülich/Raible, 1977: 54). This task was undertaken in linguistics by Elisabeth Gülich and Wolfgang Raible (1975; 1977a) as to descending analyses, by Klaus Heger (1976; 1977) as to ascending analyses and their efforts have been adapted and further developed by myself in my book on the *Shepherd of Hermas* for narrative texts, and in my essay on Romans 6 for argumentative texts (1980; 1983; see note 38).

4.2.1.3.   Here I can only give a brief summary of the most essential markers applying to narrative texts (see Hellholm, 1980: 80–95).

4.2.1.3.1.   *Delimitation markers on a meta-level (pragmatic-semantic types).*
  1) *Meta-communicative clauses.*
    These clauses function as signals for the beginning and ending of an act of communication, i.e., they make the linguistic communication situation the subject of a theme. These markers can be divided into two main groups: one with an encoding (to say, to write), the other with a decoding (to hear, to read) function. Each of these can thematicize either oral or written acts of communication. The importance of these meta-communicative clauses lies mainly in the fact that they serve as signals for changes between various levels of communication and consequently among other things also signal out different dialogue phases and dialogue structures.

2) *Substitution on the meta level.*

Contrary to the syntagmatic substitutions on the *text-level* which link sentences on the micro-syntagmatic field together, the syntagmatic substitutions on the *meta-level* are manifestations a) of various generic concepts such as "Narrative" (on the abstraction-level of "mode of writing"), "Revelatory writing" ("type of text"), "Apocalypse" ("genre"), "Apocalypse with other-worldly journey" ("subgenre"), etc. (see 3.3.4.), and b) of various textsequences of different ranks such as "vision," "letter," "scroll," etc.[45]

The substitution on meta-level functions in a two-fold but yet related way:

a) Precisely this type of substitution, through which a text or a textsequence is replaced by a meta-communicative part of a sentence, noun or verb, often plays a significant role on the surface level in delimiting the text into hierarchically arranged textsequences (Gülich/Raible, 1977: 44).

b) In connection with the first function this type of substitution also "informs the receiver of the function of the text" (Grosse, 1976: 21; Hellholm, 1980: 60, 86; see also note 39, van Dijk, 1977: 245; Austin: 75). This function is particularly important when the substitution is a manifestation of a generic concept such as "Gospel" or "Apocalypse," since a genre designation "rules the—nevertheless very many—possibilities of interpretation and curtails them: one laughs . . . at the death of an innocent man in a burlesque but one grieves therefore in a tragedy" (Raible, 1979a: 15–16; Stempel: 568). From a form-critical perspective the same function of literary genre designations has been acknowledged, e.g., by Hans Conzelmann and Andreas Lindemann: "If one reads a miracle-story as a statement of facts, one inevitably fails to recognize its own intention, since a miracle-story is not drawn up as a statement of facts but constitutes a literary product *sui generis*" (Conzelmann/Lindemann: 1980: cf. Bultmann, 1963: 57 and 1964: 41; Hartman, 1983: 331; Kubczak, 1978: 48 and 79–80; Lausberg: 224; Albrektson: 145; and 142, 144). "This is the reason," says Wolfgang Raible, "why the genre as information about the essential gestalt characteristics of a text is eminently important for its interpretation" (Raible, 1979a: 15).

3) *Substitution on abstraction-level.*

A middle position between substitutions on *text-level* and on *meta-*

---

[45] The importance of redundance in the usage of *"substitution on meta-level"* is stressed by Grosse (1976: 143 with note 4). On the importance of "Titles" see now also Hellwig.

leval is the substitution on *abstraction-level*. This type of *substituens* has a wider range of reference than the *substituendum* and frequently occurs in combination with verbs and prepositions indicating the end of a passage. The substitution on abstraction-level is often found in narrative writings as reductions of text, textsequences, or even sentences in form of "abstract nouns," "pronouns and pronominal forms," certain "adverbs and conjunctions," and "verbs on abstraction-level" (Raible, 1972: 150–51, 194–203; Hellholm, 1980: 86–87).[46] This type of substitution also serves the delimitation of texts into textsequences of different ranks, although on a lower rank than the previous markers on the meta-level.

4.2.1.3.2. *Delimitation-markers with direct textexternal analogon outside the meta-level (pragmatic-semantic types).*

1) Change in set of worlds.
  As C. J. Fillmore has pointed out,

> the discourse grammarian's most important task is that of characterizing, on the basis of the linguistic material contained in the discourse under examination, the set of worlds in which the discourse could play a role, together with the set of possible worlds compatible with the message content of the discourse. (Fillmore: 88; cf. Lewis: 175, 213ff)

Adhering to the principle of ontological neutrality (see note 1), one can, by means of reduction, arrive at the following typologization in the classification of possible worlds:

Hellholm (1980:89)	*van Dijk* (1977: 29–30)	*J. Collins* (1979a: 6–7) (cf. Olsson: 30 and Carmignac, 1979:20)
1) this-world	1) [this world];	1) this-world of human recipients
a) actual world:	a) "our actual world";	
b) fictive world;	b) "a situation where the facts are different from the real or actual facts, but compatible with the postulates (laws, principles,	

---

[46]See my forthcoming article with the preliminary title, "Problems and Importance of Substitutional Delimitationsmarkers for the Interpretation of the Gospel of Matthew."

| 2) other-world | 2) "worlds with partly or fully different laws of nature, i.e., worlds which are increasingly *dissimilar* to our 'own' world." | etc.) of the actual world";
 2) other-world of a transcendent reality and supernatural mediators. |

Among the delimitation-markers of a primarily—although not exclusively (Schmidt: 238; Schnelle: 237)—semantic nature, the "change in set of worlds" is the most important one, as can be seen from the important role it plays not only in text linguistic but also in form-critical apocalyptic research as the definition by Collins and the SBL-group reveals. The main difference, however, between this *seme/noeme* as used by Collins et alii on the one hand and the same *seme/noeme* used by Hellholm, Heger, and van Dijk on the other, is that the former only used it paradigmatically while the latter used it *syntagmatically* as well, which according to our deliberations above is a distinct advantage.

2) Episode-markers, etc.

These demarcations are signals introducing a) time and change of time and b) localization and relocalization. Both of these can be divided into aa) *absolute* episode-markers delimiting textsequences already established by preceding markers and bb) *relative* episode-markers delimiting textsequences already established by the absolute episode-markers.

3) Changes in the grouping of agents.

This marker introduces changes in the main actors regardless of whether they are active *(agens)* or passive *(patiens)* agents. More important than changes of individual actors is the switch in groups of actors, which is in line with the above-mentioned "change in set of possible worlds." Thus, the change in groups is a primary, while the change in individuals is a secondary, delimitating signal.

4.2.1.3.3. *Delimitation-markers without direct textexternal analogon (semantic-syntactic types).*

1) Renominalization

This marker reintroduces an agent who has been referred to by a pronoun, with a noun or his proper name. There seems to be a direct relationship between the change in the arrangement of actors and the renominalization; this is the reason why this marker often goes together with the previous one. This marker has only an *indirect* textexternal analogon as the "theory of mediated reference" discloses (cf. Bühler: 385ff, esp. 390; Kallmeyer et al.: 213–29; Hellholm, 1980: 41, 94), and is consequently of a semantic-syntactic character.

2) Sentence- and text-connectors: adverbs and conjunctions
    These markers with no *analoga* in the textexternal field function *per se* only on higher grades, thus delimiting sentences and textsequences on the *micro-syntagmatic* level (Dressler: 71). However, together with markers on lower levels, these signals strengthen the delimiting function of the former.

4.2.1.3.4.   From the deliberations above on delimitation-markers, three general conclusions can be drawn:
    a) There is a direct proportionate correspondence between the inclusiveness (see 3.3.3. and 4.2.1.2, #b]) of the markers and their delimiting function: the more inclusive (pragmatic-semantic) markers distinguish *communication levels* and delimit *macro-syntagmatic* structures, while the less inclusive (syntactic) markers primarily delimit the *micro-syntagmatic* structures (see 4.1.2.).
    b) As was the case with the grouping and hierarchizations of the paradigmatic *semes/noemes* (see 3.3.3.), so it is also with the syntagmatic delimitation markers: the grouping and hierarchization into pragmatic, semantic, and syntactic groups are derived *deductively* from the meta-theory applied (Hellholm, 1980: 78–79), while the specific markers (syntagmatic *semes/noemes*) within the groups are derived *inductively* from the texts themselves, thus providing a mediation between deductive and inductive methods.[47]
    c) in order to delimit not only texts but also text-sequences in a hierarchical way, these markers are to be applied recursively on the various communication levels.

4.2.1.4.   The delimitation of the Book of Visions in the *Shepherd of Hermas* on the macro-structural level resulted in the following textsequential structure (Hellholm, 1980: 136–39; 190–96):
    1) The *first grade* of textsequences consists of two parts:
        a) the brief romance story followed by b) the main visionary part;

[47] This phenomenon is to be compared to a "vision within a vision" (cf. Brashler, *passim*, esp. 135).

2) The visionary part of the *second grade* of text-sequences is delimited into four visionary reports;

3) On the *third grade* each visionary report begins by a removal to a this-worldly place of revelation and is followed by the visionary account itself;

4) The visionary account on the *fourth grade* consists of a preparation to the vision in the form of a prayer followed by the vision itself;

5) On the *fifth grade* each vision begins with an introduction followed by a dialogue between the other-worldly revealer or messenger and the human recipient *or* by listening to *or* by copying a "Heavenly book/letter."

This hierarachical ranking of different textsequences in order to arrive at the macro-structure as conceived by the author is the second striking set of syntagmatic *semes/noemes* (see 4.2.1.1. for the first set) of the generic *sememe* (concept) "Apocalypse." I break off here since my aim was only to show how the hierarchization of textsequences on the level of macro-structures works when applied to a text belonging to the genre "Apocalypse."

4.2.2.   Let me finally turn to the Apocalypse of John and see how the embedment in communication levels and the hierarchical ranking of textsequences can be established also in this text.

4.2.2.1.   I will begin by discussing the syntagmatic *seme/noeme* that, along with the change in worlds (from this-worldly to other-worldly), is the most striking macro-syntagmatic feature of the generic concept "Apocalypse," viz., the *pragmatic embedment of communication levels.* According to the hierarchy of delimitation markers this characteristic syntagmatic feature must be elaborated upon first. It is also appropriate to begin our analysis with this *seme/noeme,* since it has to do in particular with the problem of function and the relationship between function and content, i.e., between pragmatics and semantics.

4.2.2.1.1.   In analyzing the whole of the Apocalypse of John, I have discovered many more and even much more complex levels of communication than I was able to establish for *Hermas.*

On this occasion, I will merely list the most important ones and only those levels that serve as *meta-levels* for others:

a) level *one:* between the author and the general Christian audience (1:1–3 and 22:18–19) (Bousset: 183 and 459);

b) level *two:* between the author and the more specified group of seven churches (1:4);

c) level *three:* between other-worldly mediators and the author

(Jesus himself in chaps. 1–3; angelic revealers/or Jesus Christ in the rest of the book);

d) level *four:* between the "Heavenly scroll" and the author (6:1–22:5);

e) level *five:* between the other-worldly mediators and the author within the "Heavenly scroll";

f) level *six:* between God himself on the throne and the author within the "Heavenly scroll" with the command to the author to write down the words of the Supreme Divinity (21:5–8); (cf. in 1:19, Jesus' command to John: *grapson oun ha eides kai ha eisin kai ha mellei genesthai meta tauta* and on the same level of communication Hermas 6:3: *alla gnōrison tauta ta rhēmata, ktl.*).

4.2.2.1.2. Let us now take a closer look at the most embedded text, viz., the one in 21:5–8:

> And he who sat upon the throne said: "Behold, I make all things new." Also he said: "Write this, for these words are trustworthy and true." And he said to me: "It is done! I am the Alpha and the Omega, the beginning and the end. To the thirsty I will give water without price from the fountain of the water of life. He who conquers shall have this heritage and I will be his God and he shall be my son. But as for the cowardly, the faithless, the polluted, as for murderers, fornicators, sorcerers, idolaters, and all liars, their lot shall be in the lake that burns with fire and brimstone, which is the second death. (Translation from A. Collins, 1979a: 144)

From the point of view of pragmatics this is the text in the Apocalypse of John with the most profound embedment:

a) the words quoted in writing are God's own words;

b) this statement of God is written down by the human recipient at the command of the Supreme Divinity himself;

c) this textsequence is a part of the larger sequence called the "heavenly scroll";

d) this scroll could only be opened by the lamb, Jesus Christ;

e) this scroll and the breaking of its seals were shown to the author in a vision;

f) the vision took place after a heavenly journey: vision within a journey;[47]

g) this is written down in a text of a particular generic structure: an "Apocalypse";

h) the concrete text is to be read to the congregation.

Even this *simplified* description of the embedment hierarchy is in my opinion very striking and from it *three* conclusions can be drawn:

1) the *first* conclusion has to do with *virtuality*. The parallel phenomena in the *Shepherd of Hermas* and in the *Apocalypse of John* indicate that we have to do with a characteristic feature that is not accidental and variant but, on the contrary, is constitutive and invariant; it is a *seme/noeme*. This, however, does not mean that we should expect equally deep embedments of all texts of the generic concept "Apocalypse" (see 3.2.2., #[a], with note 18), but it does mean that some kind of hierarchic communication levels must be present.

2) the *second* conclusion has to do with with *function*. In my book on *Hermas* I stated that there can be no doubt regarding the reason for the hierarchic embedment: it has to do with *authorization* of the message (Hellholm, 1980: 191 with note 3). I am prepared to make the same claim now with regard to the Apocalypse of John. This claim can furthermore be substantiated by three other circumstances:

   a) The self-definition of the Supreme Divinity on the throne: *ego eimi to alpha kai to ō, hē archē kai to telos* at the end of the heavenly scroll, functioning as an introduction to the quotation of his divine words (21:6). These words correspond to a similar self-designation at the beginning of the Apocalypse of John, viz., at the end of the epistolary prescript: *ego eimi to alpha kai to ō, legei kyrios ho theos, ho ōn kai ho ēn kai ho erchomenos, ho pantokratōr* (1:8);

   b) the assurance by God himself that his words, which John is commanded to write down are *pistoi kai alēthinoi* (21:5);

   c) the direct and programmatic statement of a hierarchic revelation embedment in the title 1:1–3: from *God*, to *Jesus Christ*, to an *angelic mediator*, to *John*, to the *readers*.[48]

   d) the letter-form as utilized by the author in 1:4 and 22:21 (see Kraft: 28; Vielhauer, 1975: 500; Müller: 600–608).

   Here I am in agreement with Prof. Stegemann, when he claims that the *authorization* is *the* characteristic functional feature of the Apocalypse (504–7).

3) The *third* conclusion: there is a direct correspondence between the communication embedment on the *pragmatic* level and the content on the *semantic* level.

   a) In *Hermas the message is on the one hand* the promise (illocution) of the possibility of a second repentance for those who

---

[48] Cf. already Bousset (1906: 181): "The prophetic character of the book is emphasized with great energy (observe the *gradation of authorities*: God, Christ, the Angel, John) and it is commanded to the (ecclesiastical) lectors and to the audience: (italics mine). This passage has been analyzed along similar lines as I have pursued in this paper in Hartman, 1980. See also Apocalypse 22:18–19, and for this passage cf. Bousset, 1906: 459–60; Hartman, 1980: 148.

repent (proposition), and *on the other* a threat (illocution) of
exclusion for those who abide in their sins (proposition). This
is in fact the summary of the lengthy book by Hermas and it is
a summary by God himself in an oath of his quoted in the
"Heavenly scroll."

b) In the *Apocalypse of John the message is on the one hand* the
promise (illocution) of those who conquer that they shall live
in unity with God in the new world of his (proposition), and *on
the other hand* the threat (illocution) that the lot of the cow-
ardly and unfaithful is ultimately separation from God described by the singular concept of a "second death"
(proposition). This constitutes the summary of the Apocalypse
of John from the lips of the Supreme Divinity on the throne.

Thus, if *one function* in connection with summaries of the
Supreme Divinity is *authorization* of the message, the other
function can be defined as the *promise* of vindication and
redemption for the faithful and the *threat* of exclusion and
death to the unfaithful.[49] Both functions are furthermore in
each instance directly related to a positive and a negative
proposition. We have to keep in mind, however, that these
functions as well as propositions work on the level of *langue* or
even *langage* and consequently must be fairly general and
abstract, while the concrete exhortations and descriptions are
given *in extenso* in the separate Apocalypses as single texts on
the level of *parole*. This conclusion is in total harmony with my
observation at the beginning of this lecture that texts are
abbreviations omitting unnecessary detail.

Thus, *pragmatics* (i.e., communication embedment and
illocutions) and *semantics* (i.e., positive and negative propositions) meet in both writings at the very center of the communication hierarchy (see note 39). This is obviously a virtual
and invariant syntagmatic *seme/noeme* which together with
other syntagmatic *semes/noemes* has to be taken seriously
when syntagmatically defining the generic concept of Apocalypses and when interpreting single texts belonging to that
genre.

---

[49] On the relationship between content and function, semantics and pragmatics, cf. Ermert
(121, with note 22): "The theme of a text must not be confused with its function or with the
intention of its producer, although there are connections between the two. The latter designates
the intended impact on account of the producer, the former the subject matter of the text."
Further, see Kallmeyer et al.: 99: "Referential text-analysis—*text-semantic*—must not be confused with *text-interpretation* . . . [which] also among other things implies a *pragmatic* analysis." Cf. also van Dijk, 1979: 578ff; Kubczak, 1978: 111 (who also distinguishes between the
semantic structure of metaphors and the *interpretation* of the same); Quasthoff: 40.

4.2.2.2.   I will conclude by outlining in a preliminary way[50] the second set of syntagmatic *semes/noemes* of the generic concept "Apocalypse," viz., the delimitation of its macrostructure into hierarchically ranked textsequences.

4.2.2.2.1.   When delimiting the text of the Apocalypse of John, the markers described above in 4.2.1.3. will be utilized. The following abbreviations are being used in this analysis:

$^{1-n}$TS = textsequences of different grades;

$^{1-n}$TS^{1-n} = several textsequences of different grades;

MS = meta communicative sentences

SM = substitution on meta-level;

SM(sur) = substitution on meta-level: surrogate;

SA = substitution on abstraction level;

CSW = change in set of worlds;

EM(a/r) loc./temp. - episodemarker (absolute/relative) local and temporal

DP = dramatis personae: changes in (grouping of) agents;

RN = renominalization.

4.2.2.2.2.   Text-delimitation

^{00}TS   *[APOKALYPSIS IŌANNOU]*

  ^{0}TS   Prologue in form of a title: Apocalypse (1:1–3)

    ^{0}TS^{1} Titulus proprius (1:1–2)

    ^{0}TS^{2} Macarism (1:3)

  ^{1}TS^{1} *Epistolary prescript* (1:4–8) [Form: epistolary address; DP: John-Seven Churches]

    ^{2}TS^{11} Address (1:4–5b)

    ^{2}TS^{12} Doxology (1:5c–6)

    ^{2}TS^{13} Motto in form of a prophetic saying (1:7)

    ^{2}TS^{14} God's self-predication (1:8)

  ^{1}TS^{2} *Visionary part:* "inner story" (1:9–22:5) [CSW: this-worldly to other-worldly; SM(sur): *egenomēn en pneumati . . . ēkousa . . . eidon;* EM(a) loc: *en tę̄ nēsǭ . . . Patmǭ;* temp.: *en tę̄ kyriakę̄ hēmerạ;* RN: *egō Iōannēs*]

    ^{2}TS^{21} *Revelation without other-worldly journey* (1:9–3:22)

      ^{3}TS^{211} Pneumatic enrapture at the place of revelation (1:9–10a)

        ^{4}TS^{2111} Situation report (1:9) [DP: John alone]

          ^{5}TS^{21111} Self-presentation (1:9a)

          ^{5}TS^{21112} Report regarding place of revelation (1:9b)

---

[50] For a more definite textlinguistic analysis of the Apocalypse of John and other apocalyptic texts, see the second volume of my studies in the *Shepherd of Hermas* (in preparation).

4TS²¹¹² Report on Pneumatic enrapture (1:10a) [DP: John-Pneuma]

3TS²¹² Revelation of the message to the Seven Churches in Asia Minor (1:10b–3:20) [SM(sur): *ēkousa . . . eidon;* EM(a) temp.: *en tē̦ kyriakē̦ hēmerā̦;* DP: John-other-worldly revealers]

4TS²¹²¹ Commissionary revelation of "one like a Son of Man" as *introduction* to the copying of the seven-fold messages (1:10b–20) [DP: John-Son of Man]

5TS²¹²¹¹ Auditory revelation (1:10b–11)

5TS²¹²¹² Visionary revelation (1:12–20)

4TS²¹²² The messages to the Seven Churches (2:1–3:22) [DP: Christ-John-Angels of the Churches-the Churches themselves]

5TS²¹²²¹ To Ephesus (2:1–7)

5TS²¹²²² To Smyrna (2:8–11)

5TS²¹²²³ To Pergamon (2:12–17)

5TS²¹²²⁴ To Thyatira (2:18–29)

5TS²¹²²⁵ To Sardis (3:1–6)

5TS²¹²²⁶ To Philadelphia (3:7–13)

5TS²¹²²⁷ To Laodicea (3:14–22)

2TS²² *Revelation with other-worldly journey* (4:1–22:5) [SM(sur): *egenomēn en pneumati . . . eidon . . . idou . . . ēkousa;* SA: *meta tauta;* EM(r) temp. *meta tauta;* RN: *hē phōnē hē prōtē hēn ēkousa hōs salpingos lalousēs met' emou;*]

3TS²²¹ Pneumatic enrapture to a place of revelation (4:1–2a)

4TS²²¹¹ Situation report in form of a vision with the purpose of producing change of revelatory location (4:1) [DP: John-*hē phōnē hē prōtē*]

5TS²²¹¹¹ Vision of the open door in heaven (4:1a)

5TS²²¹¹² Audition of the command to a heavenly journey (4:1b)

4TS²²¹² Report on Pneumatic enrapture (4:2a) [DP: John-Pneuma]

3TS²²² Revelation of "that which is to come" (4:2b–22:5) [SM(sur): *Idou . . . eidon;* EM(r) loc.: *en tō̦ ouranō̦;* DP: John-Christ]

4TS²²²¹ Throne-room revelation as an *introduction* to the revelation of the "Heavenly Scroll" (4:2b–5:14) [DP: John-Christ]

5TS²²²¹¹ Vision of Supreme Divinity (4:2b–11)

5TS²²²¹² Vision of "Heavenly Scroll"; written within and on the back, and sealed (5:1)

5TS22213   Vision of angel in search of someone worthy of opening the scroll (5:2–5)

5TS2214   Vision of the Lamb as the one worthy of opening the scroll (5:6–14)

4TS2222   The revelation of the "Heavenly Scroll" (6:1–22:5) [DP: John-"Heavenly Scroll"]

5TS22221   The summary revelation as the *scriptura exterior* (*exōthen:* 5:1) (6:1–7:17) [SM: numbering of the successive seals; SM(sur): *kai eidon;* EM(r) temp.: *hote;* DP: Christ-revealer; RN: *to arnion*]

6TS222221   Vision of the first six seals pertaining to the macro-cosmic events (6:1–17)

7TS2222111   First seal (6:1–2)

7TS2222112   Second seal (6:3–4)

7TS2222113   Third seal (6:5–6)

7TS2222114   Fourth seal (6:7–8)

7TS2222115   Fifth seal (6:9–11)

7TS2222116   Sixth seal (6:12–17)

6TS222212   Supplementary vision in form of an *intercalation* pertaining to the micro-cosmic situation of the church (7:1–14) [SA: *meta tauta;* EM(r) loc.: *meta tauta;* DP: *tessares angeloi*]

7TS2222121   Sealing of the saints on earth (7:1–8)

7TX2222122   Multitude worshipping God in heaven (7:9–14)

5TS22222   The revelation as the *scriptura interior* (*esōthen:* 5:1) (8:1–22:5) [SM: numbering of the last seal; EM(r) loc. + temp.: *egeneto sigē en tọ ouranọ hōs hēmiōrion;* DP: John—*hepta angeloi* . . . n.b. not the Lamb!]

6TS222221   Vision of the first six trumpets (8:1–11:14)

7TS2222211   Introduction (8:1–5)

8TS22222111   Opening of seventh seal (8:1) [DP: John-the Lamb]

8TS22222112   Seven angels with seven trumpets (8:2) [DP: John - *allos angelos*]

8TS22222113   Preparation in throne room for trumpet sounding (8:3–5) [DP: John-*allos angelos*]

7TS2222212   Sounding of first six trumpets with woe pertaining to macro-cosmic events (8:6–9:2) [EM(r) temp: *hētoimasen;* DP: see RN; RN: *hoi hepta angeloi* . . .]

8TS22222121 Preparation to sounding the trumpets (8:6)
8TS22222122 First trumpet (8:7)
8TS22222123 Second trumpet (8:8)
8TS22222124 Third trumpet (8:10)
8TS22222125 Fourth Trumpet (8:12)
8TS22222126 *Eagle's Woe-cry* (8:13)
8TS22222127 Fifth trumpet (9:1–11)
8TS22222128 Passing of *first woe* (9:12)
8TS22222129 Sixth trumpet (9:13–21)
6TS222222   Supplementary vision in form of an intercalation: the "Little Scroll" pertaining to the micro-cosmic situation (10:1–11:14) [SM(sur): *Kai eidon;* DP: *allos angelos ischyros*]
7TS2222221 Introductory preparation for the revelation of the "Little Scroll." (10:1–11)
7TS2222222 Content of the "Little Scroll" pertaining to the micro-cosmic situation (11:1–13) [MS:*dei se palin prophēteusai . . .* (10:11)]
7TS2222223 The passing of the *second woe* and the prediction of *third woe* (11:16)
6TS222223   Vision of the seven bowls: first part: (11:15 to 22:6) [SM: numbering of last trumpet; DP:*phōnai megalai en tǭ ouranǭ; angeloi hepta echontes plēgas hepta tas eschatas*]
7TS2222231 Introduction: first part (11:15–19)
8TS22222311 Sounding of seventh trumpet (11:15a) [DP: John-seventh angel]
8TS22222312 Preparation in the throne room for the emptying of the seven bowls (11:15b–19) [DP: John-*Phōnai megalai*]
6TS222224   Supplementary vision in form of an *intercalation pertaining to the micro-cosmic situation of the church* (12:1–14:20) [SM: *sēmeion mega;* EM(r) loc: *en tǭ ouranǭ;* DP: John-*gynē*]
7TS2222241 Vision of the woman and the Dragon (12:1–18) [DP: John-*drakōn*]
7TS2222242 Vision of the beasts from the sea and from the earth (13:1–18) [DP: John-*thēria*]
7TS2222243 Vision of the Lamb on Mount Zion (14:1–5) [DP: John-*to arnion*]
7TS2222244 Vision of the three angels (14:6–13) [DP: John-three angels]
7TS2222245 Vision of the one like a Son of Man seated

on a cloud (14:14–20) [DP: John-Son of Man]

6TS222225   Vision of the seven bowls: second part pertaining to macro-cosmic events (15:1–16:21) [SM: *eidon allo sēmeion;* EM(r) loc.: *en tǭ ouranǭ;* DP: John-*angeloi hepta echontes plēgas hepta tas eschatas . . .*]

7TS2222251   Introduction: second part (15:1–8)

7TS2222252   Emptying of the seven bowls of wrath (16:1–16) [DP: John-*phōnē megalē ek tou naou—hepta angeloi*]

8TS22222521   Command to pour out the bowls on the earth (16:1)

8TS22222522   First bowl (16:2)

8TS22222523   Second bowl (16:3)

8TS22222524   Third bowl (16:4–7)

8TS22222525   Fourth bowl (16:8–9)

8TS22222526   Fifth bowl (16:10–11)

8TS22222527   Sixth bowl (16:12–16)

8TS22222528   Seventh bowl (16:17–21)

6TS222226   Supplementary visions in form of *addendum* pertaining both to micro-cosmic situation and to macro-cosmic events (17:1–22:5) [SM: *deixō soi . . . kai eidon . . . ; EM(r) loc. + temp.: kai ēlthen . . . ;* DP: *heis ek tōn hepta angelōn . . .*]

7TS2222261   Visions pertaining to the *micro-cosmic* situation of the church (17:1–19:10) [DP: John-this-worldly churches]

8TS22222611   The judgment over Babylon by an *angelus interpres* (17:1–18)

9TS222226111   The vision (17:1–6)

9TS222226112   The interpretation (17:7–18)

8TS22222612   The Fall of Babylon (18:1–24)

8TS2222213   Celebration in Heaven (19:1–10)

7TS2222262   Visions pertaining to the *macro-cosmic* events (19:11–22:5) [DP: John-godly + anti-godly powers]

8TS22222621   The final judgment (19:11–20:15) [DP: John-Christ-Satan]

9TS222226211   The victory of the equestrian on the white horse (19:11–21)

9TS222226212   The final victory over the Dragon-Satan (20:1–10)

9TS222226213   The Book of Life and the final judg-
                ment (20:11–15)
8TS22222622   The new creation (21:1–22:5) [DP: John-
                New Heaven and Earth]
9TS222226221   New Heaven and New Earth (21:1–8)
9TS222226222   New Jerusalem revealed by an *an-
                geles interpres* (21:9–22:5)
1TS3   Epilogue in form of a visionary authentication (22:6–20) [SA:
        houtoi hoi logoi . . . hoi logoi tēs prophēteias tou bibliou toutou
        etc. throughout the epilogue; EM(r): temp: *kai hote ēkousa kai
        eblepsa;* DP: John-Christ]
    2TS31   Attestation of the book and its motto on Christ's part (22:6)
    2TS32   Verification of the seer in an epiphany (22:8–9) [RN: *kagō
            Iōannēs*]
    2TS33   Paraenesis with citation of the motto on Christ's part (22:10–
            15) [DP: Christ]
    2TS34   Christ's statement of the revelatory transmission (22:16) [RN:
            egō Iēsous.]
    2TS35   Prophetic pneumatic saying with reference to the audience
            (22:17) [DP: *to pneuma kai hē nymphē, etc.*]
    2TS36   Canonization formula on Christ's part (22:18–19) [DP:
            Christ-the audience]
    2TS37   Christ's final citation of the motto with a prophetic cultic
            response (22:20) [DP: Christ-Church]
1TS4   Epistolary postscript (22:21) [DP: John-The Churches]

4.2.2.2.3.   This attempt at a delimitation of the Apocalypse of John on
the macro-structural level resulted in the following textsequential structure:
    1) The textsequence on the *nil grade* consists of the prologue func-
       tioning as a title (see 4.2.1.3.1.; #[2][b]) and is consequently
       meta-narrative in character (cf. Hartman, 1980: 132–34).
    2) The *first grade* of textsequences consists of four text parts: a) the
       epistolary prescript (Kraft: 28; Vielhauer, 1975: 500); b) the main
       revelatory part (Hartman, 1980: 140–41; Hahn: 147–48;
       Lambrecht: 78); c) the epilogue in form of a visionary authentica-
       tion by Christ (see on 21:6: Bousset: 455; Bornkamm: 220;
       Lohmeyer: 177; Strobel: 179; Kraft: 277; Hartman, 1980: 145;
       Prigent: 351; on 21:18–19 see Strobel: 179; Moe: ad loc; Hartman,
       1980: 148; Bousset: 459; Lohmeyer: 181; Kraft: 281; Prigent: 360;
       Müller: 616–18); d) the brief epistolary postscript (cf. Kraft: 282).
    3) The visionary part is on the *second grade*, divided into two major
       revelatory events (cf. Hahn: 148–49; Lambrecht: 79–80): a) the

revelation without an other-worldly journey and b) with an other-worldly journey.[51]

4) On the *third grade* each visionary report a) begins by a pneumatic enrapture on or to the place of revelation and b) is followed by the visionary account itself.

5) The visionary accounts on the *fourth grade* consist of a) introductory revelation reports (cf. Vielhauer, 1975: 497–98) ("Commissionary revelation" and "Throne-room revelation") followed by b) the messages in written form (command to write to the seven churches; the visions contained in the Heavenly Scroll [Bornkamm; Strobel: 178]).

6) On the *fifth grade* we encounter a) the separate messages to the seven churches on the one hand and b) the summary revelation as the *scriptura exterior* and the main revelation as the *scriptura interior* on the other (Bornkamm; Strobel: 178; Yadin: 222–34; Koffmahn: 10–30).

7) The most striking feature on the *sixth grade* is the appearance of "Supplementary visions" in form of either *intercalations* within or an *addendum* to the seven-visions of seals, trumpets and bowls (Lambrecht: 95–99). This leads to the openendedness of the first two seven-rows (Lambrecht: 87). This compositional feature becomes all the more interesting when one recognizes that while the seven-visions are pertaining to macro-cosmic events, the supplementary visions that are *intercalations* pertain to the micro-cosmic situation primarily of the Church, while the supplementary vision that is an *addendum* combines macro-cosmic events with micro-cosmic situations (Vielhauer, 1975: 505; Lambrecht: 99). The micro-cosmic situation is evidently the major concern of the author and the verification of these supplementary visions lies in the macro-cosmic events. The interrelationship between macro-cosmic and micro-cosmic events is, furthermore, typical of apocalypticism in general and goes as far back as to the main features of Iranian apocalypticism (Widengren: *passim*, esp. 154–56; Olsson: 33ff; Cancik: 552–53).

4.2.2.2.4. The preliminary analysis of the Apocalypse of John given above allows us to draw three conclusions:

1) The *first conclusion* has again to do with *virtuality*. The macro-syntagmatic structure of the Apocalypse of John is indeed very similar to the macro-structure of *Hermas*. This leads me to believe

---

[51] Only at the beginning of each major section do we find the SM(sur): "I was in the Spirit," which is a clear indication of the two-fold structure of the visionary part. Cf. Müller: 603.

that we have to do with a characteristic feature that is invariant and thus possesses the status of a *seme/noeme*. This, of course, does not mean that the macro-structure needs to be identical in all texts belonging to the generic concept *(sememe)* "Apocalypse," but it does mean that the macro-structure of "Apocalypses" has to be similar in all texts defined as "Apocalypses" (see 3.2.2. #[a], esp. note 18).

2) The *second conclusion* has to do with the *interrelationship* of textsequences on different levels:
   a) When delimiting texts into textsequences, one looks for markers that separate one section or unit from another (a necessary and legitimate task);
   b) By delimiting texts into textsequences of different ranks, however, the various text-units do not stand apart from, and are not unrelated to, each other, but they are in fact linked to each other; only so is it possible to discover their interrelationship and to recognize their syntagmatic function in the overall structure of the text being analyzed.

3) The *third conclusion* has to do with *coherence* and in particular with the relationship between syntactic, semantic, and pragmatic types of coherence (Hellholm, 1980: 29–31, 37–42, 46–52). A text lacking syntactic and even semantic coherence can, from a pragmatic perspective, possess a high density of coherence (see Meeks: 701). The syntactic and semantic coherence of the Apocalypse of John seems in many cases to be lacking and can probably only be fully explained by means of *diachronic* analyses. Yet one has to admit that precisely where the semantic coherence seems to be missing, i.e., where we encounter the intercalations within and the addition to different rows of seven visions, there is a high degree of pragmatic coherence (see 4.2.2.2.3.).

This phenomenon is also typical of the *Shepherd of Hermas*. This indicates that we are dealing with an invariant and virtual syntagmatic *seme/noeme*, which (together with other *semes/noemes*) ought to be subject to serious investigation when trying to define the generic concept of an "Apocalypse" syntagmatically as well as when interpreting single texts belonging to that genre.

LIST OF WORKS CONSULTED

Albrektson, B.
   1979   "Gammaltestamentlig isagogik." Pp. 121–266 in *En bok om Gamla testamentet*. 4th ed. Ed. B. Albrektson and H. Ringgren. Lund.

Allwood, J., et al.
    1977   *Logic in Linguistics*. Cambridge Textbooks in Linguistics. Cambridge: Cambridge University Press.

Althaus, H. P., et al.
    1973   *Lexicon der Germanistischen Linguistik*. Tübingen: Niemeyer.
    1980   *Lexikon der Germanistischen Linguistik*. 2nd ed., rev. and enlarged. Tübingen: Niemeyer.

Attridge, H. W.
    1979   "Greek and Latin Apocalypses." Pp. 159–86 in J. Collins, ed.

Austin, J. L.
    1975   *How to Do Things with Words*. 2nd ed. Cambridge, MA: Harvard University Press.

Bach, K., and R. M. Harnish
    1979   *Linguistic Communication and Speech Acts*. Cambridge, MA: MIT Press.

Baldinger, K.
    1980   *Semantic Theory: Towards a Modern Semantics*. Oxford/New York: St. Martin's.

Beck, G.
    1980   *Sprechakte und Sprachfunktionen: Untersuchungen zur Handlungsstruktur der Sprache und ihren Grenzen*. Reihe Germanistische Linguistik 27. Tübingen: Niemeyer.

Berger, K.
    1974   "Apostelbrief und apostolische Rede/ Zum Formular frühchristlicher Briefe." *ZNW* 65: 190–231.

Bornkamm, G.
    1959   "Die Komposition der apokalyptischen Visionen in der Offenbarung Johannis." Pp. 204–22 in G. Bornkamm, *Studien zu Antike und Urchristentum*. Gesammelte Aufsätze, Vol. 2; BEvT 28. Munich: C. Kaiser.

Bousset, W.
    1906   *Die Offenbarung des Johannis*. MeyerK 16. Reprint, 1966. Göttingen: Vandenhoeck & Ruprecht.

Brashler, J.
    1977   *The Coptic Apocalypse of Peter: A Genre Analysis and Interpretation*. Ph.D. dissertation. Claremont.

Brinker, K.
    1983   "Textfunktionen: Ansätze zu ihrer Beschreibung." *ZGL* 11: 127–48.

Bühler, K.
    1934   *Sprachtheorie: Die Darstellungfunktion der Sprache*. Ullstein 3392. Frankfurt am Main: Klostermann.

Bultmann, R.
1928   "Evengelien, gattungsgeschichtlich (formgeschichtlich)." *RGG²*. 2: 418–22. Tübingen: Mohr.
1963   *History of the Synoptic Tradition*. Oxford/New York: Harper and Row.
1964   *Die Geschichte der synoptischen Tradition*. FRLANT 29, 6th ed. Göttingen: Vandenhoeck & Ruprecht.

Cancik, H.
1983   "Libri fatales: Römische Offenbarungsliteratur und Geschichtstheologie." Pp. 549–76 in Hellholm, ed.

Carmignac, J.
1979   "Qu'est-ce que l'Apocalyptique? Son emploi à Qumrân." *RevQ* 10: 3–33.
1983   "Description du phénomène de l'Apocalyptique dans l'Ancien Testament." Pp. 163–70 in Hellholm, ed.

Chomski, N.
1965   *Aspects of the Theory of Syntax*. Cambridge, MA: MIT Press.

Collins, A. Yarbro
1979   "The Early Christian Apocalypses." Pp. 61–121 in J. Collins, ed.
1979a   *The Apocalypse*. New Testament Message 22. Wilmington, DE: Michael Glazier.
1983   "Persecution and Vengeance in the Book of Revelation." Pp. 729–49 in Helholm, ed.
1984   *Crisis and Catharsis: The Power of the Apocalypse*. Philadelphia: Westminster.

Collins, J. J., ed.
1979   *Apocalypse: The Morphology of a Genre*. Semeia 14. Missoula: Scholars Press.

Collins, J. J.
1979a   "Introduction: Towards a Morphology of a Genre." Pp. 1–20 in J. Collins, ed.
1979b   "The Jewish Apocalypses." Pp. 21–59 in J. Collins, ed.
1981   "Apocalyptic Genre and Mythic Allusions in Daniel." *JSOT* 21: 83–100.
1982   "The Apocalyptic Technique: Setting and Function in the Book of Watchers." *CBQ* 4: 91–111.

Conzelmann, H., and A. Lindemann
1980   *Arbeitsbuch zum Neuen Testament*. Uni-Taschenbücher 52. 5th rev. ed. Tübingen: Mohr.

Coseriu, E.
1964   "Pour une sémantique diachronique structurale." *Travaux de linguistique et de la littérature* (TraLiLi) II,1: 139–86. German

trans.: Pp. 90–163, *Strukturelle Bedeutungslehre*. WdF 426. Ed. H. Geckeler. Darmstadt: Wissenschaftliche Buchgesellschaft.

1974   *Synchronie, Diachronie und Geschichte*. Internationale Bibliothek für allgemeine Linguistik 31. Munich: Fink.

1980   "Vom Primat der Geschichte." *Sprachwissenschaft* 5: 125–45.

1981   *Textlinguistik: Eine Einführung*. Tübinger Beiträge zur Linguistik, 109. Tübingen: Gunter Narr.

Davidson, D., and G. Harman, eds.

1972   *Semantics of Natural Language*. Synthese Library 40. Dordrecht/Boston: Reidel.

van Dijk, T. A., and J. S. Petöfi, eds.

1977   *Grammars and Descriptions*. Research in Text Theory/Untersuchungen in Texttheorie 1. Berlin/New York: W. de Gruyter.

van Dijk, T. A.

1977   *Text and Context: Explorations in the Semantics and Pragmatics of Discourse*. Longman Linguistics Library 21. London/New York: Longman.

1979   "New Developments and Problems in Textlinguistics." Pp. 509–23 in Petöfi, ed., 1979b.

Dressler, W.

1973   *Einführung in die Textlinguistik*. Konzepte der Sprach- und Literaturwissenschaft 13. 2nd ed. Tübingen: Niemeyer.

Dressler, W., ed.

1978   *Current Trends in Textlinguistics*. Research in Text Theory/Untersuchungen in Texttheorie 2. Berlin/New York: W. de Gruyter.

Ermert, K.

1979   *Briefsorten: Untersuchungen zu Theorie und Empire der Textklassifikation*. Reihe Germanistische Linguistik 20. Tübingen: Niemeyer.

Fallon, F. T.

1979   "The Gnostic Apocalypses." Pp. 123–54 in Collins, ed.

Fillmore, Ch. J.

1976   "Pragmatics and the Description of Discourse." Pp. 83–104 in Schmidt, ed.

Grosse, E. U.

1976   *Text und Kommunikation: Eine linguistische Einführung in die Funktionen der Texte*. Stuttgart: Kohlhammer.

1979   "Von der Satzgrammatik zum Erzähltextmodell. Linguistische Grundlagen und Differenzen bei Greimas und Bremond." Pp. 595–617 in Petöfi, ed., 1979b.

Gülich E., and W. Raible

1975   "Textsorten-Probleme." Pp. 144–97 in Moser, ed.

1977   *Linguistische Textmodelle: Grundlagen und Möglichkeiten.* Uni-
            Taschenbücher 130. Munich: Fink.

1977a   "Ueberlegungen zu einer makrostrukturellen Textanalyse: J.
            Thurber, The Lover and his Lass." Pp. 132–75 in van Dijk/
            Petöfi, eds.

Gunkel, H.
1924   "Jesaia 33, eine prophetische Liturgie. Ein Vortrag." *ZAW* 42:
            177–208.

1925   "Letter from Hermann Gunkel to Adolf Jülicher from 8 Sep-
            tember 1925." Pp. 281–86 in Rollmann.

1928   "Fundamental Problems of Hebrew Literary History." Pp. 57–
            78 in H. Gunkel, *What Remains of the Old Testament and Other
            Essays.* London/New York: Macmillan.

Hahn, F.
1979   "Zum Aufbau der Johannesoffenbarung." Pp. 145–54 in *Kirche
            und Bibel: Festgabe für Bischof Eduard Schick.* Paderborn:
            Schönigh.

Hanson, P. D.
1971   "Jewish Apocalyptic Against its Near Eastern Environment."
            RB 78: 31–58.

Harnisch, W.
1983   "Der Prophet als Widerpart und Zeuge der Offenbarung: Er-
            wägungen zur Interdependenz von Form und Sache im IV Buch
            Esra." Pp. 461–93 in Hellholm, ed.

Hartman, L.
1980   "Form and Message: A Preliminary Discussion of 'Partial Texts'
            in Rev 1–3 and 22:6ff." Pp. 129–49 in Dressler, ed.

1983   "Survey of the Problem of Apocalyptic Genre." Pp. 329–43 in
            Hellholm, ed.

Harweg, R.
1973   "Text Grammar and Literary Texts: Remarks on a Grammatical
            Science of Literature." *Poetics* 9: 65–91.

1978   "Substitution Linguistics." Pp. 247–60 in Dressler, ed.

1979   *Pronomina und Textkonstitution.* Beihefte zu Poetica 2. 2nd rev.
            and enlarged ed. Munich: Fink.

Hayes, J. H.
1980   *An Introduction to Old Testament Study.* 2nd ed. Nashville:
            Abingdon.

Heger, R.
1976   *Monem, Wort, Satz und Text.* Konzepte der Sprache-und Liter-
            aturwissenschaft 8. 2nd enlarged ed. Tübingen: Niemeyer.

1977   "Sigmenränge und Textanalyse." Pp. 260–313 in van Dijk/Petöfi, eds.

1979   "Text und Textlinguistik." Pp. 49–62 in Petöfi, ed., 1979a.

1979a   "Ungenauigkeiten in der angeblichen Ungenauigkeit sprachlicher Zeichen." Pp. 22–37 in *Festschrift Kurt Baldinger zum 60 Geburtstag; 17 Nov. 1979*. Ed. M. Höfler, et al. Tübingen: Niemeyer.

Hellholm, D.
1980   *Das Visionenbuch des Hermas als Apokalypse: Formgeschichtliche und texttheoretische Studien zu einer literarischen Gattung*. Vol. 1: Methodologische Vorüberlegungen und makrostrukturelle Textanalyse. *ConNT* 13:1. Lund: Gleerup.

1983   "Paul's Argumentation in Romans 6." In process of publication.

1984   *Makrostrukturelle Delimitationsheirarchie und kommunikative Einbettungshierarchie als gattungsspezifische Merkmale apokalyptischer Texte: Eine generische Untersuchung zu Lukian von Samosatas Ikaromenippus*. Paper read in the Seminar on the Apocalypse at the SNTS-meeting in Basel, Aug. 20–25, 1984.

Hellholm, D., ed.
1983   *Apocalypticism in the Mediterranean World and the Near East*. Proceedings of the International Colloquium on Apocalypticism, Uppsala, August 12–17, 1979. Tübingen: Mohr.

Hellwig, P.
1984   "Titulus oder über den Zusammengang von Titeln und Texten: Titel sind ein Schlüssel zur Textkonstitution." *ZGL* 12: 1–20.

Hempfer, K.
1973   *Gattungstheorie: Information und Synthese*. Uni-Taschenbücher 133. Munich: Fink.

1977   "Zur pragmatischen Fundierung der Texttypologie." Pp. 1–26 in Hinck, ed.

Hendricks, W. O.
1973   "Methodology of Narrative Structural Analysis." Pp. 175–95 in Hendricks, *Essays on Semiolinguistics and Verbal Art*. Approaches to Semiotics 37. The Hague/Paris: Mouton.

Hengel, M.
1983   "Messianische Hoffnung und politischer 'Radikalismus' in der 'jüdisch-hellenistischen Diaspora.'" Pp. 655–86 in Hellholm, ed.

Hinck, W.,. ed.
1977   *Textsortenlehre-Gattungsgeschichte*. Medium Literatur 4. Heidelberg: Winter.

Hirsch, E. D.
1967   *Validity in Interpretation*. New Haven: Yale University Press.

von Humboldt, W.
1836   *Ueber die Verschiedenheit des menschlichen Sprachbaues und ihren Einfluss auf die geistige Entwicklung des Meschengeschlechts*. Berlin: Druckerei der Koniglichen Akademie der Wissenschaften.

Husserl, E.
1970   "Zur Logik der Zeichen (Semiotik)." Pp. 340–73 in *Philosophie der Arithmetik: Logische und psychologische Untersuchungen. Mit ergänzenden Texten (1890–1901)*. Gesammelte Werke, Vol. 12. Ed. Lothar Eley. The Hague: Nijhoff.

Kallmeyer, W., et al.
1977   *Lektürekolleg zur Textlinguistik*. Band 1: Einführung. Fischer Athenäum Taschenbücher 2050. 2nd ed. Kronberg: Athenäum-Verlag.

Kallmeyer, W., and R. Meyer-Hermann.
1973   "Textlinguistik." Pp. 221–31 in Althaus et al., eds., 1973.
1980   "Textlinguistik." Pp. 242–58 in Althaus et al., eds., 1980.

Kamlah, W., and P. Lorenzen.
1973   *Logische Propädeutik: Vorschule des vernünftigen Redens*. Mannhein: Bibliographisches Institut.

Knierim, R.
1973   "Old Testament Form Criticism Reconsidered." *Int* 27: 435–67.

Koch, K.
1972   *The Rediscovery of Apocalyptic*. SBT 22. Naperville, IL: Allenson.
1983   "*Vom profetischen zum apokalyptischen Visionsbericht*." Pp. 413–46 in Hellholm, ed.

Koester, H.
1971   "One Jesus and Four Primitive Gospels." Pp. 158–204 in *Trajectories Through Early Christianity*. Eds. J. M. Robinson and H. Koester. Philadelphia: Fortress.

Koffmahn, E.
1968   *Die Doppelurkunde aus der Wüste Juda*. STDJ 5. Leiden: Brill.

Kraft, H.
1974   *Die Offenbarung Johannes*. HNT 16a. Tübingen: Mohr.

Kubczak, H.
1975   *Das Verhältnis von Intension und Extension als sprachwissenschaftliches Problem*. FbIdS 23. Tubingen: Narr.
1978   *Die Metapher: Beiträge zur Interpretation und semantischen Struktur der Metapher auf der Basis einer referentialen Bedeutungsdefinition*. Heidelberg: Winter.

1984   "Bühlers 'Symptomfunktion.'" *ZRPh* 100: 1–25.

von Kutschera, F.
1975   *Philosophy of Language.* Synthese Library 71. Dordrecht/
Boston: D. Reidel.

Lambrecht, J., ed.
1980   *L'Apocalypse johannique et l'Apocalyptique dans le Nouveau
Testament.* BETL 53. Louvain: University Press.

Lambrecht, J.
1980   "A Structuration of Revelation 4:1–22:5." Pp. 77–104 in
Lambrecht, ed.

Lausberg, H.
1973   *Handbuch der literarischen Rhetorik: Ein Grundlegung der
Literaturwissenschaft.* 2nd enlarged ed. Munich: Hueber.

Lewis, D.
1972   "General Semantics." Pp. 169–218 in Davidson/Harman, eds.

Lohmeyer, E.
1953   *Die Offenbarung des Johannes.* HNT 16. 2nd enlarged ed.
Tübingen: Mohr.

MacRae, G. W.
1983   "Apocalyptic Eschatology in Gnosticism." Pp. 317–325 in
Hellholm, ed.

Meeks, W. A.
1983   "Social Functions of Apocalyptic Language in Pauline Christianity." Pp. 687–705 in Hellholm, ed.

Menne, A.
1973   *Einführung in die Logik.* Uni-Taschenbücher 34. 2nd ed.
Munich: Francke.

Moe, O.
1963   *Johannes Uppenbarelse: Bibelns sista bok.* Tolkning av Nya Testamentet 11. Stockholm: Diakomstyrelsens.

Moser, H., ed.
1975   *Linguistische Probleme der Textanalyse.* Jahrbuch des Instituts
für deutsche Sprache 35. Dusseldorf: Pädagogischer Verlag Sch-
wamm.

Müller, U. B.
1983   "Literarische und formgeschichtliche Bestimmung der Apokalypse des Johannes als einem Zeugnis früchristlicher
Apokalyptik." Pp. 599–619 in Hellholm, ed.

Olsson, Tord.
1983   "The Apocalyptic Activity: The Case of Jāmāsp Nāmag." Pp. 21–
49 in Hellholm, ed.

Petöfi, J. S., ed.
1979a   *Text vs Sentence: Basic Questions of Textlinguistics, First Part.*

Papiere zur Textlinguistik/Papers in Textlinguistics, 20,1. Hamburg: Buske.

1979b   *Text vs Sentence: Basic Questions of Textlinguistics, Second Part.*
         Papiere zur Textlinguistik/Papers in Textlinguistics, 20,2. Hamburg: Buske.

Piaget, J.
1970   *Structuralism.* New York: Harper and Row.

Plett, H.
1975   *Einführung in die rhetorische Textanalyse.* 2nd ed. Hamburg: Buske.

Plett, H., ed.
1977   *Rhetorik: Kritische Positionen zum Stand der Forschung.* Kritische Information 50. Munich: Fink.

Plett, H.
1977a   "Die Rhetorik der Figuren: Zur Systematik, Pragmatik und Asthetik der 'Elocutio.'" Pp. 125–65 in Plett, ed.

Prigent, P.
1981   *L'Apocalypse de Saint Jean.* CNT 14. Lausanne/Paris: Delachaux & Niestle.

Quasthoff, U.
1980   *Erzählen in Gesprachen.* Kommunikation und Institution 1. Tübingen: Narr.

Raible, W.
1972   *Satz und Text: Untersuchungen zu vier romanischen Sprachen.* Beihefte zur Zeitschrift für die romanische Philologie 132. Tübingen: Niemeyer.

1979a   "Gattungen als Textorten." Unpublished paper. The author kindly provided the present writer with a copy. For this favor I hereby express my sincere gratitude.

1979b   "Zum Textbegriff und zur Textlinguistik." Pp. 63–76 in Petöfi, ed. 1979a.

1981   "Von der Allgegenwart des Gegensinns (und einiger anderer Relationen): Strategien zur Einordnung semantischer Information." *ZRPh* 97: 1–40.

Robinson, J. M.
1971   "LOGOI SOPHON: On the Gattung of Q." Pp. 71–113 in *Trajectories Through Early Christianity.* Ed. J. M. Robinson and H. Koester. Philadelphia: Fortress.

Rollman, H.
1981   "Zwei Briefe Hermann Gunkels an Adolf Jühlicher zur religionsgeschichtlichen und formgeschichtlichen Methode." *ZTK* 78:276–88.

Rosengren, I.
    1980   "Texttheorie." Pp. 275–86 in Althaus et al., ed.

Sanders, E. P.
    1983   "The Genre of Palestinian Jewish Apocalypses." Pp. 447–59 in
                Hellholm, ed.

de Saussure, F.
    1916   *Cours de linguistique générale.* Geneva: Georg.

Schenk, W.
    1984   *Die Philipperbriefe des Paulus.* Stuttgart: W. Kohlhammer.

Schmidt, S. J.
    1973   "Texttheorie, Pragmalinguistik." Pp. 233–44 in Althaus et al.,
                eds.

Schmidt, S. J., ed.
    1976   *Pragmatik/Pragmatics 2: Zur Grundlegung einer expliziten Prag-
                matik.* Kritische Information 23. Munich: Fink.

Schnelle, H.
    1973   *Sprachphilosophie   und   Linguistik: Prinzipien   der
                Sprachanalyse a priori und a posteriori.* Rororo Studium 30.
                Reinbek/Hamburg: Rowahlt.

Seiler, H.
    1960   *Relativstaz, Attribut und Apposition.* Wiesbaden: O. Har-
                rassowitz.

Smith, J. Z.
    1975   "Wisdom and Apocalyptic." Pp. 131–56 in *Religious Syncretism
                in Antiquity: Essays in Conversation with Geo Widengren.* Ed.
                B. A. Pearson. Missoula: Scholars Press.

Sökeland, W.
    1980   *Indirektheit von Sprechhandlung: Eine linguistische Unter-
                suchung.* Reihe Germanistische Linguistik 26. Tübingen:
                Niemeyer.

Stegemann, H.
    1983   "Die Bedeutung der Qumranfunde für die Erforschung der
                Apokalyptik." Pp. 495–530 in Hellholm, ed.

Stone, M.
    1976   "Lists of Revealed Things in the Apocalyptic Literature."
                Pp. 414–52 in *Magnalia Dei: The Might Acts of God: Essays on
                the Bible and Archaeology in Memory of G. E. Wright.* Ed.
                F. M. Cross, et al. Garden City: Doubleday.

Stempel, W.-D.
    1971   "Pour une description des genres littéraires." Pp. 565–70 in
                *Acele celui de-al XII-lea congres international de ligvistică si
                filologie romanică.* Vol. II. Bucharest.

Strobel, A.
1978   "Apokalypse des Johannes." Pp. 174–89 in *Theologische Real-enzyklopädie (TRE)*. Vol. III. Berlin/New York: De Gruyter.

Theissen, G.
1971   *Ergänzungsheft to Rudolf Bultmann: Die Geschichte der synoptischen Tradition*. Göttingen: Vandenhoeck & Ruprecht.

Ullmann, S.
1962   *Semantics: An Introduction to the Science of Meaning*. Oxford: Blackwell.

Vielhauer, P.
1965   "Apocalypses and Related Subjects: Introduction." Pp. 581–607 in *New Testament Apocrypha*. Vol. II. Ed. E. Hennecke, et al. Philadelphia: Westminster.
1975   *Geschichte der urchristlichen Literatur: Einleitung in das Neue Testament, die Apokryphen und die Apostolischen Väter*. De Gruyter Lehrbuch. Berlin/New York: De Gruyter.

Widengren, G.
1983   "Leitende Ideen und Quellen der iranischen Apokalyptik." Pp. 77–162 in Hellholm, ed.

Wunderlich, D.
1979   *Foundations of Linguistics*. Cambridge Studies in Linguistics 22. Cambridge: Cambridge University Press.

Yadin, Y.
1971   *Bar-Kokhba: The Rediscovery of the Legendary Hero of the Last Jewish Revolt Against Imperial Rome*. New York: Random House.

Zimmermann, K.
1978   *Erkundigungen zur Texttypologie*. Tübingen: Narr.

THE APOCALYPSE OF JOHN AND THE PROBLEM OF GENRE[1]

David E. Aune

Saint Xavier College, Chicago

ABSTRACT

During the last few years several important contributions have been made to the problem of defining the apocalyptic genre. These include the contribution of the SBL Apocalypse Group, chaired by J. J. Collins, the work of D. Hellholm, and several papers read at the International Colloquium on Apocalypticism held in Uppsala in 1979. After a summary of these contributions, some of the distinctive characteristics of ancient literature are discussed to illustrate the existence of significant qualitative differences between ancient and modern literary assumptions and procedures. The areas discussed include orality and textuality, the relationship between the whole and the part and the connections between literature and cult. It is also argued that apocalypses (extended vision reports), are a distinctive type of religious literature which must be understood in light of texts usually associated with ancient revelatory magic, and in light of the "reveal/conceal" dialectic characteristic of revelatory literature. Apocalypses are generically described in terms of form, content and function in a manner intended to synthesize previous contributions to the discussion. In *form*, an apocalypse is an autobiographical prose narrative reporting revelatory visions experienced by the author and structured to emphasize the central revelatory message. The *content* of an apocalypse is the communication of a transcendent, often eschatological, perspective on human experience. In *function*, an apocalypse legitimates the transcendent authority of the message by mediating a new revelatory experience for the audience to encourage them to modify

[1]The original version of this paper was presented to the SBL Seminar on Early Christian apocalypticism on December 19, 1983 in Dallas, Texas. A number of suggestions made by Hans Dieter Betz, the main respondent, and Adela Yarbro Collins (the chair of the Seminar) as well as other members of the Seminar have been incorporated into this version of the paper.

their cognition and behavior in conformity with transcendent
perspectives.

I. Approaching the Problem of Genre

Genre criticism is that aspect of comparative literature which attempts to understand literary works in relation to one another, both
diachronically and synchronically. A literary genre consists of a group of
texts which exhibit a coherent and recurring pattern of features constituted by the interrelated elements of form, content and function.[2]
Satisfactory definitions and descriptions of particular genres are rare, not
only because there has been so little agreement among literary critics
regarding which specific literary qualities are generically significant, but
also because of the diversity of perspective brought to specific types of
texts by scholars. The notion of "genre" has for the most part been based
on intuitive or phenomenological judgments that particular groups of
texts have closer affinities with each other than with texts which appear to
belong to other groups. Consequently definitions of genres exhibit wide
differences. In a useful article summarizing modern theoretical discussion of the problem of genre W. G. Doty concludes:

> Generic definitions ought not be restricted to any one particular
> feature (such as form, content, etc.), but they ought to be widely
> enough constructed to allow one to conceive of a genre as a
> congeries of (a limited number of) factors. The cluster of traits
> charted may include: authorial intention, audience expectancy,
> formal units used, structure, use of sources, characterizations,
> sequential action, primary motifs, institutional setting, rhetorical
> patterns, and the like. (439–40)

Although this synthesis of possible generic features represents the state
of genre research a decade ago, its very lack of specificity and systemic
integrity militates against its usefulness. At this point in research, it
appears that real progress will be made only through the careful generic
analysis of individual members of affiliated texts. The first part of the
discussion below focuses on recent research on the apocalyptic genre, an
area in which important strides have been made in the last decade. The
second section argues that significant qualitative differences between
ancient literature and modern (western) literature should make critics
wary of forcing ancient texts to conform to modern expectations. The
third part of the paper suggests that by their very nature ancient apoc-

---

[2]The necessity of defining a particular genre in terms of form, content and function is argued
persuasively by D. Hellholm. "The Problem of Apocalyptic Genre and the Apocalypse of John,"
(SBLASP, 1982), 157–63.

alypses exhibit a special literary character which necessitates a consideration of related revelatory genres as well as the phenomenology of ancient
revelatory experience, and part four proposes a definition of the apocalyptic genre.

Before moving into the first part of the discussion two important
preliminary points need to be made. First, the conception of "mixed
genres" is theoretically infelicitous and should be used only as a court of
last resort, for if the notion of a *mixtum compositum* is too quickly applied
to a problematic text, the possibility of achieving a generic understanding
of the structure of the entire text is given up without a struggle. Second,
the three-fold distinction between "apocalypses" (as literature), "apocalyptic eschatology" (as a world view), and "apocalypticism" (as a socio-
religious movement) proposed recently by a number of scholars is an
important step forward in the discussion of the genre of apocalypses and
should be retained (Stone: 439–42; Hanson: 29–31). It can no longer be
assumed that apocalypses were produced by apocalyptic groups who
espoused a distinctive type of apocalyptic eschatology. The central concern of the writers of apocalypses was not apocalyptic eschatology so
much as speculative knowledge generally, in which cosmology figured
prominently (Stone; Rowland, 1983: 49–72). It is therefore critically
important to derive the content of the apocalypses, not from an external
conception of apocalyptic eschatology, but rather from the study of the
texts considered "apocalypses" themselves.

II. Recent Research on the Genre of Apocalypses

In a paper published in 1976, M. E. Stone observed:

> Recent years have not seen any particularly great advances in the
> study of the apocalypses as a genre, although criticism of various
> individual works has been advanced at diverse points. (439)

That assessment is no longer accurate. First, the work of the Society
of Biblical Literature's Apocalypse Group, part of the SBL Genres Project, published the results of its collaborative research in Volume 14 of
Semeia (1979), edited by the Group's chairman John J. Collins, with the
title: "Apocalypse: The Morphology of a Genre." Second, the International Colloquium on apocalypticism, held in Uppsala in 1979, consisted
of thirty-four papers (twelve on the problem of genre), published under
the editorship of David Hellholm with the title *Apocalypticism in the
Mediterranean World and the Near East*. Third, there is the significant
work of David Hellholm himself, first in his published Uppsala dissertation (1980), and more recently his paper on "The Problem of Apocalyptic
Genre and the Apocalypse of John" discussed in the SBL Seminar on

Early Christian apocalypticism in 1982 in New York and included in this volume. Since all of these contributions to the discussion were made (or appeared) between 1979 and 1983, there has not been a sufficient interval for the contributors to interact critically with each other, or for their work to be assessed adequately by a broader spectrum of scholarship. In this section of the paper, I propose both to summarize and assess critically the contributions of J. J. Collins and D. Hellholm and then to point out some of the more significant contributions to the discussion made by participants in the 1979 International Colloquium on apocalypticism.

1. *The Proposal of J. J. Collins*

Professor Collins has formulated a definition of the genre apocalypse which consists of what he considers the constant or invariable features of the genre:

> "Apocalypse" is a genre of revelatory literature with a narrative framework, in which a revelation is mediated by an otherworldly being to a human recipient, disclosing a transcendent reality which is both temporal, insofar as it envisages eschatological salvation, and spatial insofar as it involves another, supernatural world. (1979a:9)

Although the core elements of the genre are described in this definition, no specific apocalypse, Collins claims, can be understood properly without reference to a master paradigm which he has constructed, consisting of a lengthy list of the constituent features of apocalypses, divided into the following major categories, each of which describes an aspect of the form or content of apocalypses: (1) Manner of Revelation (i.e., form), (2) Content: Temporal Axis (i.e., content), (3) Content: Spatial Axis (i.e., content), (4) Paraenesis (i.e., content), and (5) Concluding Elements (i.e., form). Further, in addition to the core definition and the master paradigm of elements which are frequently, but not always, found in individual apocalypses, Collins proposes two main types of apocalypses, those with and those without an otherworldly journey (Types I and II respectively). Each type may be further specified by one of three features: (a) Those with a historical review, (b) Those with cosmic or political eschatology, and (c) Those with only personal eschatology.

This definition, master paradigm and typological grouping focus on the generic dimensions of *form* and *content*. On the relationship of the dimension of function to generic definition, Collins observes:

> Further, while a complete study of a genre must consider function and social setting, neither of these factors can determine the definition. At least in the case of ancient literature our knowledge of function and setting is often extremely hypothetical and cannot

provide a firm basis for generic classification. The only firm basis
which can be found is the identification of recurring elements
which are explicitly present in the texts. (1979a:1–2)

While this description of the genre apocalypse is probably the most
complete and systematic attempt to define the genre at the pragmatic
level, it has not gone without criticism. David Hellholm, for example,
who insists that the three dimensions of form, content and function must
be integrated for a successful definition of a given genre (Hellholm,
1982:167; in this volume: 26), accepts Collins' definition (as a paradigmatically established definition), but proposes adding a statement dealing with *function:* "intended for a group in crisis with the purpose of
exhortation and/or consolation by means of divine authority" (1982:168; in
this volume: 27). Further, Hellholm claims that while Collins himself has
properly presented a hierarchization of recurring features of apocalypses
(designated *semes/noemes* by Hellholm) in his master paradigm, he has
failed to carry this insight out in practice. Although Hellholm's insistence
on including the element of function is well-taken, I think he is wrong in
claiming that Collins' master paradigm is hierarchically arranged, so that
when he criticizes Collins for hierarchical inaccuracies in his paradigm he
criticizes him for what he did not set out to do. Collins' master paradigm
is only "hierarchically arranged" in the sense that it is in outline form,
and the function of an outline, with its infinite capacity for subordination,
is by definition "hierarchic."

Both Lars Hartman and E. P. Sanders have criticized Collins' proposal from different perspectives. Hartman lists four groups of genre
constituents: (1) linguistic/stylistic constituents, (2) propositional constituents, (3) illocutionary features, and (4) socio-linguistic function (329–43),
and claims that all the elements of Collins' master paradigm belong to the
category of propositional constituents. Hartman thinks that in dealing
with propositional constituents one must not only consider such features
as plot, themes and motifs (as Collins does), but also take into consideration the hierarchic structure and literary interrelations of those elements.
Another critic of Collins' proposals is E. P. Sanders, who discusses the
difficulties of regarding "genre" as a term appropriate for entire literary
works when applied to texts which are compiled (447–59). Thus, he
points out, Collins does not consider *1 Enoch* 91–104 an apocalypse, even
though the other sections of 1 Enoch are so categorized. Similarly, claims
Sanders, Collins considers only *Jubilees* 23 an apocalypse, while other
scholars (notably J. Carmignac) consider the entire document an apocalypse. He concludes that "a lot of the material is left out of the description. The questions of the whole and the parts and of composite works
still leave problems for students of genre" (454). Sanders further criticizes
Collins by noting the fact that the definition of what ought to constitute

the basic elements in defining a genre proposed by W. G. Doty, part of which is quoted above (413–48), has little relationship to the elements included by Collins (Sanders: 454–55). However, this criticism erroneously assumes that Doty's synthesis of generically salient literary features is anything more than an eclectic summary of possibilities.

In sum, Collins' proposals represent an important step forward in research on the genre of ancient apocalypses, though two problematic features have surfaced: the problem of the *function* of the genre, and the problem of the hierarchical arrangement of various generically salient literary features of apocalypses. Further, despite the comprehensive character of Collins' definition, it remains inductive and descriptive. Thus is cannot deal with the virtualities or potentialities of the apocalyptic genre and shows little hermeneutical promise.

2. The Proposal of David Hellholm

The work of David Hellholm, mentioned above, constitutes another important step forward in genre research generally, and may provide a complement to the work of John J. Collins. Hellholm utilizes text-linguistic methodology, particularly as developed in Germany during the past two decades. His discussions and analyses are exceedingly complex, but the results are so important that New Testament scholars should become aware of his work and its implications. Hellholm is fully cognizant that language has paradigmatic as well as syntagmatic relations (i.e., form as well as content must be considered), and so he insists that the paradigmatic approach to defining the genre of apocalypses be supplemented by a syntagmatic approach (1982: 172; in this volume: 33). Hellholm must make this concession since formal linguistic structures (syntagmatics) *have no intrinsic meaning* (pragmatics), and it is difficult to imagine a generic definition which ignored text-pragmatics.

In this macro-syntagmatic approach to the analysis of generic structures, Hellholm proposes two necessary and complementary steps in text analysis: (1) Division of the text into hierarchically arranged communication levels (the text-pragmatic aspect), and (2) Division of the text into hierarchical textsequences (the text-semantic aspect). The communication levels are of two types, those external to the text (between the sender and receiver, author and readers), and those internal to the text (between *dramatis personae*). Textsequences are signalled by several types of markers: (a) changes in "world" (this world; other world), (b) episode markers indicating time and change of time, localization and relocalization, (c) changes in grouping of actors, (d) renominalization (an actor referred to by a pronoun is reintroduced with a noun or name), (e) adverbs and conjunctions which relate clauses to each other. The identification of communication levels and textsequences together constitute the generic structures of the text.

Hellholm has analyzed two apocalypses in this way, the *Shepherd of Hermas* (*Vis.* 1–4) in great detail,[3] and Revelation in considerably less detail. For *Herm. Vis.* 1–4, Hellholm proposes six levels of communication (from lowest to highest), excluding the title: (1) Between author and addressees, (2a) Between mediators of revelation and author, (2b) Between the bearers of revelation and addressees, (3) Between quotations from revealed books in the text and author, (3a) Between quotations from revealed books in the text and addressees, (4) Between the quoted saying of God and a quoted apocryphal prophetic book and addressees (1980: 190–91). The texts which constitute the highest communication level are the most profoundly embedded texts in the apocalypse. Hellholm's next complementary step, the hierarchical ranking of textsequences, produces a scheme in five "grades," extending from the general to the particular (1980: 190–96):

1. Introductory narrative
    Main visionary part
2.   Four vision reports
3.   Movement to place of this-worldly revelation
          Vision account
4.   Preparation for vision
              Vision
5.   Dialogue between revealer and human recipient
                  Listening to or copying heavenly book/letter

Hellholm shows that the most embedded text on the communication level coincides with the location of the same embedded text at the fifth, or highest, grade of the textsequential structure. The most embedded texts in *Herm. Vis.* 1–4 which Hellholm has identified are *Herm. Vis.* 2.2.5 and 2.3.4:

> (For the Master has sworn to his elect by his glory that) if there is still sin after this day has been fixed, they shall find no salvation; for repentance for the just has an end; the days of repentance have been fulfilled for all the saints, but for the heathen repentance is open until the last day.

> The Lord is near those that turn to him, (as it is written in the book of Eldad and Modat, who prophesied to the people in the wilderness). (*LCL* translation)

Hellholm proposes that the function of this hierarchical embedment is the *authorization* of the message, and it is true that the first passage

---

[3] Hellholm (1980:11–13) regards these four visions as constituting a unified apocalypse; the fifth vision is judged a redactional introduction to the *Man.*.

constitutes a clear expression of the central message of *Hermas*. He promises to discuss the genre of *Hermas* and the interpretation of specific texts in a forthcoming volume. Further, he intends to present an analysis of the levels of the macro-structure and functional communcation levels of other apocalyptic texts (1980: 197).

Yet some of Hellholm's conclusions are available, if only in a preliminary way in connection with his discussion of the genre of the Apocalypse of John in comparison with the earlier analysis of the *Shepherd of Hermas*. In presenting his analysis of the hierarchical communication levels in the Apocalypse of John, Hellholm proposes six such levels or grades (1982: 181; in this volume: 43–44):

1. Prologue functioning as a title
2.   Epistolary prescript
     Main revelatory part
     Epilogue in form of a visionary authentication by Christ
     Brief Epistolary postscript
3.   Revelation without an other-worldly journey
       Revelation with an other-worldly journey
4.   Pneumatic enrapture
         Visionary account itself
5.   Introductory revelation reports
           Messages in written form
6.   Separate message to the seven churches
             Summary revelation as *scriptura*
               exterior and the main revelation as
               scriptura interior

As in the case of *Herm. Vis.* 1–4, Hellholm finds that the text most profoundly embedded at the functional communication level coincides with the sixth, or highest, grade of the macro-structure of the Apocalypse of John. This text is Rev 21:5–8, a passage which expresses the book's central message:

> And he who sat upon the throne said, "Behold, I make all things new." Also he said, "Write this, for these words are trustworthy and true." And he said to me, "It is done! I am the Alpha and the Omega, the beginning and the end. To the thirsty I will give water without price from the fountain of the water of life. He who conquers shall have this heritage, and I will be his God and he shall be my son. But as for the cowardly, the faithless, the polluted, as for murderers, fornicators, sorcerers, idolaters, and all liars, their lot shall be in the lake that burns with fire and brimstone, which is the second death. (RSV translation)

In comparing his analyses of the Apocalypse of John and the *Shepherd of Hermas*, Hellholm claims that the phenomenon of embedment is a constitutive and invariant feature of the apocalyptic genre and that while equally deep embedments in other apocalypses cannot be expected, ". . . it does mean that some kind of hierarchic communication levels must be present" (1982: 182; in this volume: 45). In both apocalypses the most deeply embedded level of communication coincides with the highest grade of hierarchically ranked text sequences (1982: 188–89; in this volume: 52–53).

Hellholm's syntagmatic approach to the description of generically salient features of ancient apocalypses is a methodologically sophisticated generic analysis of both the Apocalypse of John and the *Shepherd of Hermas* which has yielded some striking results. Hellholm's demonstration of the existence of parallel phenomena in the macro-structures of both texts suggests that he has made an important contribution to our knowledge of these texts as well as of the genre of ancient apocalypses generally. There are a number of issues which must be raised in connection with some of his proposals, however. The most obvious problem concerns the comparative nature of genre criticism. One or two syntagmatic analyses, striking though they may be in their convergences, cannot be generalized to include all the texts of that type until all (or at least many) have been syntagmatically analyzed. This is Hellholm's ultimate intention, but whether the results will support his claims regarding the two apocalypses he has already analyzed remains to be seen. Further, texts which are *not* commonly regarded as "apocalypses" must also be subject to syntagmatic analysis, for comparisons can be made confidently only when contrasts are clearly drawn as well.

A second problem lies in the relationship between paradigmatic and syntagmatic definitions of the apocalyptic genre. If the paradigmatic model must be supplemented by syntagmatic analysis (as Hellholm insists), what is the precise relationship between these two approaches to formulating a generic definition of apocalypses? This issue will be taken up again below, for one of the purposes of this paper is the integration of the results of Hellholm's syntagmatic analysis within the framework of a paradigmatic description of the apocalyptic genre.

Yet a third problematic area is the matter of determining just what degree of embedment and what degree of hierarchically arranged partial texts should be regarded as constitutive for the apocalyptic genre. Any ancient text which recounts a visionary experience within which statements by a revealer or a dialogue occur will exhibit several grades of embedment. In the NT this phenomenon is found not only in Revelation but also in the gospels, Acts and letters as well (e.g., 2 Cor 12). By way of illustration, let me propose a preliminary analysis of one of the acts of the martyrs not normally considered an apocalyptic text, the *Martyrdom of Perpetua and Felicitas*.[4] Excluding the title, this text exhibits three levels of communication: (1) Between the author and the addressees, (2) Between the martyrs and the addressees, and (3) Between the principal figures in the visions and the martyrs. In attempting to rank partial texts in a hierarchical series of grades, I propose the following levels (with references in parentheses):

1. Prologue (1)
   Narrative introduction (2)
   Visionary part (3–13)
   Narrative conclusion (14:1–21:10)
   Epilogue (21:11)
2.   Revelation without an otherworldly journey
      Revelation with an otherworldly journey
3.   Five vision reports (4:1–10; 7:1–10; 7:11–8:4;
            10:1–12; 11:1–13:8)
         Narrative interludes (3:1–9; 5:1–6:8; 9:1–3)
4.   Autobiographical written vision reports
5.   Prayer preceding vision
               Vision report
               Explication of vision

In this analysis the fifth grade of hierarchically arranged text sequences coincides with the third level of communication, yet this phenomenon occurs frequently within the text at no apparently significant junctures. Despite the tentative nature of this analysis, two mutually exclusive observations can be made: either this analysis suggests that the syntagmatic analysis which Hellholm regards as constitutive for apocalypses is also exhibited in other types of ancient texts, or, the *Martyrdom of Perpetua and Felicitas* should be regarded as belonging to the apocalyptic genre.

3. *Relevant Contributions from the Uppsala Colloquium*.

Four of the twelve essays in the section entitled "The Literary Genre of Apocalypses" in the volume of the Uppsala Colloquium proceedings are particularly relevant to the present discussion. The essays by

[4] This text is not considered in the survey of early Christian apocalypses by A. Y. Collins: 61–121. The omission of this text from consideration is based on Professor Collins' view (expressed at the Seminar mentioned in note 1), that a supernatural revealer, a necessary feature of apocalypses, is missing. This phenomenon, however, is present in the fifth vision report (11:1–13:8), though not in the first four vision reports. Professor Collins also regards apocalypses as first-person reports of revelatory experiences; since the author of the *Martyrdom* is relating the visionary experiences of *others* the work is not an apocalypse. Musurillo (xxv) regards the composition as an apocalypse.

Hartman and Sanders have already been discussed briefly above. The essay by John J. Collins also makes an important contribution to the discussion (1983). Reiterating the definition discussed above, he focuses on 2 (Slavonic) *Enoch*, 3 (Greek) *Baruch* and the *Testament of Abraham* (Rec. A, 10–15; Rec. B, 8–12). He concludes that the function of 2 *Enoch* is hortatory, 3 *Baruch* gives a perspective on the fall of Jerusalem minimizing its importance in the light of an individualized eschatology, and the *Testament of Abraham* gives a perspective on death in light of God's mercy. All, however, have a significant parenetic aspect. Collins makes the following generalization

> The coherence of these works does not lie in their precise function, but in their underlying conceptual structure: the belief in another, heavenly, world, already existing and in a definite judgment of every individual after death. This structure constitutes the premises for more specific argument. (1983:544)

While only 3 *Baruch* can be related to a political crisis, all the texts appeal to transcendent reality as the most profound reality and as the final goal of humanity. The universalism of these apocalypses suggests that they cannot be identified with the sectarian views of particular conventicles.

In another significant essay, Hans Dieter Betz examines the literary sources on the ancient oracle of Trophonius and shows how afterlife mythology exerted an increasingly strong influence on accounts of consultations (1983:577–97). Betz proposes that the oracular dialogue, or *erotapokrisis*, found in literary accounts of consultations, developed from simpler oracular inquiries. In Plutarch's *De genio Socratis* 589F-592E, the story *(mythos)* of Timarchus' inquiry at the oracular grotto of Trophonius (his descent-and-return reflects the death-and-rebirth experience of mystery initiations) is preceded by a *logos* and concluded by a paraenetic interpretation of the *mythos*. Betz shows that an elaborate underworld mythology, influenced by Orphic-Pythagorean mythology, had become attached to many Greek oracles. Betz observes that *mythos* refers to a specific literary genre attested in Plato and thereafter only fragmentarily until it reappears in Plutarch (1983:585–95). In Plato, *mythos* has a particular nature and function: (1) *Mythos* can do what *logos* cannot do, namely, speak of matters beyond the human world in human language. (2) The notion of the immortality of the soul, impossible to deal with in rational speech, "requires a confrontation with the destiny of one's own soul, and to bring this about is the purpose of *mythos*" (1983:588). (3) The experience of fear, generated by the *mythos* (including, e.g., the punishment of the wicked in the underworld), motivates people to live good lives. (4) "Like a magical charm the *mythos* must be

told again and again" (1983:588). Plutarch's eschatological myths, argues
Betz, are representative of the genre *mythos* at the end of the first
century A.D., and the changes since Plato lie primarily in the areas of:
(1) the increasing influence of Orphic-Pythagorean netherworld mythology, (2) the growing importance of cosmic visions, and (3) recent
developments in ideas about the soul, divination and supernatural
beings. *Mythos* is oracular narrative which stimulates man to explore its
meaning. For Plutarch eschatological myths, which must be allegorically
interpreted, function in several ways: (1) They explain the cause of conversion (here the case is Aridaeus-Thespesius in *De sera num. vind.*
563Bff.), and confront the hearer with the ancient notion that "responsibility belongs to the chooser; God is not responsible" (Plato *Rep.*
10.617E). (2) The shock-like experience of fear motivates man to live a
good life. (3) *Mythos* produces the correct view of the gods, i.e., faith,
while *logos* has functioned to awaken rational thought in the soul.

III. Special Features of Ancient Mediterranean Literature

Modern analyses of ancient texts usually proceed under the assumption that literature, particularly "good" literature, possesses certain
essential qualities which transcend the specific culture and circumstances of its origin and reflect matters universal to human experience.
On that basis, literary critical methods and perspectives which "work"
with modern literature are automatically assumed to apply to ancient
texts as well. But when an entire period in the history of Greco-Roman
literary culture (the second century A.D.), can be labeled "mediocre"
and "decadent," it is readily apparent that modern tastes and perspectives have precluded a sympathetic understanding and evaluation of
ancient literature (Van Groningen: 41-56). The scholarship of Peter Brown
has done much to rescue late antiquity from such pejorative labels and
shown it instead to be an era of remarkable cultural change and
creativity. Further, dramatic differences between archaic and modern
society and thought have been amply demonstrated in the work of Moses
I. Finley on ancient economy and democracy (ix–xxvi). Models based on
modern assumptions, when applied to ancient society and culture, may
serve to mask the distinctive features of ancient life and thought. The
purpose of this section is to suggest that the problem of the genre of
ancient texts must be approached in a manner sensitive to the ancient
cultural systems which such literature reflects. Four major areas of
concern involve the problem of orality and textuality (involving the
relationships between literature and rhetoric and texts and performance),
the relationship between the whole and the part in literary texts, and the
possible connections between literature and religious cults.

1. *Orality and Textuality*

Literature and rhetoric were so closely connected in the ancient world that many modern assumptions about the nature of ancient texts are misleading. It can be said, without exaggeration, that "all classical Greek authors composed for the ear" (Stanford: 4). The numerous (and entertaining) excurses in the first six books of Herodotus' *History of the Persian Wars*, for example, appear to be included precisely because the author wrote with the intention of public recitation, and indeed polished his material by delivering the same lectures many times.[5] Further, Thucydides' reliance upon speeches as a primary means for understanding the motivations of great men and their role in influencing historical events is scarcely conceivable in isolation from the great development in rhetoric and oratory in the Athens of his day. The dramatic effect created by the oral performance of these works, using first-person narratio, capitalized on the illusion of the author's actual presence (Fornara: 31, 130; Plutarch *De gloria Ath.* 347A-B). Ancient authors normally composed aloud (Balogh: 213), and the advice of Dio Chrysostom (end of first, beginning of second centuries A.D.) illustrates the continuing affinity between oratory and writing:

> Writing, however, I do not advise you to engage in with your own hand, or only very rarely, but rather to dictate to a secretary. For, in the first place, the one who utters his thoughts aloud is more nearly in the mood of a man addressing an audience than one who writes, and, in the second place, less labour is involved. (Dio Chrysostom *Or.* 18.18; LCL translation)

One of the features of ancient reading which closely links literature to rhetoric is the fact that texts were almost always read aloud, and authors knew that their works would be "performed" in such a manner and could design them accordingly. Ancients who read "silently" (i.e., making no audible sound, but with their lips moving) were an elite minority including Aristotle, Julius Caesar, Ambrose and Augustine.[6] Thus in many ancient texts, the terms "hear" and "read" are often used as synonyms, a phenomenon which occurs in Rev 1:3.[7] The intimate relationship, not

[5] For an impressive analysis of Herodotus' style and compositional techniques, see Immerwahr.

[6] On Julius Caesar, cf. Plutarch *Brutus* 5.3; on Ambrose, cf. Augustine *Conf.* 6.3; on Augustine, cf. Augustine *Conf.* 8.12, where it states that he read Romans "i silentio." On the subject of ancient reading, see (in addition to Balogh) Hendrikson, McCartney, Knox, where he corrects certain exaggerations found in Balogh.

[7] Herodotus 1.48; Augustine *Ep.* 147; *Conf.* 10.3; Cassiodorus *Inst. div. lec.* 1.29; Balogh: 206–210; Hendrikson: 182–90.

only between writing and rhetoric but also between literature and oral
performance suggests the importance of the rhetorical handbooks of
antiquity for students of ancient literature.[8] It is likely that all of the
compositions in the NT were written expressly for public, oral performance. Even the *Shepherd of Hermas,* a cumbersome text by any account,
was intended for public presentation (*Herm. Vis.* 2.4.3; cf. 1.3.3–4).
Orality played an explicit role in the composition of the Apocalypse of
John, for the entire document was written expressly for public performance (Rev. 1:3; 22:18), and each of the seven proclamations of Rev 2–3 are
presented as dictated to the author, as are many other segments of the
book (cf. Rev 21:5). The fact that both the Apocalypse of John and the
Shepherd of Hermas were intended for oral performance before Christian congregations *constitutes a unique feature of these two apocalypses.*
There is some evidence from late Jewish apocalypses to suggest that an
audience is envisaged, e.g. the use of plural forms of address,[9] but
parallels to the specific prescriptions for performance found in the Apocalypse of John and the *Shepherd of Hermas* are notably absent. The
feature of dramatic public performance, then, appears to be an innovative
factor in the function of early Christian apocalypses. Types of ancient
literature (such as apocalypses) which utilize "first-person" narratives are
a particularly appropriate vehicle for reenacting the original speech
experience within the framework of a public performance.

2. *The Whole and the Part.*

The composite character of some apocalypses necessitates a consideration of the problem of the whole and the part in ancient literature. J. J.
Collins, for example, does not regard *1 Enoch* 91–104 as an apocalypse
(though the rest of *1 Enoch* is), and he considers *Jub* 23, *T. Levi* 2–5 and *T.
Abr.* 10–15 as apocalypses, though not the rest of those documents
(1979b:21–49). David Hellholm regards only *Herm. Vis.* 1–4 as an apocalypse, and not *Herm. Vis.* 5 or the rest of the *Shepherd of Hermas*
(1980:11–13). Generally, apocalyptic vision reports are constituent elements of larger texts in Greco-Roman literature (Attridge: 159), while in
Jewish and Christian tradition they tend to exist in discrete form. Since
modern genre theory (representing many literary and linguistic perspec-

[8]The value of these handbooks for exegesis is demonstrated in Cairns on Greek and Roman
poetry, and for Paul's letter to the Galatians in the commentary by Betz (1979); for an extensive
review see Huebner. For a comprehensive overview of rhetorical criticism and its possibilities,
see Kennedy.

[9]Public recitation is implied in *Apocalypse of Zephaniah* 8:5: "Now, moreover, my sons, this is
the trial because it is necessary that the good and evil be weighed in the balance" (Charlesworth:
514). Public recitation however, is not enjoined by the author, a *prima facie* impossibility if the
fiction of pseudonymity was to be retained. Lebram (173) has observed that the post-Biblical
apocalypses are "a *literary* revelation, . . . a revelation intended to be read and not heard."

tives) tends to emphasize the "gestaltist" unity of literary texts (i.e., the whole is greater than the sum of its parts),[10] there is no satisfactory framework with which to deal with "compilations" other than resorting to the view of "mixed genres."

In ancient Greek and Israelite literature, tension existed between literary compositions which exhibited a striking degree of unity of both plot and structure (e.g., epic, tragedy, comedy, and Biblical books such as Ruth, Esther and Jonah), and those which exhibited a looser, more episodic structure or were used as vehicles to frame other, shorter, literary forms (examples from Greco-Roman literature include history, biography, and "antiquities," and in the Bible the "historical" section, running continuously from Genesis through 2 Kings). These two styles of literary macrostructures may be designated *periodic* and *paratactic* respectively, following a useful distinction made by Aristotle.[11] The periodic (or, hypotactic) style has a beginning and an end and is the style reflecting the influence of oratory on writing.[12] The paratactic style, on the other hand, has no natural stopping places and ends when there is no more to say on the subject. The effect of parataxis is discontinuity, since the integrity of various members of the chain are preserved at the expense of the unity of the whole. Herodotus and the early Greek logographers, like the historical books of the OT, exhibit paratactic macrostructure.

During the Hellenistic and Roman periods the tension between the

[10] The "gestaltist" character of texts is treated in great detail by Guettgemanns: 259–97. E. D. Hirsch's notion of "intrinsic genre," is "that sense of the whole by means of which an interpreter can correctly understand any part in its determinacy" (86). The same credo is articulated by a very different literary critic, J. M. Ellis: "An interpretation, then, is a hypothesis about the more general organization and coherence of all the elements that form a literary text. The most satisfying interpretation will be that which is the most inclusive" (202). Text-linguists too ascribe to this conception as this quotation from W. Raible suggests; Raible claims that neither sentences nor text sequences of various degrees "have *per se* any function but only obtain their function from a superior totality, e.g. (with regard to tones) within a melody or, as far as texts are concerned, within a superior unit of meaning" (quoted in Hellholm, 1982:175; in this volume: 000).

[11] Aristotle uses the phrases *eiromene lexis*, i.e., "continuous" or "running style," and the *periodos lexis*, i.e., "periodic style" (*Rhet.* 1409A–B). Norden (367–79) derived the style of early literature from two types of grammatical relationships, *kai*-sentences (i.e., paratactic), and *de*-sentences (i.e., periodic). For a discussion of paratactic composition in Herodotus, see Immerwahr: 1–16, 46–78. For a comparison between the paratactic styles of the Greek historians and OT literature, see Van Seters: 35–38.

[12] *Narratio*, when used in contexts other than forensic oratory, e.g., historiography, can be structured in terms of a drama according to Cicero *De inventione* 1.27; cf. *Ad. Herennium* 1.12–13. Historians could give dramatic unity to their narratives if they wrote monographs on very restricted sequences of related events. Polybius is an opponent of such "tragic history" (2.56.1–16), and looks down on those who write historical monographs instead of universal history, as he does (cf. Sacks: 96–121. For the influence of drama on narrative fiction, the novel, see Perry: 140–48.

two styles of composition continued. While rhetorical theory exerted a powerful influence on literature, a number of types of prose narratives continued to be composed paratactically, including dialogues, various types of history and biography and the novel. Unfortunately, modern scholars have virtually ignored macrostructural composition techniques in these and other ancient narrative genres. Some of the more characteristic features of paratactic composition, such as ring composition, or chiasmus (i.e. close correspondence between statements which frame a literary unit in a composition), and related devices such as *inclusio*, are *never discussed in the rhetorical handbooks*, though they were important structuring devices. Paratactic macrostructure was more characteristic of popular literature (such as the Greek novel and the NT gospels and Acts), though even among educated writers it was used (such as the historians Polybius, Dionysius of Halicarnassus and Josephus, and some of the dialogues of Plutarch and Lucian).[13]

There was a greater exploitation during this period of the elastic and framing qualities inherent in the paratactic character of particular genres, and the inclusion of a wide variety of constituent literary forms within larger, more encompassing "host" or "inclusive" genres became commonplace.[14] Under such circumstances, notions of an overall gestaltic unity are anachronistic, for in texts exhibiting a paratactic macrostructure, the constituent literary forms (or *logoi*) of which the whole is constructed have their own disconcerting dominance. An apocalypse, then, can exist as an independent text or as a constituent part of a host genre, and must be recognized on its own terms in either setting.[15]

3. Literature and Cult

In describing the function of a given text and the genre to which is belongs, it is often helpful (though often difficult) to reconstruct the socio-religious setting of author and readers. The quest for the original *Sitze im Leben* of ancient religious texts in particular has proven a vexing problem for scholars, and "solutions" have often been excessively speculative. Of special concern here are texts which may "encode" cultic practices, i.e., transform them into a system of symbolic equivalents fully comprehensible only to members. One such theory, proposed by Karl Kerenyi (1962, originally published in 1927), broadened by Reinhold

---

[13] Lucian's emphasis on a smoothly progressing historical narrative in which each unit is like a link in a chain (*Hist. conscr.* 55; cf. Avenarius: 105–164), suggests that the historians he implicitly criticizes were clumsily paratactic.

[14] Dubrow: 116, coins the phrase "host genre" for a genre, "one of whose roles is to provide a hospitable environment for the other form or forms that are regularly incorporated within them."

[15] The argument of Sanders, that partial texts should not be regarded as apocalypses is therefore without substance (454).

Merkelbach, and all but universally rejected by scholars, discerns an intimate relationship between the ancient novel and Hellenistic mystery religions. Merkelbach proposed that the novel was in fact a mystery text, completely comprehensible only to initiants. The themes of separation, wandering, trials, apparent death and ultimate reunion (characteristic of all Greek novels), reproduce the myth of Isis and Osiris. Yet the theory founders on the fact that human experience exhibits basic patterns which are reflected in ritual and myth as well as in the novel.[16] A similar theory has been proposed for the Jewish novel *Joseph and Aseneth*, that it reflects a Jewish mystery initiation, but this too has not been well received.[17] Evidence for the existence of a Jewish mystery cult has also been proposed for the dream of Moses in the *Exogoge* of the Jewish tragedian Ezekiel (lines 68–89), but this too has met with resistance.[18]

Less well-known, perhaps, is Richard Reitzenstein's proposal that *Corpus Hermeticum* 13 constitutes a *Lese-Mysterium*, i.e., a "literary mystery" (as a surrogate for an actual mystery cult), in which the author acts as a mystagogue and the reader can experience initiation (i.e., regeneration) through the use of imagination (Reitzenstein: 51–52, 64–65, 242–45). While nothing in the tractate suggests that it is intended to effect regeneration in the reader (the injunctions to secrecy in 13.13, 22 militate against it), it does appear to serve both as a reminder of a past experience of regeneration and perhaps of the cultic setting in which it occurred (Grese: 201–2).

These examples suggest that while the relationship between literary texts and cults may be complex and speculative, it is a factor which cannot be ignored. The Apocalypse of John and the *Shepherd of Hermas*, both explicitly intended for public presentation, possibly within the setting of Christian worship (revelation is part of worship, 1 Cor. 14:26), potentially can be described generically in terms of their cultic function.

IV. The Generic Virtualities of Apocalypses and the Apocalypse of John

1. The Special Character of Apocalypses

One of the reasons that it has proven so difficult to move from theoretical discussions of genre constituents to the description of discrete genres is that each genre must be analyzed in its own terms and not in terms of an eclectic list of literary qualities derived from the description of many individual genres (such as that proposed by W. G. Doty). In the

---

[16] For two short but telling critiques of Merkelbach's hypothesis, see Reardon: 393–399, and Haegg: 101–104.

[17] This view is favored by Philonenko: 89–98. For a comprehensive critique, see Saenger.

[18] This was proposed by Cerfaux: 1.85–88 and accepted by Goodenough: 289–91. For a critique see J. J. Collins, 1983a:207–211. A recent introduction and commentary on this work reflects no awareness of this theory: Jacobson.

preceding section the apocalyptic genre was placed in its ancient literary
setting. At this point I will describe some of the special features of
apocalypses which must be considered in any generic description of
apocalypses.

Vision Reports and Revelatory Magic

A crucial issue in understanding the generic character of ancient
apocalypses is the problem of determining the literary parameters within
which a comparative analysis may be carried out fruitfully. There are two
types of literature relevant for an investigation of the generic affinities of
the Apocalypse of John: (1) ancient vision reports, commonly designated
"apocalypses," including Christian, Greco-Roman, Greco-Egyptian, Iranian and Greco-Persian apocalypses in addition to Jewish apocalypses,
and (2) ancient ritual prescriptions describing the techniques, possibilities and benefits of visionary revelatory experience, including (on
the Jewish side), the texts dealing with Merkavah mysticism and (on the
Greco-Roman side), the magical papyri whose chief concern is revelatory
magie.[18a] *Both* types of ancient revelatory literature are relevant for
understanding the genre of the Apocalypse of John.

First, regardless of the problem of the authenticity of revelatory
experiences narrated in apocalypses (in my view an insoluble problem),
they were composed in conformity with ancient cultural patterns and
expectations. This suggests that regardless of the stereotypical literary
formulations, structures and imagery, the context in which such texts
must be understood is that of the *phenomenology of revelatory experience*. Texts describing the ritual techniques for achieving revelatory
visions and those which narrate revelatory visions, describe two complementary phases of revelatory experience. To be sure, the apocalyptist is
never overeager to publish his revelatory techniques along with the
account of his visions, but we cannot on that account assume (using the
argument from silence) that the author of an apocalypse did not employ
such techniques. Nor should scholars succumb to the temptation to
formulate theological judgments which value spontaneity and disapprove
of "apocalyptogenic" technique.[19] The Merkavah literature and the
Greek magical papyri provide the ritual procedures for achieving revelatory visions without including a narrative of the visions themselves.

[18a]Magical divination was a major concern of ancient Greco-Roman magic to judge by the
many magical procedures which deal with this type of magic. The most comprehensive discussion of the subject remains that of Hopfner. For an overview of the role of the magical diviner,
see Aune: 44–47.

[19]Maier (17), for example, claims that the revelatory experiences typical of those narrated in
apocalypses occurred spontaneously, while the visions anticipated in the Merkavah literature
and the magical papyri were obviously based on the initiative of man and induced through
complex theurgic techniques cf. Smith: 155–56.

Apocalypses, on the other hand, narrate the vision while generally omitting all but brief references to the preparatory ritual procedures. Some apocalypses do provide hints of the ritual techniques preparatory to the reception of visionary revelations, but these hints merely suggest that the authors knew more than they chose to reveal.[20]

Second, there are important phenomenological similarities between the literature containing preparatory ritual procedures for receiving revelations and apocalyptic literature. A number of scholars have emphasized the relationship between Jewish apocalypses and Merkavah mysticism in particular.[21] In spite of differences in emphasis (apocalypses tend to focus more on eschatological and cosmological themes, while Merkavah literature focuses on the mysteries of heaven and the throne of God), there is tentative agreement that Merkavah mysticism emerged from Jewish apocalypticism (Alexander, 1983:235). Further, in addition to the apparently close relationship between the Merkavah texts, particularly the Hekalot literature[22], and Jewish apocalypses, it is important to recognize the close phenomenological relationship between the Merkavah texts and the Greek magical papyri (Scholem: 75–83; Smith: 142–60), and now made even more apparent by the Jewish magical text *Sepher ha-Razim*.[23]

Third, the texts prescribing ritual procedures for procuring revelatory visions and those narrating such visions (i.e. apocalypses) in addition to sharing a similar conceptual world, also share similar constituent literary forms. One example is the oracular dialogue, commonly found in both Greco-Roman and Jewish apocalypses, a form suggested in prescriptions for magical revelation found in the magical papyri. Here are two examples of this phenomenon from a Demotic magical papyrus:

> You cause him (i.e., the boy medium) to say to Anubis "The god who will inquire for me to-day, let him tell me his name." When

---

[20] 4 Ezra 3:1–36 narrates a long preparatory prayer for revelation (cf. Dan 9:3; 10:2–3), and the preparatory procedure of fasting and mourning for seven days, concluded by a preparatory prayer are found in 4 Ezra 5:20–30; 6:31–59; 9:23–37; 13:50–51. In *Herm. Vis.* 2.1.1, Hermas is seized by the Spirit after prayer, and fasting and prayer precede revelatory experiences in *Herm Vis.* 2.2.1; 3.1.1–2. In Greek apocalypses, preparatory rituals are also only briefly mentioned; cf. Betz, 1983:581.

[21] Gruenwald, 1974:37–46; 1979:29–72; Rowland, 1983:271–348 (where he treats esoteric Judaism within the framework of apocalyptic); Alexander, 1983:235. Elsewhere Alexander suggests that Gnosticism and Merkavah mysticism have a common ancestor in Jewish apocalyptic and a mediator in syncretistic magic (1984:17). The *Apocalypse of Abraham*, according to Scholem, "more closely resembles a Merkabah text than any other in Jewish apocalyptic literature" (23), and Rowland (1983:15, 344–45).

[22] The Hekalot literature is surveyed in Scholem: 1–8. The contents of many of these documents is summarized by Gruenwald, 1979:127–234.

[23] Gruenwald, 1979:225–34, summarizes the content of *Sepher ha-Razim*, even though he claims that "magic as such does not directly belong to our subject matter" (225). This Jewish magical text is now available in English translation by Morgan.

he stands up and tells you his name, you ask him concerning
everything you wish.

"The god who will ask for me, let him put forth his hand to me
and let him tell me his name." When he tells you his name, you
ask him as to that which you desire. When you have ceased asking
him as to that which you desire, you send him away. (Griffith and
Thompson: 33, 123)

The revelatory dialogue anticipated in these introductory preparations
was to have begun with a question regarding the identity of the inspiring
divinity (clearly a more pressing question in a pagan than in a Jewish or
Christian setting, given the crowd of possibilities), and an answer introduced with the phrase "I am," a self-disclosure formula occurring frequently in the magical papyri. When we turn to apocalyptic literature,
the same phenomenon occurs occasionally at the beginning of the composition. In Jewish apocalypses it occurs in *Apoc. Abr.* 9:1–4 and *3 Enoch*
3:1–3; in Greek apocalypses it occurs in *Corpus Hermeticum* 1.2: Lucian
Icar. 13; in Gnostic apocalypses in *Apoc. Paul* 18:21 and *Apocry. John*
2:11–15. The three narrative vision accounts of Paul's conversion in Acts
all begin with a similar question-and-answer dialogue (*erotapokrisis*), in
which the revealer identifies himself with an "I am" formulation. Finally,
in Revelation, the "I am" self-disclosure formula plays a significant role in
the opening chapter (Rev. 1:8, 17–20), where it is oracular and functions
both to identity and to legitimate the revealer and the revelations which
follow.

The Reveal/Conceal Dialectic

Although revelatory texts from antiquity must be interpreted within
the structural framework of the particular religious traditions of which
they are expressions, it is nevertheless possible to speak of a "reveal"/"conceal" dialectic which pervades ancient Mediterranean revelatory literature. It consists of the paradox that the hidden, now revealed,
nevertheless remains concealed, a phenomenon described by Paul
Tillich:

Only what essentially is concealed, and accessible by no mode of
knowledge whatsoever, is imparted by revelation. But in thus
being revealed it does not cease to remain concealed, since its
secrecy pertains to its very essence; and when therefore it is
revealed it is so precisely as that which is hidden. (Tillich: 406;
quoted in Van der Leeuw: 2.565)

This dialectic finds frequent expression in ancient apocalypses. Despite
the fact that the "hidden" now appears "revealed," the literary presentation of revelation is expressed in obscure modes so that the substance of

the revelation is not clarified once-and-for-all. Rather, it becomes a vehicle capable of providing new revelations for the audience (when the apocalypse is orally performed), or for the individual reader (when studied). This is a generic feature characteristic of apocalypses including the Apocalypse of John and the *Shepherd of Hermas*. One of the generic virtualities of apocalyptic genre is the possibility of maximizing audience/reader participation in the revelatory experience.

A recent study of the parables in *1 Enoch*, *4 Ezra* and *2 Baruch* concludes that they "function as a means of revealing and concealing divine truths." The author, P. Patten, goes on to observe:

> They [parables] are used to illustrate a point in a message, but their intended meaning is not clear until an inspired word of interpretation or application is made, for mortal man is incapable of understanding the ways of God. This inspired word of interpretation is restricted to only a few chosen people who are characterized as the "wise." (Patten: 252)

Though parables, as such, are not utilized in the Apocalypse of John, they do play a prominent role in the *Shepherd of Hermas*, where the term itself in its various forms occurs thirty-two times. The view of parables reflected in *Hermas*, where they are particularly emphasized in the section called "Similitudes" *(parabolai)*, is very similar to that found in Mark 4:11–12 in terms of their function: both to reveal and conceal divine truth (cf. *Herm. Mand.* 10.1.3–6). While it is commonly held that *Hermas'* use of parables is dependent upon synoptic tradition, it is more likely that there was an apocalyptic convention in Judaism which preferred parables for their paradoxical ability both to reveal and conceal divine truth. This suggests that one of the literary forms constituting the apocalyptic repertoire, the parable, was used in apocalypses precisely because of their essential affinity and mutual compatibility.

In the Apocalypse of John, the reveal/conceal dialectic comes to expression in the phenomenon that only rarely are visions accompanied by explanations (Rev 1:20; 7:13–17; 17:6b-18), an uncommon characteristic in apocalypses in which revelatory dialogues *(erotapokriseis)* between the revealer and the visionary, which are explicitly explanatory, are the rule. Further, in the Apocalypse of John the three passages which contain explanations do not reveal much. Rev 1:20 discloses just two basic equivalencies (seven stars = seven angels of the churches; seven lampstands = seven churches). Rev 7:13–17 simply explains that the great host in white are those who have come out of the great tribulation, i.e., martyrs, and Rev 17:6b-18 interprets the great harlot seated upon many waters in such enigmatical terms that the interpretation is made obviously pertinent only to political matters. This minimal use of explanation in the rehearsal of visionary sequences suggests that the ingenuity and imagination of the audience is allowed greater challenge and fuller scope than in the case of most apocalypses. This in turn suggests that the author wanted to achieve the fullest possible degree of audience participation. Though extensive visionary scenes are narrated, the author's only real literary control over the direction of the audience's response (aside from the negligible impact of the three passages just discussed), is exerted through his creative utilization of hymns and hymn-like choral passages to develop a commentary on the direction and significance of the narrated eschatological visions.

Yet another expression of the reveal-conceal motif in revelatory literature is through explicit references to the *limitations* of revelatory knowledge. There is a tendency in oracular dialogues, and hence in apocalypses which incorporate this form, to emphasize the fact that an oracular question is either improper, should not be answered at all, should be delayed, or that the answer given to the seer should not be relayed to his audience. In Rev 10:4, we read: "And when the seven thunders had sounded, I was about to write, but I heard a voice from heaven saying, 'Seal up what the seven thunders have said, and do not write it down.'" Here John is put into a position of claiming to know more than he can reveal, much as Paul "heard things that cannot be told, which man may not utter" (2 Cor 12:4). The statement in Rev 10:4 is significant, because a refusal to reveal all lends credibility to what is disclosed, placing as it does a limit on what can be revealed, i.e., revelation never involves full disclosure. Similar passages occur in a wide range of Christian, Jewish and Greco-Roman apocalypses and revelatory literature (*Herm. Vis.* 1.3.3; 3.3.4; T. Sol. 6:6; Lucian *Alex.* 43; Plutarch *De genio Socratis* 22; 4 Ezra 4:10f., 21, 52). These occurrences of apocalyptic secrecy are phenomenologically related to the necessity of maintaining secrecy in connection with initiation into mystery religions (an initiation which could often include various stages of revelatory experience). One is not the *source* of the other, but both are expressions of the phenomenology of revelatory experience. In cultic experience as well as in revelatory literature, the revealed/concealed dialectic is a pervasive phenomenon in ancient perceptions of revelatory experience.

2. The Genre of the Apocalypse of John

In any specification of a genre, the definition, if possible, should be formulated in terms of form, content and function. Although the description of the form or function or content of the apocalyptic genre may, if taken separately, apply to other types of literature, when taken together they should describe only apocalypses. The proposed definition of the apocalyptic genre, with special reference to the Apocalypse of John, is as follows: (1) *Form:* an apocalypse is a prose narrative, in autobiographical form, of revelatory visions experienced by the author, so structured that the central revelatory message constitutes a literary climax, and framed by a narrative of the circumstances surrounding the revelatory experience(s). (2) *Content:* the communication of a transcendent, often eschatological, perspective on human experience. (3) *Function:* (a) to legitimate the transcendent authorization of the message, (b) by mediating a new actualization of the original revelatory experience through literary devices, structures and imagery, which function to "conceal" the message which the text "reveals," so that (c) the recipients of the message will be encouraged to modify their cognitive and behavioral stance in conformity with transcendent perspectives. Each of these aspects will now be discussed in greater detail.

The Form of Apocalypses.

Three aspects of the definition of the form of apocalypses proposed above require special comment, autobiographical style, the structuration or segmentation of vision reports, and the central revelatory message as a literary climax. First, the autobiographical style of apocalypses requires emphasis since this feature is an important aspect of the *legitimation* of the revelatory experience (see under function), and the first-person style in oral performance enables the audience to experience the vividness and vitality of the original revelatory experience. Unlike pseudonymous apocalypses in the eastern Mediterranean tradition, two Christian apocalypses, the Apocalypse of John and the *Shepherd of Hermas*, were written by persons personally known to their addressees so that the intended public recitation of these revelatory writings would take on a different significance than the recitation of a pseudonymous work. The historical reviews, presented as predictions, which form a central structural feature of many Jewish apocalypses (together with pseudepigraphy), enables the reader to see the predictions as applicable to his own day and situation. John and Hermas accomplish this in an alternate way without recourse to either pseudepigraphy or historical reviews (J. J. Collins, 1977). Second, the notion that the literary climax of an apocalypse coincides with the central message is one of the virtualities of the apocalyptic genre, the successful execution of which lies in the abilities and skill of the individual author. Segmentation can refer to a variety of literary strategies. Such apocalypses as the *Shepherd of Hermas*, sections of *1 Enoch*, *2 Baruch* and *4 Ezra*, utilize a sequence of vision reports which are kept distinct from each other through literary markers, whereas a single, extensive vision report dominates the body of the Apocalypse of John, 4:1–22:5 (Hanson: 1422–23). If the segmented or episodic presentation of vision narrative is a generically salient feature of apocalypses generally, the literary segmentation used by the author of the Apocalypse of John appears generically imposed. Another common form of segmentation in apocalypses is achieved by successive movement through the heavens to the highest heaven of all (usually the seventh). This obtains for the dreams which constitute *2 Enoch* 1-38, *3 Enoch,* the conceptual world of Merkavah mysticism, *Sepher ha-Razim,* and others.

The assertion that the central message of an apocalypse coincides with a literary climax expresses in paradigmatic terms the proposal of Hellholm that the texts of the Apocalypse of John and the *Shepherd of Hermas* in which the most embedded text at the highest communication level coincides with the highest grade of hierarchically arranged textsequences constitute the central messages of these apocalypses. Ring composition and chiasmic structures are also used in apocalypses to direct the attention of the audience to the texts within such frames. Apocalypses use these surface markers to enable the audience to progress from the periphery of the revelatory experience to the "innermost" or highest mystery which the author wishes to communicate. One of the more common devices used for this purpose in ancient apocalypses is the otherworldly journey whereby the seer ascends through the various spheres or heavens to the uppermost heaven where the crowning revelation is found, usually the vision of God himself (Rowland, 1983:84). In the Apocalypse of John, of course, this culminating revelatory experience is delayed, for in John's vision of the throneroom in Rev 4–5, the one sitting upon the throne is described only with vague imagery (4:3), and 5:1 mentions only that a scroll was in his hand. Thus the vision of God is skillfully delayed until the penultimate chapter, when the one seated upon the throne finally speaks (21:5–8). These formal structures for highlighting the central message of the author closely relate to an aspect of the *function* of apocalypses discussed below.

The Content of Apocalypses

The content of apocalypses, considered at an appropriately abstract level, overlaps with the content of other forms of ancient revelatory literature. Thus ancient revelatory literature communicates a *transcendent* perspective on human experience. The revelatory message is necessitated by the perception of discrepancy between ideology and reality perceived by the author and communicated to his audience. Apocalypses belong to a narrower grouping of revelatory literature which includes an *eschatological* in addition to a transcendental perspective on human affairs. Cosmic or individual eschatology is characteristic of Jewish, Christian, and Greco-Roman apocalypses, and some revelatory discourses (e.g. the *Sibylline Oracles*). J. Carmignac omits any reference to eschatological salvation in his definition of the apocalyptic genre, which he describes as "a literary genre which presents, through characteristic symbols, revelations either concerning God, or concerning angels or demons, or concerning their supporters, or concerning the instruments of their activity" (20). Carmignac expresses general agreement with the

definition proposed by J. J. Collins except that he does not regard
eschatological salvation as essential to apocalypses. It is apparent that he
errs by defining eschatology too narrowly so that individual eschatology is
left out of consideration.

The Function of Apocalypses
In most discussions of the function of apocalyptic literature, the
notion of "function" is frequently understood, explicitly or implicitly, as
"*social* function," i.e., as a quest for the original *Sitz im Leben,* or life
setting of apocalypses. Apocalypses are often, and not incorrectly, understood as a form of protest literature in which the oppressed rights of a
minority are legitimated by divine revelation. Yet it is precisely this
aspect of apocalyptic literature most often hidden from the view of
modern scholars and in many cases irrecoverable. The concept "function," however, has many meanings, necessitating a distinction between
literary function and *social* function (J. J. Collins, 1982:92–94, 110–11).
The literary function of an apocalypse is concerned only with the implicit
and explicit indications within the text itself of the purpose or use of the
composition. The social function of an apocalypse, from this perspective,
would include not only its original (implicit and explicit) purpose (if
recoverable), but also the entire history of varied utilization which it (as
any other literary text) has experienced.
The description of the function of apocalypses in the definition above
proposes three complementary literary functions of apocalypses, of which
the first is the legitimation of the transcendent authorization of the
message. This is a very important aspect of the function of apocalypses (as
perhaps of all revelatory literature), for in many cases it suggests that an
appeal to transcendent authority is necessitated by either the impossibility or ineffectiveness of an appeal to more rational or mundane
structures of thought or authority. It is certainly true sociologically that
persons or groups on the margins of society have sought to appeal to the
transcendent through various forms of vision-trance and possession-
trance to receive enhanced status, justification for innovative social pro-
grams and ideologies (Lewis).
The second aspect of our functional definition proposes that apocalypses mediate a new actualization of the original revelatory experience
through literary devices, structures and imagery which function to "conceal" the message which the text purportedly "reveals." That is, the
skillful apocalyptic writer may portray the revelatory experience which
he purportedly had with such literary skill (particularly enhanced
through public performance) that the intended audience may indeed
participate in the original experience to such an extent that the experience is "re-presented" or re-actualized for them. Further, the peculiar
idiom of apocalypses (perhaps more characteristic of those in the east

than the west) is to thinly conceal what it purports to reveal so that the audience may themselves have the experience of decoding or deciphering the message. Apocalypses stand in a unique relationship to revelatory experience, for it is they which provide continuing access to a past, ordinarily irretrievable, type of religious experience. Just as cults can protect and isolate the sacred from the profane by placing it at the center of both ritual and spatial barriers, so the central message of an apocalypse can lie at the center of or at the climax of a series of literary devices intended to protect the sacred character of the revelatory message from the profane hearers and readers. Just as an initiant makes his way through various cultic barriers into the *adyton* where the focal religious experience will be staged, so the audience of such revelatory literature as the Apocalypse of John is brought through various literary structures and devices into the innermost recesses of the secrets which an apocalypse is designed to convey. The phenomenon of profound embedment of the focal message of the Apocalypse functions to conceal, as it were, that message within the innermost recesses of the composition. The movement from one level of communcation to another, then, is a device utilized by the author to replicate the original revelatory experience in a literary, rather than a ritual or spatial, idiom, thereby maximizing the participation of the audience in the performance of the Apocalypse within the framework of public performance, possibly within framework of worship. That is, the author does not merely *narrate* the substance of the divine revelation he has received to his audience, he provides the audience with a literary vehicle so that they can, in effect, relive the experience of the seer and thereby appropriate for themselves the revelatory message.

The third aspect of our functional definition of the apocalyptic genre focuses on the purpose of apocalypses in terms of their role in encouraging cognitive and behavioral modifications based on the message communicated from the transcendent world. In this sense apocalypses are basically ideological, and are basically paraenetic even though the specifically paraenetic features appear at first sight to be in short supply (Lebram: 173). Viewed from this perspective, paraenesis, though existing in its own distinctive literary forms, exhibits an affinity for apocalypses which are particularly concerned with behavioral aspects of human experience. Hans Dieter Betz has shown that one of the theoretically explicit functions of Greco-Roman apocalypses is to motivate changes in life-style through the shock-like experience of fear based on a journey to the afterlife or the nether world, an experience which can be shared by those who hear the story (Betz, 1983: 595). Apocalyptic vision reports in Judaism and early Christianity function analogously. The message of the Apocalypse of John centers on the promise of final salvation for believers and terrible punishment which will be meted out to unbelievers (Rev

21:5–8). The author who wrote Rev 22:18–19 (though there are compositional problems at this point), wanted to threaten those who might add to or delete from the book. A central purpose of the author was to motivate the audience to pursue a life of faithfulness and purity in order to avoid the punishments awaiting those who follow the wrong path.

V. Conclusions

Recent research on the problem of the genre of ancient apocalypses has made important strides. In particular, the paradigmatic description of the genre by John J. Collins and the syntagmatic analysis of the macrostructure of two Christian apocalypses by David Hellholm have provided two very different yet comlementary approaches to the problem. In this article I have implicitly rejected Hellholm's proposal that the addition of "exhortation and/or consolation" to J. J. Collins' definition provides an adequate statement on function, and proposed instead a more comprehensive description of the function of the Apocalypse of John, based on what I consider the implications of Hellholm's own proposals. The profound embedment of the speech of God summarizing the central message of the Apocalypse (Rev 21:5–8) is the core of a literary structure which is a surrogate for the cultic barriers which separate the profane from the sacred, the hidden from the revealed. The Apocalypse of John is a literary replication of the original and unique revelatory experience of John the Seer which, when performed in a public, probably even a cultic setting, communicates the author's paraenetic message with divine authority.

WORKS CONSULTED

Alexander, P.
    1983   "3 (Hebrew Apocalypse of) Enoch." Pp. 223–315 in *The Old Testament Pseudepigrapha*, Vol. 1: *Apocalyptic Literature and Testaments*. Ed. J. H. Charlesworth. Garden City: Doubleday.
    1984   "Comparing Merkavah Mysticism and Gnosticism." *JJS* 35:1–18.
Attridge, H. W.
    1979   "Greek and Latin Apocalypses." *Semeia* 14:159–86.
Aune, D. E.
    1983   *Prophecy in Early Christianity and the Ancient Mediterranean World*. Grand Rapids: Eerdmans.
Avenarius, G.
    1956   *Lukians Schrift zur Geschichtsschreibung*. Meisenheim/Glan: Anton Hain.

Balogh, J.
1927 "'Voces Paginarum:' Beitraege zur Geschichte des lauten Lesens und Schreibens." *Philologus* 82:84–109, 202–40.

Betz, H. D.
1979 *Galatians*. Philadelphia: Fortress Press.
1983 "The Problem of Apocalyptic Genre in Greek and Hellenistic Literature: The Case of the Oracle of Trophonius." Pp. 577–97 in *Apocalypticism in the Mediterranean World and the Near East*. Ed. D. Hellholm. Tuebingen: Mohr.

Brown, P.
1978 *The Making of Late Antiquity*. Cambridge: Harvard University Press.

Cairns, F.
1972 *Generic Composition in Greek and Roman Poetry*. Edinburgh: University Press.

Carmignac, J.
1979 "Qu'est-ce que l'apocalyptique? Son emploi à Qumran." *RevQ* 10:3–33.

Cerfaux, L.
1954 "Influence des Mystères sur le Judaisme Alexandrin avant Philo." Vol. 1, pp. 65–112 in L. Cerfaux, *Recueil Lucient Cerfaux*. BETL, 6–7. Gembloux: J. Duculot.

Collins, A. Y.
1979 "The Early Christian Apocalypses." *Semeia* 14:61–121.

Collins, J. J.
1977 "Pseudonymity, Historical Reviews and the Genre of the Revelation of John." *CBQ* 39:329–43.
1979a "Introduction: Towards the Morphology of a Genre." *Semeia* 14:1–20.
1979b "The Jewish Apocalypses." *Semeia* 14:21–49.
1982 "The Apocalyptic Technique: Setting and Function in the Book of Watchers." *CBQ* 44:91–111.
1983a *Between Athens and Jerusalem: Jewish Identity in the Hellenistic Diaspora*. New York: Crossroad.
1983b "The Genre Apocalypse in Hellenistic Judaism." Pp. 531–48 in *Apocalypticism in the Mediterranean World and the Near East*. Ed. D. Hellholm. Tuebingen: Mohr.

Doty, W. G.
1972 "The Concept of Genre in Literary Analysis." Pp. 413–48 in *SBL 1972 Proceedings*. 2 vols. Ed. L. C. McGaughy. SBL.

Dubrow, H.
1982 *Genre*. New York and London: Methuen.

Ellis, J. M.
1974 *The Theory of Literary Criticism: A Logical Analysis.* Berkeley and Los Angeles: University of California Press.

Finley, M. I.
1982 *Economy and Society in Ancient Greece.* New York: Viking.

Fornara, C. W.
1983 *The Nature of History in Ancient Greece and Rome.* Berkeley and Los Angeles: University of California Press.

Goodenough, E. R.
1935 *By Light, Light: The Mystic Gospel of Hellenistic Judaism.* New Haven: Yale University Press.

Grese, W. C.
1979 *Corpus Hermeticum XIII and Early Christian Literature.* SCHNT, 5. Leiden: Brill.

Griffith, L. and H. Thompson
1904 *The Demotic Magical Papyrus of London and Leiden.* London: H. Grevel. Republished under the title *The Leyden Papyrus: An Egyptian Magical Book.* New York: Dover, 1974.

Groningen, B. A. van.
1965 "General Literary Tendencies in the Second Century A.D." *Mnemosyne* 18:41–56.

Gruenwald, I.
1974 "The Jewish Esoteric Literature in the Time of the Mishnah and the Talmud." *Immanuel* 4:37–46.
1979 *Apocalyptic and Merkavah Mysticism.* Leiden: Brill.

Guettgemanns, E.
1979 *Candid Questions Concerning Gospel Form Criticism.* Pittsburgh: Pickwick Press.

Haegg, T.
1983 *The Novel in Antiquity.* Berkeley and Los Angeles: University of California Press.

Hanson, J. S.
1980 "Dreams and Visions in the Graeco-Roman World and Early Christianity." Section II, Vol. 23, Part 2, pp. 1395–1427 in *Aufstieg und Niedergang der roemischen Welt.* Ed. H. Temporini and W. Haase. Berlin: W. de Gruyter.

Hanson, P. D.
1976 "Apocalypticism." Pp. 29–31 in IDBSup. Nashville: Abingdon.

Hartman, L.
1983 "Survey of the Problem of Apocalyptic Genre." Pp. 329–43 in *Apocalypticism in the Mediterranean World and the Near East.* Ed. D. Hellholm. Tuebingen: Mohr.

Hellholm, D.
1980   *Das Visionenbuch des Hermas als Apokalypse: Form-
              geschichtliche und texttheoretische Studien zu einer
              literarischen Gattung*. ConBNT 13/1. Lund: Gleerup.
1982   "The Problem of Apocalyptic Genre and the Apocalypse of
              John." Pp. 157–98 in *SBL 1982 Seminar Papers*. Ed. K. H.
              Richards. Chico: Scholars Press. A revised form of this paper is
              contained in this volume.

Hendrikson, G. L.
1929/30   "Ancient Reading." *Classical Journal* 25: 182–90.

Hirsch, E. D.
1967   *Validity in Interpretation*. New Haven: Yale University Press.

Hopfner, T.
1921–24   *Griechisch-aegyptischer Offenbarungszauber*. 2 vols. Leipzig:
              R. Haessel.

Huebner, H.
1984   "Der Galaterbrief und das Verhaeltnis von antiker Rhetoric und
              Epistolographie." *TLZ* 109:241–50.

Immerwahr, H. R.
1966   *Form and Thought in Herodotus*. American Philological Associa-
              tion Monographs, 23. Cleveland: American Philological
              Association.

Jacobson, H.
1983   *The "Exogoge" of Ezekiel*. Cambridge: The University Press.

Kennedy, G. A.
1984   *New Testament Interpretation Through Rhetorical Criticism*.
              Chapel Hill and London: University of North Carolina Press.

Kerenyi, K.
1962   *Die griechisch-orientalische Romanliteratur in re-
              ligionsgeschichtlicher Beleuchtung*. 2. Aufl. Darmstadt:
              Wissenschaftliche Buchgesellschaft.

Knox, B. M. W.
1968   "Silent Reading in Antiquity." *GRBS* 9:421–35.

Lebram, J. C. H.
1983   "The Piety of the Jewish Apocalypses." Pp. 171–210 in *Apoc-
              alypticism in the Mediterranean World and the Near East*. Ed.
              D. Hellholm. Tuebingen: Mohr.

Leeuw, G. van der.
1963   *Religion in Essence and Manifestation*. 2 vols. New York and
              Evanston: Harper & Row.

Lewis, I. M.
1971   *Ecstatic Religion: An Anthropological Study of Spirit Possession
              and Shamanism*. Boston: Penguin Books.

Maier, J.
  1964   *Vom Kultus zur Gnosis*. Salzburg: Otto Mueller.

McCartney, E. S.
  1948   "On Reading and Praying Audibly." *Classical Philology*. 43:184–87.

Merkelbach, R.
  1962   *Roman und Mysterium in der Antike*. Muenchen and Berlin: C. H. Beck.

Morgan, M.
  1983   *Sepher Ha-Razim: The Book of Mysteries*. Chico: Scholars Press.

Musurillo, H.
  1972   *The Acts of the Christian Martyrs*. Oxford: The Clarendon Press.

Norden, E.
  1956   *Agnostos Theos: Untersuchungen zur Formengeschichte religioeser Rede*. Darmstadt: Wissenschaftliche Buchgesellschaft.

Perry, B. E.
  1967   *The Ancient Romances: A Literary-Historical Account of Their Origins*. Sather Classical Lectures, 37. Berkeley and Los Angeles: University of California Press.

Philonenko, M.
  1968   *Joseph et Aseneth: introduction, texte critique, traduction et notes*. SPB, 13. Leiden: Brill.

Reardon, B. P.
  1971   *Courants littéraires grecs des IIe et IIIe siècles après J.-C*. Annales littéraires de l'Université de Nantes, 3. Paris: Les Belles Lettres.

Reitzenstein, R.
  1927   *Die hellenistische Mysterienreligionen nach Ihren Grundgedanken und Wirkungen*. 3. Aufl. Stuttgart: B. G. Teubner.

Rowland, C.
  1980   "The Vision of the Risen Christ in Rev. 1:13ff.: The Debt of an Early Christology to an Aspect of Jewish Angelology." *JTS* 31:1–11.
  1983   *The Open Heaven: A Study of Apocalyptic in Judaism and Early Christianity*. New York: Crossroad.

Sacks, K.
  1981   *Polybius On the Writing of History*. Classical Studies, 24. Berkeley and Los Angeles: University of California Press.

Saenger, D.
  1980   *Antikes Judentum und die Mysterien: Religionsgeschichtliche*

Untersuchungen zu Joseph und Aseneth. WUNT 2/5. Tuebingen: Mohr.

Sanders, E. P.
1983   "The Genre of Palestinian Jewish Apocalypses." Pp. 447–59 in *Apocalypticism in the Mediterranean World and the Near East.* Ed. D. Hellholm. Tuebingen: Mohr.

Scholem, G.
1965   *Jewish Gnosticism, Merkabah Mysticism, and Talmudic Tradition.* New York: Jewish Theological Seminary.

Seters, J. van.
1983   *In Search of History: Historiography in the Ancient World and the Origins of Biblical History.* New Haven: Yale University Press.

Smith, M.
1963   "Observations on Hekhalot Rabbati." Pp. 142–60 in *Biblical and Other Studies.* Ed. A. Altmann. Cambridge: Harvard University Press.

Stanford, W. B.
1967   *The Sound of Greek: Studies in the Greek Theory and Practise of Euphony.* Berkeley and Los Angeles: University of California Press.

Stone, M. E.
1976   "Lists of Revealed Things in Apocalyptic Literature." Pp. 441–52 in *Magnalia Dei: The Mighty Acts of God.* Ed. F. M. Cross, W. E. Lemke and P. D. Miller, Jr. Garden City, Doubleday.

Tillich, P.
1927   "Die Idee der Offenbarung." *ZTK* 35:403–12.

THE EXPERIENCE OF THE VISIONARY AND GENRE IN THE ASCENSION OF ISAIAH 6–11 AND THE APOCALYPSE OF PAUL

Martha Himmelfarb

Princeton University

ABSTRACT

The 1979 volume of *Semeia* (*Apocalypse: The Morphology of a Genre*) offers a categorization of apocalypses that places the *Ascension of Isaiah* 6–11 and the *Apocalypse of Paul* in the same sub-grouping, otherworldly journeys with cosmic and/or political eschatology (II b). Yet the experience of the visionary differs dramatically in the two works. In the *Ascension of Isaiah* the prophet is transformed as he ascends through the heavens until he has achieved a status higher than that of the angels. The *Apocalypse of Paul* rejects the idea of transformation. It borrows from the *Apocalypse of Zephaniah* an episode during which Zephaniah undergoes a transformation and takes his place among the angels, but omits the transformation. This difference in orientation opens the question of the suitability of placing these two apocalypses in the same category.

Another problem with the *Semeia* categories is that they separate the *Apocalypse of Paul* from some of the other tours of hell, with which it shares both form and content. The basis for the separation is the presence of "cosmic and/or political eschatology" in the *Apocalypse of Paul* and some of the other tours of hell and its absence in others. Yet such eschatology does not play an important role in the *Apocalypse of Paul* or in any of the other tours of hell (with the exception of the *Apocalypse of Peter*, which differs from the rest of the tours in important ways). Since the absence or presence of such eschatology is of minor importance for the meaning of the tours of hell, it is not a useful criterion for categorization.

The centrality of cosmic and/or political eschatology for the *Semeia* volume shows the continued influence of the traditional scholarly view of such eschatology as the most important aspect of apocalyptic literature. The volume can be read as a reaction against this emphasis, but it is not entirely free of his influence.

> The influence can also be seen in the relatively small space in the
> master paradigm for the apocalypses allotted to "otherworldly
> elements" (10). Greater attention to these elements would allow a
> more helpful categorization of apocalypses involving otherworldly
> journeys like the *Ascension of Isaiah* 6–11 and the *Apocalypse of
> Paul*.

The lively discussion of apocalyptic genre in recent years is in part an
attempt to do justice to the many apocalypses that are not interested
primarily in the imminent and cataclysmic end of the world. These
apocalypses contain tours of the heavens or of paradise and hell, and they
are at least as interested in the angelic realm, cosmological phenomena,
or reward and punishment as in the end of the world.

Students of the tour apocalypses are very much in the debt of the
authors the 1979 *Semeia* volume on the genre apocalypse (ed. Collins). In
offering some suggestions for refining its categories, I hope that I am
proceeding in the spirit of the volume, which speaks of itself as a first
step. I shall concentrate here on the *Ascension of Isaiah* 6–11 and the
Apocalypse of Paul, which are treated as members of the same sub-
grouping, otherworldly journeys with cosmic and/or political eschatology
(II b), by Adela Yarbro Collins in her chapter on early Christian apocalypses in the *Semeia* volume. I intend to take a careful look at the
treatment of the theme of the visionary's transformation in the two
apocalypses and to examine the implications for the question of genre.

The Ascension of Isaiah

As it was transmitted in Ethiopic, the *Ascension of Isaiah* consists of
two sections, the martyrdom of Isaiah at the hands of Manasseh (chs. 1–
5), and Isaiah's ascent to heaven during the reign of Manasseh's father
Hezekiah (chs. 6–11). The two sections were originally independent
works; the second section, with which we are concerned, circulates on its
own in Latin and Slavonic (Fleming and Duensing, 642–44; all quotations
are taken from this translation). It is clearly a Christian work, culminating
in Isaiah's vision of Christ's descent to earth and subsequent ascent, but
there is reason to believe that it drew on a Jewish apocalypse involving
Isaiah's ascent to heaven (Himmelfarb: 137).[1] The work probably belongs
to the first two Christian centuries when its picture of the heavens and its

---

[1] I am not alone in claiming a written Jewish source for this part of the *Ascension of Isaiah*.
Ithamar Gruenwald writes, "There are good reasons to believe that the book as a whole is of
Jewish origin and that all the clear Christian references belong to a later editor or interpolator"
(1980: 62, n. 119). Unfortunately Gruenwald does not tell us the reasons. In this he follows
Scholem, who claimed, without argument, that the Ascension of Isaiah "is based on a Jewish
text" (1954: 45).

Christology would not yet have seemed heretical (Fleming and Duensing, 643).[2]

The prophetic claim to participation in the divine council forms the background to the ascent in the *Ascension of Isaiah*.[3] Several passages in biblical literature describe the prophet as he overhears or joins in the deliberations of the divine council (Cross: 186–88; Mullen: 209–26). In Isaiah 6 and 1 Kings 22, the divine council is actually seen: God appears enthroned in the midst of his angelic courtiers.[4] The vivid descriptions of God enthroned in Ezekiel 1 and 8–11 are also indebted to this tradition. The *Ascension of Isaiah*'s picture of seven heavens full of angels singing hymns of praise stands in a direct line of descent from these visions.

With the rise of apocalyptic literature, it becomes standard practice for the visionary to ascend to the council. Enoch in *1 Enoch* 14 (third century BCE) is the first to do so (Nickelsburg, 1981a: 576–82). In the earlier apocalypses there is only one heaven. By the time of the *Ascension of Isaiah*, the idea of seven heavens is well established, although it exists side by side with the older conception, as in the Book of Revelation.

In claiming to stand in the divine council, the prophet claims for himself the status of one of the heavenly host. The *Ascension of Isaiah* goes even farther. In each of the first five heavens, Isaiah sees a throne with an angel on it.[5] When Isaiah falls on his face in the second heaven to worship the angel enthroned there, his angelic guide tells him, "Worship neither throne nor angel which belongs to the six heavens . . . , for above all the heavens and their angels is thy throne set, and thy garments and thy crown which thou shalt see" (7:21–22).

At his first appearance Isaiah's angelic guide was described as more glorious than the angels Isaiah was used to seeing. When in the sixth heaven Isaiah addresses him as "my Lord," the guide responds, "I am not thy Lord, but thy companion" (8:1–5). In the sixth heaven Isaiah is awed by the glory of the angels there, so much greater than that of the angels of the heavens below, yet he joins his guide and the other angels in their

[2] Duensing (1965b: 1. 190) points out that the *Ascension of Isaiah*'s story of Christ's descent in the form of an angel to prevent the angels from recognizing him finds a parallel in the *Epistle of the Apostles*, which seems likely on other grounds to date from the second century.

[3] The *Ascension of Isaiah* apparently alludes to Isaiah of Jerusalem's vision of the divine council in session in the temple when it has Isaiah describe the angel who guides him during his ascent as more glorious than the angels he was accustomed to seeing (7:2). The journey and vision recounted in the Ascension of Isaiah, then, are being presented as greater than the vision of Isaiah 6.

[4] Daniel 7 is another such passage. It exerted a strong influence on later apocalypses because of its canonical status, but from the point of view of the history of apocalyptic literature, it is a beneficiary of the tradition, like *1 Enoch* 14–16.

[5] Gruenwald (1980: 59) notes that *Re'uyot Yehezqel*, a midrash on the merkavah from perhaps the fourth century, contains a chariot throne in each of its seven heavens.

song of praise, noting that his praise is like theirs (8:17). Now the angel explains that Isaiah is being taken to the seventh heaven to see the "unnamed one . . . and his Elect one: (8:7). The angel assures Isaiah that no other man who must return to the body has ever seen what he will see.

Isaiah's entrance into the seventh heaven is challenged by an angel of the sixth heaven.[6] "How far should he ascend who dwells among aliens?"[7] But Christ's voice is heard permitting Isaiah to enter because "his garment is here" (9:2). What this means becomes clear almost immediately when Isaiah enters the seventh heaven and sees heroes of the Hebrew Bible and the other righteous "stripped of the garment of the flesh, . . . in their higher garments, . . . like the angels who stand there in great glory" (9:9). The righteous are not yet seated on their thrones, nor have they put on their crowns of glory. For these they await Christ's ascent following his mission on earth (9:10–18).

In the course of Isaiah's sojourn in the seventh heaven he joins the righteous in their praise of Christ and the Holy Spirit, and he observes their praise of God himself.[8] It is the righteous who offer praise first, followed by the angels, and while the angels and Isaiah are capable only of glancing at God, the righteous are able to "[behold] with great power the glory of that One" (9:37–38). Isaiah's distinction, then, is that he is able to see while still alive; after their deaths all the righteous share a status higher than that of the angels.

Isaiah achieves a level between the angels and the righteous dead. It is the righteous, not the angels, whom Isaiah joins in offering praise to Christ, and his "song of praise was like theirs" (9:28). Upon entering the third heaven, Isaiah had noted, "The glory of my countenance was being transformed as I ascended from heaven to heaven. . ." (7:24). When Isaiah undergoes his final transformation in the seventh heaven, he is said to become like an angel (9:30).[9] After this Isaiah sees the Holy Spirit and again joins the righteous in their praise, but his "glory was not transformed in accordance with their appearance" (9:33).[10] This transforma-

---

[6] Although we are told that there is no throne in the sixth heaven and thus no angels on the left or right (8:7, 16), the angel who calls out here is described as the one who "(is placed) over the praise of the sixth heaven" (9:4).

[7] While this challenge may echo Isa 6:5, "For I dwell among a people of unclean lips," David Halperin points out to me that similar angelic complaints about human beings who ascend to heaven appear in rabbinic discussions of Moses' ascent to receive the Torah (*Midrash haGadol*) to Exodus 19:20, *b. Shabbat* 88b, *Pesiqta Rabbati* 20:4; see Shäfer, 1975: 127–31) and in *3 Enoch* 6:2.

[8] Isaiah does not join even the angels in the praise of God (9:40–42).

[9] This is according to the Slavonic and Latin 2 (Charles: note to 9:30). The Ethiopic seems to suggest that Christ is transformed into an angel at this point.

[10] Again there are textual problems. Although Slavonic, Latin 2, and Ethiopic all read "his

tion apparently must await Isaiah's death. This explains why Isaiah was not able to look upon God or to praise him as the righteous do. Why he was able to join the righteous in offering praise to Christ and the Holy Spirit is not clear. But the hierarchy of the inhabitants of the heavens is quite clear: the righteous dead are at a higher level than the angels, while the seer before his death stands between them.

Other Physical Transformations

Parallels to the physical transformation of the visionary as he travels through the heavenly world can be found elsewhere in apocalyptic literature. One such parallel appears in the *Apocalypse of Zephaniah*. This text, preserved primarily in a single Coptic manuscript, appears to be a Jewish work from the turn of the era (Wintermute, 1:499–501). Unfortunately the passage describing the transformation follows a lacuna of two pages in the manuscript. Before the lacuna Zephaniah has been terrified by the Accuser and awed by the angel Eremiel, who rules over Hades. He has seen the scroll on which all his sins are recorded, and an angel has announced to him that he has triumphed.

After the lacuna we read, "They helped me and set me on the boat. Thousands of thousands and myriads of myriads of angels gave praise before me. I, myself, put on an angelic garment. I saw all of those angels praying. I, myself, prayed together with them, I knew their language, which they spoke with me" (8:2–4; tr. Wintermute). The angel blows his trumpet to announce Zephaniah's triumph once again, as he had before the lacuna, and Zephaniah meets the righteous heroes of the Hebrew Bible. Apparently he is now in paradise.

After he has been judged righteous, then, Zephaniah enjoys fellowship with the angels. He "put[s] on an angelic garment." With the garment on, Zephaniah can join the angels in prayer and speak their language.

It is not clear whether the seer in the *Apocalypse of Zephaniah* is to be understood as one of the dead[11] or as a privileged visitor who will return to the body at the end of his travels. If Zephaniah is one of the righteous dead, the apocalypse may be claiming angelic status for all of the righteous dead.

Like the *Apocalypse of Zephaniah*, *2 Enoch* is preserved only in a Christian language (in this case, Slavonic), but appears to be a Jewish work from first-century CE Egypt (Nickelsburg, 1981b; 188; all quotations

---

[the Holy Spirit's] glory," Charles and Fleming and Deunsing emend to "my [Isaiah's] glory." This emendation makes sense of an otherwise extremely problematic passage, and it fits well with Isaiah's inability to behold God steadily as the righteous do.

[11] The fragmentary opening scene is about a burial.

from Andersen). In *2 Enoch*, when Enoch reaches the seventh heaven, he is removed from his "earthly clothing," anointed with oil, and dressed in the "clothes of [God's] glory."[12] Then, he tells us, "I looked at myseslf, and I had become like one of the glorious ones, and there was no observable difference" (22:8–10).[13] At this point Enoch begins to serve as scribe in heaven.

This tradition about Enoch obviously contributes to the story of Enoch's transformation into the angel Metatron, the heavenly scribe who is God's angelic vice-regent, in *3 Enoch*. As its use of Enoch traditions suggests, *3 Enoch* stands closest of all of the hekhalot texts to apocalyptic literature, and it is the only hekhalot text that contains a physical transformation of the visionary (Schäfer, 1980, 221). It probably dates from the fifth or sixth century, perhaps in Babylonia (Alexander: 1:225–29).

Two different accounts of Enoch's physical transformation are preserved in *3 Enoch*. In ch. 9 Enoch grows to the size of the world and sprouts wings in the process of becoming Metatron. In ch. 15 Enoch's body becomes fire when he is taken to serve before the throne of glory. "My flesh turned to flame, my sinews to blazing fire, my bones to juniper coals, my eyelashes to lightning flashes, my eyeballs to fiery torches, the hairs of my head to hot flames, all my limbs to wings of burning fire, and the substance of my body to blazing fire" (15:1 [= Schäfer, 1981: #19 (= 855)], tr. Alexander).[14]

Schäfer takes these accounts of transformation as further evidence that in this work the traditions of ascent to the chariot have reached an

---

[12] The garments of the *Ascension of Isaiah*, the *Apocalypse of Zephaniah*, and *2 Enoch* constitute an interesting parallel, but as the passages quoted make clear, they function in somewhat different ways.

[13] MS A, the shorter text printed by Andersen, contains no mention of the dressing. It goes directly from the removal of the earthly clothes to Enoch's report of his transformation.

[14] When the mystic gazes on the garment of God in *Hekhalot Rabbati* (4:3 [= Schäfer, 1981: # 102]), "Whirling gyration grip the balls of his eyes. / And the balls of his eyes cast out and send forth torches of fire / And these enkindle him and these burn him" (tr. Scholem, 1965: 60). On the basis of the parallel to the passage quoted above from *3 Enoch*, Scholem considers this an example of transformation, but David Halperin points out to me that its context suggests that it is an instance of a danger the visionary must face. So too, I think, is R. Ishmael's report that when he looked on the prince of the first gate, "my hands were burned, and I stood without hands and without feet," which Scholem also takes as a transformation similar to Enoch's (1954: 52, 361 n. 42; Schäfer, 1981: #420). An almost identical experience is attributed to R. Ishmael in the geniza fragments of a hekhalot text published by Gruenwald (1968–69): ". . . he burned my hands and feet from me, and I sat without hands and feet. . . ." (A/2: 40). Halperin has drawn my attention to a number of instances in the Sar Torah materials where the initiate speaks of his eyes or heart being enlightened to describe the psychological or spiritual transformation that follows on learning the secret for mastering the study of Torah (Schäfer, 1981: # 279 [= # 678], # 309, # 680). The relationship of the body imagery of these passages to the physical transformation of the apocalypses requires further consideration. The magical papyri too may provide pertinent parallels.

entirely literary stage (1980: 224). The fact that the influence of the apocalypses is most evident in the hekhalot work that stands at the end of the hekhalot tradition requires further consideration.

The Experience of the Visionary

The experience of fellowship with the angels is by no means restricted to texts in which physical transformation plays a role (Collins, 1974: 21–43). Enoch serves as mediator between God and the angels in the *Book of the Watchers* (*1 Enoch* 1–36), for example, and in the *Similitudes of Enoch* (*1 Enoch* 37–71), Enoch becomes the heavenly son of man. The physical transformation of the visionary is a particularly dramatic expression of an experience known and desired in a wide range of Greco-Roman literature, from the apocalypses discussed here to gnostic texts to magical papyri to the platonic tradition.

It is not always clear whether the experience of the visionary in the apocalypses is meant to represent an experience available to others. Did the author of *2 Enoch*, for example, imagine that he or his readers could ascend to God's throne as Enoch did?

For the hekhalot texts the answer is clear. The hekhalot texts in general are concerned with instructions; they contain instructions for invoking the aid of the angels for all kinds of practical ends.[15] Like the magical papyri but unlike the apocalypses, the hekhalot texts also provide instructions for ascent.[16] The experience of participation in the angelic realm is presented as available to any initiate, not only to the pseudonymous protagonists of the ascents like R. Aqiba and R. Ishmael.

For the *Ascension of Isaiah*, too, it is clear that the experience of the visionary is understood as available to all of the righteous, after death. Isaiah is special only because he is able to attain temporary angelic status before his death. But the *Ascension of Isaiah* promises the righteous not fellowship with the angels, but superiority to them. And the promise is to all the righteous. The righteous of the seventh heaven are not only great heroes. The text emphasizes this: "And then I saw all the righteous from Adam. And I saw the holy Abel and all the righteous. And there I saw Enoch and all who were with him . . ." (9:7–9).

We know that the community at Qumran understood itself as living with the angels (Collins, 1974: 35–37). Angels were present in the camp

---

[15] The correlation of ascent with ends that are not practical is not perfect. The instructions for ascent in *Hekhalot Zutrati* (Schäfer: # 413–17) culminate in the prayer the mystic is to use to ask God to put all his servants at his disposal (# 418–19). The practical implications of this request are spelled out in the paragraph that follows (# 420). On this passage, see Halperin: 549–50.

[16] Indeed the goal of ascent in the hekhalot literature can probably be illumined by the passages in the magical papyri in which the magician identifies himself with a god or provides spells for becoming a god.

on earth and the community pictured itself as present when the angelic priests performed the liturgy in the heavenly temple (Newsom). The emphasis in the *Ascension of Isaiah* on "all the righteous" suggests a similar communal transcendence.

The *Apocalypse of Paul*

The experience of the visionary in the *Apocalypse of Paul* is very different. The *Apocalypse of Paul* was probably the most popular of all Christian apocalypses outside the canon. It is preserved in seven languages, and it spawned many descendants, apocalypses with other heroes that borrowed from it liberally and often literally, as well as a number of medieval Latin redactions (Silverstein: 1–14; Himmelfarb; 19–24). The original language was Greek, and the work was probably written in Egypt. The preserved Greek is an abridgment; the Latin is the version closest to the original. The Tarsus introduction (chs. 1–3 in the Latin) gives a precise date, 388 CE, for the work, but the introduction is probably not original; it appears at the end of the Syriac version rather than at the beginning, and it is missing altogether in the Coptic. Origen appears to have known the apocalypse, and the early third-century date this requires fits well the picture of Christianity the work presents (Casey: 27–28, 31; Himmelfarb: 18–19).

The theme of fellowship with the angels is not absent from the *Apocalypse of Paul*. The righteous soul is greeted at death by a chorus of encouraging angels (ch. 14). Most of the heroes of the Hebrew Bible Paul meets on his second visit to paradise are accompanied by angels (chs. 46–51), and Paul and his angelic guide even discuss this fact. "'Does then each of the righteous have an angel as his companion?' . . . 'Each of the saints has his own angel who helps him and sings a hymn, and the one does not leave the other'" (ch. 49) (tr. Duensing: 1965a; all quotations are from this translation).

This is the strongest statement about fellowship with the angels in the *Apocalypse of Paul*. Unlike the angelic guide in the *Ascension of Isaiah*, Paul's guide never tells him to stop calling him "Lord."[17] Paul experiences no transformation, physical or otherwise, in the course of the tour. This is particularly striking in view of the fact that the *Apocalypse of Paul* uses the *Apocalypse of Zephaniah* as a source (Himmelfarb 147–51; Wintermute, 1:506), and its borrowings include the episode from the *Apocalypse of Zephaniah* that contains the transformation quoted above.

This incident is part of Paul's tour of paradise. After he has seen the land of promise, Paul is taken to the city of Christ. "And he [the angelic

---

[17] The Latin is "dominus" in both works. In his version of the *Apocalypse of Paul*, Duensing translates "sir."

guide] put me in a golden boat and about three thousand angels were singing a hymn before me until I reached the city of Christ" (ch. 23). The boat of the *Apocalypse of Zephaniah* is now golden, while the number of angels is more modest, but the scene in the *Apocalypse of Paul* is easily recognized as corresponding to the one in the *Apocalypse of Zephaniah*. The most significant change is the angelic garment, which has been entirely eliminated from the account in the *Apocalypse of Paul*. Paul is no more one of the angels when he reaches the city than he was when he began his journey.

The elimination of the transformation of the visionary into an angel is part of the *Apocalypse of Paul*'s rejection of all aspects of the *Apocalypse of Zephaniah* that might seem questionable from a later point of view (Himmelfarb, 151). It is an especially clear example of this tendency because the scene in which the transformation takes place is retained.

For the author of the *Apocalypse of Paul*, the boundaries between divine and human are firmly fixed. Despite the role of angels in greeting and escorting righteous souls in the period between their death and judgment, the ordinary righteous dwell in the city of Christ without angelic companions. Indeed in the visit to the city of Christ even the heroes of the Hebrew Bible live without angelic company in contradiction to the picture of the second visit to paradise.

The *Apocalypse of Paul*'s concern is sin and punishment, righteousness and reward. As the *Apocalypse of Zephaniah* shows, there is nothing about the subject itself that prevents fellowship with the angels. Rather the *Apocalypse of Paul*'s unwillingness to allow human entry into the realm of the angels is related to the way the *Apocalypse of Paul* understands the community to which it is addressed. The example of Qumran is instructive here.

At Qumran, identification with the angels, even during life, is possible because of the acute sense of the contrast between the righteousness of those inside the community and the wickedness of those outside. Membership in the community defines righteousness, and there is no continuity between righteousness and unrighteousness. The view of the world of most apocalypses is not unlike that of the community at Qumran, with a strong distinction between those inside the community and those outside.[18] The Ascension of Isaiah seems to manifest just such a view.

The *Apocalypse of Paul*, on the other hand, admits degrees of righteousness. When Paul has seen the land of promise, his guide tells him that what he has seen is for the married righteous; even greater things await virgins (ch. 22). The angel's comments make it clear that at least

---

[18] Collins (1983: 531–48) has recently argued that *2 Enoch*, *3 Baruch*, and the *Testament of Abraham* are quite universalist in their outlook.

some of the inhabitants of the land of promise were guilty of at least minor sins. ". . . When the righteous have come forth from the body and see the promises and good things which God has prepared for them, they will sigh and weep yet again, saying: Why did we utter a word from our mouth to irritate our neighbour even for a single day?" (ch. 22). Outside the city of Christ Paul sees penitents who will be able to enter the city only at Christ's coming; despite their asceticism, they were guilty of pride (ch. 24).

The *Apocalypse of Paul* is a document of the third century. Its church includes both righteous and sinners living side by side. Membership in the community does not determine moral status, nor are human beings divided neatly and emphatically into two classes. For people who believe that the righteous sometimes sin, the boundary between human beings and angels is likely to be well defined.

The Question of Genre

It is clear, then, that the *Apocalypse of Paul* and the *Ascension of Isaiah* 6–11 offer very different understandings of the nature of the experience of the visionary and of the righteous after death. Is this difference adequately represented by the classification of these two works as members of the same sub-group?

The discussion of genre in *Semeia* makes a largely successful attempt to overcome the scholarly habit of concentrating on historical apocalypses. But in the end the categories it delineates are not entirely free of the influence of that habit. For Collins in his introduction to the volume (1979: 9–10), transcendence is at the center of the definition of the genre. The different understandings of transcendence are then organized under headings of "cosmic and/or political eschatology" (with historical review, type a; without such a review, type b) and "only personal eschatology" (type c). Yet I think that it can be shown that the presence or absence of cosmic or political eschatology is often not of great significance, and that each of the headings can include views so widely divergent that the categories are not very useful.

The *Apocalypse of Paul* is a tour of paradise and hell. I have argued elsewhere at length that there is a recognizable genre, or perhaps for our purposes here subgenre, of tours of hell in apocalyptic literature. Explanations of the sights the visionary sees that begin with a demonstrative pronoun or adjective, often in response to a question from the visionary that also uses a demonstrative, are the formal features that unite these tours (Himmelfarb: 45–50). There are also impressive similarities of content from tour to tour in the descriptions of the sins and punishments (Himmelfarb, 68–126). Some of these apocalypses contain tours of paradise with demonstrative explanations. These tour apocalypses are related to each other in a variety of ways, ranging from direct literary dependence to use of a common stock of imagery for describing paradise and hell (Himmelfarb: 127–68).

Those tours of hell that Yarbro Collins considers in her chapter in *Semeia* appear in three different categories. The *Apocalypse of Peter,* the earliest of the tours of hell, is placed in category Ib, apocalypses of cosmic and/or political eschatology with neither historical review nor otherworldly journey. It is placed in this category because the tour of hell in the *Apocalypse of Peter* takes place in a vision. The first half of the apocalypse, before the vision of hell, is concerned with predictions of the second coming that make veiled allusions to the author's time. Hell and paradise are to be the fate of souls at the final judgment. In this the *Apocalypse of Peter* stands apart from later tours of hell, and I shall leave it aside in my discussion of the *Semeia* categories.

In category IIb, otherworldly journey with cosmic and/or political eschatology, we find three tours of hell, the *Apocalypse of Paul,* the *Apocalypse of Esdras* (the *Apocalypse of Ezra* in Himmelfarb), and the *Apocalypse of the Virgin Mary* (the *Ethiopic Apocalypse of Mary* in Himmelfarb). In category IIc, apocalypses with an otherworldly journey and only personal eschatology, there appear two other tours of hell, the *Testament of Isaac* 5–6, and the *Apocalypse of the Holy Mother of God Concerning the Punishments* (the *Greek Apocalypse of Mary* in Himmelfarb).

With the exception of the chapters from the *Testament of Isaac,* all of these texts are complete works devoted to tours of hell and in some cases of paradise as well with demonstrative questions and explanations clearly marked. Both the *Apocalypse of the Virgin Mary* and the *Apocalypse of the Holy Mother of God* draw on the *Apocalypse of Paul* for their sins and punishments (Himmelfarb: 122–26), while the *Apocalypse of Esdras* shows similarities to other tours of hell in its sins and punishments (Himmelfarb, 160–65). In the *Testament of Isaac,* the formal features are not as developed, and the sins and punishments are related in only a general way to those of the other tours (Himmelfarb: 46 (chart), 167–68).

For the *Apocalypse of Peter* the vision of hell and paradise will become a reality at the end, which is near at hand (Yarbro Collins: 72). In the later tours the orientation is very different. There is no indication that the end is near. In response to their complaints against mankind in the *Apocalypse of Paul* (chs. 4–7), God forbids the sun, the moon, the stars, and the sea to bring disaster upon the earth. "I know all these things," God says of the sins reported to him, "for my eye sees and my ear hears, but my patience bears with them until they are converted and repent. But if they do not return to me I will judge them all." (This response appears in both ch. 4 and ch. 5; a very similar one appears in ch. 6.) This is hardly a statement fraught with eschatological expectation. The description of the land of promise (ch. 22) is introduced by the angelic guide's explanation that the land will appear at Christ's second coming, but there is no hint that that coming is any time soon. Aside from the Tarsus introduction, which serves only to place the publication (or one stage of the publication) of the work, there are no references to contemporary events in the *Apocalypse of Paul*.[19] The heroes of the Hebrew Bible, in whom there is considerable interest, are used as exempla, not for historical purposes, as Yarbro Collins notes (86). The purpose of the *Apocalypse of Paul* is to encourage proper behavior among Christians. The author surely believed, like other Christians, that Christ would one day come again, but he does not seem to have been particularly concerned with that coming, probably because he did not expect it any time soon.

The absence of cosmic or political eschatology in an early Jewish apocalypse is significant; it may mean that the author of the text had no such expectations.[20] But in works like the *Apocalypse of Paul* and the later Christian tours of hell, a belief in the second coming, though probably not intense expectation, can be assumed even if it is never expressed. Thus the absence or presence of an explicit statement of that belief may not mean very much. To assign categories based on the fact that the *Apocalypse of the Virgin Mary* mentions in passing the second coming while the *Apocalypse of the Holy Mother of God* does not obscures the more important resemblances between them.

The *Ascension of Isaish* probably has a better claim to be considered an "otherworldly journey with cosmic and/or political eschatology" than the tours of hell. The climax of the *Ascension of Isaiah* 6–11 is a vision of the descent of Christ through the seven heavens and his subsequent triumphant ascent. The central events of Christian eschatology, then, are far more prominent here than in the tours of hell, and the eschatological content of the vision of Christ's descent has been integrated into the picture of the heavens, for the righteous will not receive their thrones and crowns until Christ has ascended (9:16–18). Still I hope that our discussion of the experience of the visionary supports Yarbro Collins' claim that the *Ascension of Isaiah* is interested in the contents of the heavens not merely as the setting for the vision but for their own sake (85).

There is no clearly definable sub-genre of apocalyptic literature like the tours of hell to which the *Ascension of Isaiah* belongs, but we can place it in relation to other apocalypses and ascents. It shares the schema of seven heavens with a number of other apocalypses like *2 Enoch*, the *Testament of Levi* 2–7, and the *Apocalypse of Abraham*. But these apocalypses do not share their picture of the heavens as the tours of hell

[19]There are reflections of contemporary practices and beliefs (Casey: 28; Himmelfarb: 18–19).
[20]See Collins' discussion of *3 Baruch* (1983: 539–40).

share their picture of hell. To consider only the examples just named, these apocalypses have in common with the *Ascension of Isaiah* an understanding of heaven, or rather some of the heavens, as temple, an understanding they share with some of the hekhalot literature. Yet this understanding receives quite different degrees of emphasis from text to text. In *2 Enoch*, each heaven contains a different set of phenomena, cosmology plays a prominent role, and only in the two highest heavens is the angelic liturgy prominent. In the *Testament of Levi*, the lower heavens are devoted to cosmology and eschatology, while the higher heavens are the scene of the angelic temple service. The *Apocalypse of Abraham* pays little attention to the contents of any of its heavens except the highest, in which songs of praise are offered by the angelic creatures of the chariot throne itself.

We have seen that Isaiah's transformation has parallels in a number of other texts, and this too suggest a possibility for categorizing apocalyptic ascents. The way in which the relationship of the hero of the apocalypse to angels and men is conceived is an important aspect of the outlook of a work, and one that has received relatively little attention.

If transcendence is the key to the apocalypses, we still need to ask, what kind of transendence? How is the heavenly realm in which transcendence is experienced conceived? The master paradigm in *Semeia* offers no way of introducing the quality of the visionary's experience as a factor in the categorization of apocalypses, and it provides far more differentiation in the discussion of the temporal axis (items 4–9) than for the spatial axis (item 10) (Collins: 6–8). "Otherworldly elements" (item 10) is subdivided into "otherworldly regions" (10.1) and "otherworldly beings" (10.2). The message of our discussion here has been that the nature of the visionary's experience and the specifics of those regions and beings matter.[21]

WORKS CONSULTED

Alexander, Philip.
    1983   "3 (Hebrew Apocalypse of) Enoch." Pp. 223–315 in Vol. 1, *Old Testament Pseudepigrapha*. Ed. James H. Charlesworth. Garden City, NY: Doubleday.

Andersen, Francis I.
    1983   "2 (Slavonic Apocalypse of) Enoch." Pp. 91–221 in Vol. 1, *Old Testament Pseudepigrapha*. Ed. James H. Charlesworth. Garden City, NY: Doubleday.

[21] I would like to thank David Halperin for his helpful comments on this paper, which go beyond the observations that could be individually acknowledged. Responsibility for the content of the paper is, of course, mine alone.

Casey, Robert.
    1933   "The Apocalypse of Paul." *JTS* 34: 26–31.

Charles, R. H.
    1900   *The Ascension of Isaiah*. London: Adam and Charles Black.

Collins, John J.
    1974   "Apocalyptic Eschatology as the Transcendence of Death." *CBQ*
                 36: 21–43.
    1979   "Introduction: Towards the Morphology of a Genre." Pp. 1–19 in
                 John J. Collins, ed.
    1983   "The Genre Apocalypse in Hellenistic Judaism." Pp. 531–48 in
                 Apocalypticism in the Mediterranean World and the Near East.
                 Ed. David Hellholm. Proceedings of the International Collo-
                 quium on Apocalypticism, Uppsala, August 12–17, 1979.
                 Tübingen: J. C. B. Mohr (Paul Siebeck).

Collins, John J., ed.
    1979   *Apocalypse: The Morphology of a Genre. Semeia* 14.

Cross, Frank Moore.
    1973   *Canaanite Myth and Hebrew Epic*. Cambridge, Mass: Harvard.

Duensing, H.
    1965a   "The Apocalypse of Paul." Pp. 755–98 in Vol. 2. *New Testament
                 Apocrypha*. Eds. Edgar Hennecke, Wilhelm Schneemelcher,
                 and Robin McL. Wilson. Philadelphia: Westminster.
    1965b   "Epistula Apostolorum." Pp. 189–227 in Vol. 2, *New Testament
                 Apocrypha*. Eds. Edgar Hennecke, Wilhelm Schneemelcher,
                 and Robin McL. Wilson. Philadelphia: Westminster.

Fleming, J. and Duensing, H.
    1965   "The Ascension of Isaiah." Pp. 642–63 in Vol. 2, *New Testament
                 Apocrypha*. Eds. Edgar Hennecke, Wilhelm Schneemelcher,
                 and Robin McL. Wilson. Philadelphia: Westminster.

Gruenwald, Ithamar.
    1968–69   "New Passages from *Hekhalot* Literature" (Hebrew). *Tarbiz* 38:
                 354–72.
    1980   *Apocalyptic and Merkavah Mysticism*. Leiden: Brill.

Halperin, David.
    1984   "A New Edition of the Hekhalot Literature." *JAOS* 104: 543–52.

Himmelfarb, Martha.
    1983   *Tours of Hell: An Apocalyptic Form in Jewish and Christian
                 Literature*. Philadelphia: University of Pennsylvania.

Mullen, E. Theodore, Jr.
    1980   *The Assembly of the Gods*. Harvard Semitic Monographs 24.
                 Chico, CA: Scholars Press.

Newsom, Carol
    forthcoming   *The Qumran Songs of the Sabbath Sacrifice: Edition, Translation, and Commentary.* Harvard Semitic Monographs. Atlanta: Scholars Press.

Nickelsburg, George W. E.
    1981a   "Enoch, Levi, and Peter: Recipients of Revelation in Upper Galilee." *JBL* 100: 576–82.
    1981b   *Jewish Literature from the Bible to the Mishnah.* Philadelphia: Fortress.

Schäfer, Peter.
    1975   *Rivalität zwischen Engeln und Menschen.* Berlin and New York: de Gruyter.
    1980   "Engel und Menschen in der Hekhalot-Literatur." *Kairos* 22: 201–25.
    1981   *Synopse zur Hekhalot-Literatur.* In collaboration with Margarete Schlüter and Hans Georg von Mutius. Texte und Studien zum Antiken Judentum 2. Tübingen: J. C. B. Mohr (Paul Siebeck).

Scholem, Gershom G.
    1954   *Major Trends in Jewish Mysticism.* 3rd ed. New York: Schocken.
    1965   *Jewish Gnosticism, Merkabah Mysticism, and Talmudic Tradition.* 2nd rev. ed. New York: Jewish Theological Seminary.

Silverstein, Theodore.
    1935   *Visio Sancti Pauli.* Studies and Documents 4. London: Christophers.

Smith, Morton.
    1978   *Jesus the Magician.* San Francisco: Harper and Row.

Wintermute, O. S.
    1983   "The Apocalypse of Zephaniah." Pp. 497–507 in Vol. 1, *Old Testament Pseudepigrapha.* Ed. James H. Charlesworth. Garden City, NY: Doubleday.

Yarbro Collins, Adela.
    1979   "Early Christian Apocalypses." Pp. 61–121 in John J. Collins, ed.

THE GENRE AND FUNCTION OF THE *SHEPHERD OF HERMAS*

Carolyn Osiek
Catholic Theological Union

ABSTRACT

Discussions of form and content of apocalyptic literature cannot be dissociated from discussion of *function*, since the latter is the key to understanding an apocalypse within its own context. In spite of some questioning to the contrary, *Hermas* meets the qualifications of apocalyptic literature. The key to its difference from much apocalyptic literature is in its function. The function of apocalypticism is to address a crisis of some kind. Just as Revelation responded to a perceived crisis of one kind, so too did *Hermas*. In the case of *Hermas* the crisis is not one of political persecution, nor certainly is it the need to contribute to the discipline of ecclesiastical penitence. Rather, the crisis concerns the vitality of the Christian community through the quality of its inner relationships. Far from being apocalypticism failed, *Hermas* represents a new adaptation of a literary form to meet changing needs in changing situations.

Speaking about the *Shepherd of Hermas* is something like speaking about the Letter of Jude—not in regard to length of the document, certainly, but in regard to the type of response it usually provokes: a short attention span and a long yawn. Indeed its length, monotony, and the pedantic style of large sections of it pose serious obstacles to all but the most devoted reader. My own interest in *Hermas* began not through a study of apocalypticism but rather through pursuit of the social history of early Christianity, hence a different approach and different expectations. As I pursued my study of the document, I became convinced that not in spite of but because of its literary form, it has much to tell us about the life and problems of Christians in a given situation.

For this reason both questions of form and content as well as questions of function need to be considered. This paper will briefly review the question of the apocalyptic genre of *Hermas*, then go on to join the current discussion of the *function* of apocalyptic genre as it appears in *Hermas*.

The recent work of D. Hellholm, *Das Visionenbuch des Hermas als Apokalypse,* is encouraging in that it represents a new attempt to tackle the old problem of the relationship of *Hermas* to the apocalyptic literary tradition. This ambitious undertaking aims by a semiotic analysis of the *Visions* to establish the relationship between form critical method and modern text theory. Since only volume I of a two-volume work has so far appeared, we do not yet have the total picture of this attempt. Thus its final outcome is yet to be evaluated. Unfortunately it does not seem that vol. II will appear in the near future.

Earlier studies have generally tended to decide for multiple authorship of the work as a whole, thus allowing for a plurality of genres and original contexts (exceptions: Joly: 11–16; Hilhorst: 19–31). The most extreme theory of diverse authorship is that of Coleborne who would divide the whole book into as many as seven sections from six different authors on the basis of linguistic analysis. This seems unnecessarily complicated, whereas the proposal of S. Giet seems the most reasonable in terms of divisions in the book and assumption of different authorship, even if everyone cannot go along with his theories of who the authors may have been.

Giet proposes that *Vis.* 1–4 were written by the original Hermas, contemporary with Clement of Rome in the late first century (*Vis.* 2.4.3.); *Sim.* 9, which recapitulates the theme of the tower from *Vis.* 3, by the brother of Pius in the middle of the second century (Muratorian Canon); and *Vis.* 5–*Sim.* 8 and *Sim.* 10 by an unknown author sometime later.

Using Giet's thesis as a framework provides a reasonable way of assessing stylistic and thematic differences in the material. As even the manuscript evidence suggests, there is a clean break between *Vis.* 4 and *Vis.* 5. The latter serves as an introduction to the *Mandates* which follow, while the first four visions are characterized by considerably more apocalyptic elements of form: a heavenly revelatory agent, a mystified and inquiring recipient, visions and symbols, instructions about dissemination of the revelation, a sense of urgency because of the impending *thlipsis* (*Vis.* 2.2.8; 4.1.1, 2.5, 3.6, etc.; see further descriptions in A. Y. Collins, 1979: 74–75). Paraenesis, an unusual but not unknown component of apocalyptic literature, is also an important part of the content of the *Visions*.

The *Mandates* and *Similitudes* lay less stress on urgency and imminence, far more on paraenesis, but the difference is one of degree, not kind. The literary devices of revelatory agent and symbolic visions are sustained throughout, though the visions are usually explained by the revealer in prolonged and (to the modern reader) often boring detail. There is elaborate use of allegory in the explanations; indeed, the author

sometimes seems to delight in making the allegories as long and complicated as possible. Yet the eschatological symbol of the building of the
tower, begun in the *Visions* to signify the time when repentance is
possible (*Vis.* 3.3.3, 5.5, 8.9, 9.5), is picked up again in *Sim.* 9 and 10 as a
basis for expanded allegory and a continued exhortation to repentance
while there is time (*Sim.* 9.32.1). The final exhortation (*Sim.* 10.4.4)
returns to the image of the tower. Thus in spite of the sustained emphasis
in this very long document on this-worldly existence and its ethical
exigencies, the overall framework of the book envisages a limited time in
which earthly action is possible.

Because of ambiguities of content and theology as well as form, the
classification of *Hermas* as apocalypse has long been disputed. As has
already been mentioned, much of the content is devoted to paraenetic
instruction, often in the form of commandments, to the extent that the
eschatological perspective seems frequently to get lost. Some parts of the
book (especially *Sim.* 9) contain various and often peculiar elements of
Christology that send students of the development of doctrine reeling.
The recurring and insistent theme of repentance, even though laced with
a certain eschatological urgency, is an unfamiliar element in apocalypticism. The historical and political concerns associated with Jewish apocalypticism seem to be lacking in *Hermas* (Synder: 9–10), but this
expectation needs to be carefully evaluated in comparison with other
Christian apocalypses and the degree and type of "political" content in
any early Christian writings (this will be taken up again under function,
below). A. Y. Collins in her survey of early Christian apocalypses in
Semeia 14 concludes that "since Herm is characterized both by apocalyptic eschatology and by revelation mediated by otherworldly beings, there
is no good reason to exclude it from the genre 'apocalypse'" (A. Y.
Collins, 1979: 75). I concur in that judgment. For those impressed by
statistics, of the 28 elements suggested as constitutive of apocalyptic
form, *Hermas* possesses 16, in a list of Christian apocalypses whose
average number is 13.3. In regard to its "deviant" content, perhaps more
discussion is needed about the boundaries of a genre, the kind of discussion launched in *Semeia* 14, and the differences not only of form and style
but of content and scope between Jewish and Christian apocalypses.

Let us now turn our attention to the function of the apocalyptic genre
in *Hermas*, a direction that is at present being pursued more widely in
the study of early Christian apocalypticism and one which usually
provokes more interest. Recently several studies have tackled this question in regard to the "favorite" Christian apocalypse, the Book of Revelation (Gager: 49–65; Aune; A. Y. Collins; Thompson). I would like to
extend this kind of discussion to *Hermas*.

P. Hanson speaks of the dialectic between vision and reality which is
at the heart of all ethical religions, a dialectic which must be maintained

if there is to be vitality in a religious tradition. The vision calls institutions and structures (and I would add, people) to judgment, while the realism maintains those institutions and structures and assures continuity (Hanson: 21–22, 29–30). Jewish apocalyptic eschatology, he suggests, discloses to the elect in usually esoteric form the cosmic vision of God's sovereignty. In contrast to its precursor, prophetic eschatology, it has largely ceased to translate the revelation into history, politics, and human action because of its historical pessimism. Instead, it provides a means of escape "from the growing contradiction between glorious promise and harsh reality" (11–12, 27). Another interpretation would be that it provides a vision strong enough to *sustain* a community in its present harsh reality. Such would be the traditional understanding of the function of the Book of Revelation, for example.

More recent investigation of the function of Revelation in light of its sociohistorical context would suggest something different, however. Close study of the contextual historical information (A. Y. Collins, Thompson) is hard put to produce evidence of Domitianic persecution of Christians. What then is the harsh reality in which the author wishes to sustain the community? If crisis and deprivation theory are no longer adequate to explain the function of a piece of apocalyptic literature like Revelation, what is? If there is no actual (that is, external political) crisis behind Revelation, says Collins, there must be at least a *perceived* crisis with a sociohistorical dimension that has something to do with the social identity of Christians, with Nero's persecution, and with the destruction of Jerusalem (A. Y. Collins, 1984: 84–110).

Is a "perceived" crisis any less a crisis if it is shared by a large enough group of people, even if it has more to do with their response to their situation than with a threat imposed directly from outside? Let us remember that the seven letters of Rev 2–3 raise far more concerns about false teachers and religious clashes than they do about civil persecution (reflected only in Rev 2:10, 13). A perceived crisis can be brought about by internal as well as external factors.

In the *Visions* of Hermas there is repeated warning about the coming of a great *thlipsis* (*Vis.* 2.2.7, 3.4; 4.1.1, 2.5, 3.6. *Vis.* 3.6.5 may refer to the same kind of context, as well references to those who have suffered in *Vis.* 3.1.9, 2.1, 5.2; *Sim.* 8.3.6–7). If it is difficult from historical sources to establish a persecution under Domitian to fit Revelation, it is equally so with *Hermas* whose earliest section, the *Visions*, presumably comes from about the same time. A Neronic persecution, which in the limited location of Rome may well have impressed itself on Christian memory, was nearly a generation earlier. It is therefore difficult to suppose that the warnings of *thlipsis* to come, understood as civil persecution, are prophecy-after-the-event intended for a contemporary audience, though the references to past problems may well be historical reminiscences. The coming eschatological conflict must be envisioned here.

What can with some assurance be reconstructed about the context of *Hermas* is that the final edition of the book comes from Rome or its environs as far as Campania, probably no later than the third quarter of the second century, though the composition of its earlier parts may span more than half a century previous. There is no reason to doubt that the principal author's name is Hermas, any more than that the name of the author of Revelation is John. The main biographical data in the *Visions*— that Hermas is a freedman who once belonged to a woman named Rhoda, and that his family are a source of scandal in the Church—are variously disputed or accepted. Inasmuch as they make no substantial contribution to the theological structure, I see no reason to doubt them, since they serve no obvious purpose.

The situation of Christians in early and middle second-century Rome is not well attested. The time of the apostles and Clement's letterwriting lies in the past and the liturgical and christological controversies of later in the century are yet to blossom. It is the time of Justin, Marcion, and Valentinus, a trio of names indicative of both external and internal conflict. There is not a shred of solid evidence relating what we know of them to *The Shepherd*, the bulk of which may have been written only a few years before their prominence. Hermas' concerns do not seem to be theirs. This difference need not be attributed to a discrepancy of time or place, but simply to diversity of perspective and concern.

I would dispute the usual assumption that the principal concern of Hermas as a whole is the promulgation of a second repentance, and that the book is thus most properly catalogued as a step along the way to later penitential discipline. That it serves this function in the development of ecclesiastical penitence may be true, but this neither exhausts nor even properly names the function and importance of *The Shepherd* for its contemporaries or for the vitality of the early church.

It becomes clear in the analysis of certain passages (*Vis.* 1.1.8, 3.1; 2.3.1; 3.6.5–7, 9.4–5, 11.3; *Man.* 3.5; 5.2.2; 6.2.5; 8.3; 10.1.4–5; 12.2.1; *Sim.* 1.8–10; 2 throughout; 4.5.7; 8.8.1–2; 8.9.1; 9.19.3; 9.20.1–2, 30.4–5, 31.2) that preoccupation with material comforts and business affairs comes under heavy criticism by Hermas, and that *dipsychia*, on occasion explicitly associated with these material distractions but more often not, is a major target of criticism, inveighed against more than 50 times. Both of these issues are identified as reasons for the repentance of Christians, but neither has to do with a *doctrine* of second repentance. The teaching about these and other shortcomings and social evils has little to do with history and politics in the usual sense. It has to do rather with ethics and morality—some would say moralizing. The whole of *The Shepherd* is a call to a change of heart, within a perspective of a limited time frame. Recent studies of the function of paraenesis for both external and internal propaganda purposes (e.g. D. Balch and J. Elliott on 1 Peter) have enhanced our appreciation of the usefulness of this type of literature for community building, especially in a situation where there is no perceived imminent crisis impending from outside.

Such, I believe, is the case with *Hermas*. The perceived crisis originates rather in the degeneration of quality of life in a milieu in which many Christians are economically comfortable, upwardly mobile, and inclined to find vigorous fidelity to the demands of religious visionaries uninteresting if not downright threatening. Indeed, we might suppose that the yawns of modern readers had ancient precedents. In such an atmosphere, where are the historical and political dimensions of apocalypticism, such as they may be? These are not people caught up in world affairs, but rather in the daily events of busines-as-usual in the Roman streets. Their history is the story of their church; their politics concern church leadership and the allegiances demanded by their faith (*Vis.* 1.4.2; 2.2.6; 3.5.1; *Man.* 10.1.4; *Sim.* 1.8–11). The secular is certainly not intrinsically evil, but it is a threat to the well-being of Christians. A type of privatized religion, perhaps; at least a severe narrowing of the horizon, but one which met the needs of the time.

The overall framework remains one of cosmic eschatology, involving ultimate destruction of the world and divine retribution (*Vis.* 4.3; *Sim.* 4.4; 6.5.7; 8.7.3–6; 9.14.1–2; et al). The heavenly revealers convey the bulk of the message. The elderly lady of the *Visions* who rejuvenates with the passage of time and is the symbol of the Church suggests the external nature of the Church as bridge between heaven and earth. The Shepherd who takes over her role in *Vis.* 5 is sent by "the distinguished angel" (*Vis.* 5.2), a manifestation of the Holy Spirit, the Son of God (*Sim.* 9.1.1–3). The major unifying image is the cosmic tower built upon water (*Vis.* 3.2.4), another aspect of the Church (3.3), whose building process is the movement toward the consummation of time, whose completion is the end and terminates the chance for repentance (*Vis.* 3.5.5, 8.9, 9.5; *Sim.* 9.32.1; 10.4.4).

The "comprehensive definition of the genre" of apocalypse in *Semeia* 14 is perfectly coherent with *Hermas:* "a genre of revelatory literature with a narrative framework, in which a revelation is mediated by an otherworldly being to a human recipient, disclosing a transcendent reality which is both temporal, insofar as it envisages eschatological salvation, and spatial insofar as it involves another, supernatural world" (J. Collins: 9). What causes problems in terms of genre is the centrality of repentance and paraenesis in *Hermas*. It is here that we need to focus attention on function and purpose rather than on form; here, I suggest, we have a proving ground for the way in which function modifies form.

Either we can judge that departure from conventional apocalyptic form and content is departure from apocalyptic genre, in a sense, apocalypticism failed; or we can ask whether such modifications of form and content as are present in *Hermas* open apocalyptic genre to new possibilities because it is able to adapt to a changed role in a changed situation. To go in this latter direction, we need to ask new questions about the function of ethical teaching within apocalypticism. Here it is helpful to recall again the tension between realism and vision that Hanson sees at work in the growth of the genre. The ethical, paraenetic content gives shape to the realism just as much as the apparitions of Church, beast, Shepherd, and tower give shape to the vision. The tension between realism and vision achieves a new synthesis. I would maintain that the purpose of *The Shepherd of Hermas* is neither the proclamation of a second repentance nor the opportunity to perpetrate moralization in apocalyptic garb, but the translation of eschatological vision into realistic terms.

J. Gager remarks of the aftermath of the failure of prophecy that "the remarkable fact that the majority remains should prompt us to ask whether the millennium has in some sense come to life in the experience of the community as a whole." He goes on to suggest that "various elements of early Christian ethics can best be understood as efforts to capture in the present the conditions of the future" (Gager: 49–50) through such means as asceticism and the elimination of social distinctions and injustice. It is here that the poles of realism and vision meet in the ethical exhortations and eschatological projections of *Hermas*.

It has been asserted that apocalyptic myth, rather than simply responding to social reality and providing a means of escape from it, may also serve to shape heavily a community's perception of reality, and that the symbiosis of apocalyptic myth and social reality forms a fluid mutuality of cause and effect (Thompson: 12–16). This dynamic is operative in *Hermas* as well as in *Revelation*, with the added factors of repentance and paraenesis. The social reality prompts a response of ethical exhortation within a framework of apocalyptic myth; at the same time, apocalyptic myth gives meaning and shape to a prophetic and paraenetic interpretation of the social reality. In these varied ways an author or group of authors speak their concerns to their second-century community and carry on in their present a vision of the future through a tradition from the past by which they can interpret their world.

WORKS CONSULTED

Aune, David E.
1981   "The Social Matrix of the Apocalypse of John." *BR* 26: 16–32.

Balch, David L.
1981   *Let Wives Be Submissive: The Domestic Code of I Peter.* SBLMS
            26. Chico, CA: Scholars.

Coleborne, W.
1969   "A Linguistic Approach to the Problem of Structure and Com-
            position of the Shepherd of Hermas." *Colloquium* 3: 133–42.
1970   "The *Shepherd* of Hermas: A Case for Multiple Authorship and
            Some Implications." Berlin: *Studia Patristica* 10:1 = TU 107: 65–
            70.

Collins, Adela Y.
1979   "The Early Christian Apocalypses." *Semeia* 14: 61–121.
1981   "Dating the Apocalypse of John." *BR* 26: 33–45.
1984   *Crisis and Catharsis: The Power of the Apocalypse.* Phila-
            delphia: Westminster.

Collins, John J.
1979   "Introduction: Towards the Morphology of a Genre." *Semeia* 14:
            1–20.

Elliott, John H.
1981   *A Home for the Homeless: A Sociological Exegesis of 1 Peter.*
            Philadelphia: Fortress.

Gager, John G.
1975   *Kingdom and Community: The Social World of Early Chris-
            tianity.* Englewood Cliffs, NJ: Prentice-Hall.

Giet, Stanislas
1963   *Hermas et les pasteurs: les trois auteurs du Pasteur d'Hermas.*
            Paris: Presses Universitaires de France.

Hanson, Paul D.
1975   *The Dawn of Apocalyptic: The Historical and Sociological Roots
            of Jewish Apocalyptic Eschatology.* Philadelphia: Fortress.

Hellholm, David
1980   *Das Visionenbuch des Hermas als Apokalypse: Form-
            geschichtliche und texttheoretische Studien zu einer
            literarischen Gattung.* Vol. I: Methodologische
            Vorüberlegungen und makrostruckturelle Textanalyse.* ConBNT
            13:1. Lund: C. W. K. Gleerup.

Hilhorst, A.
1976   *Sémitismes et latinismes dans le Pasteur d'Hermas.* Graecitas
            Christianorum Primaeva 5. Nijmegen: Dekker and Van de Vegt.

Joly, Robert
    1958   *Hermas le Pasteur*. Introduction, critical text, translation, and notes. SC 53. Paris: Editions du Cerf.

Snyder, Graydon F.
    1968   *The Shepherd of Hermas*. Translation and commentary. Apostolic Fathers 6. Ed. R. M. Grant. Camden, NJ: T. Nelson.

Thompson, Leonard
    1986   "A Sociological Analysis of Tribulation in the Apocalypse of John." In this volume, pp. 147–74.

.

THE FOLLOWERS OF THE LAMB: VISIONARY RHETORIC AND SOCIAL-POLITICAL SITUATION*

Elisabeth Schüssler Fiorenza
Episcopal Divinity School

ABSTRACT

Using Rev 14:1–5 as an example, this article explores some conditions and possibilities for interpreting the language used by John. First, as a poetic work with a symbolic universe and language, Rev requires the interpreter to acknowledge different layers of meaning rather than a single definite one. Second, as a rhetorical work, it calls for the examination of the strategic position and textual relations of the symbols and images within the entire book, as well as the analysis of specific markers John used to ensure that his audience would understand these symbols and images in a particular way and be moved by them. Finally, the article applies these structural principles to the book as a whole, pointing out how its symbolic universe was a fitting response to the social-historical-political situation faced by the Christians of Asia Minor. Although John could not change the brute realities of their world, he could control their destructive effects by taking his audience on a dramatic-cathartic journey. The article then closes with some suggestions on understanding Rev in a society such as ours where a different rhetorical situation exists.

> Our visions, stories and utopias
> are not only aesthetic:
> they engage us.
> Amos Wilder

In his summary of the overall outline and analysis of the Apocalypse W. Bousset stresses that Rev 14:1–5 was not taken over from a source but that it is formulated as "contrast-image" by the author. However he

*This essay was originally published in *The Book of Revelation—Justice and Judgement* (Philadelphia: Fortress Press, 1985) and *Discipleship in the New Testament*, ed. Fernando Segovia (Philadelphia: Fortress Press, 1985), and is used here by permission of the publisher.

concludes: "Ganz klar wird es nicht was der Apk. sich bei der Szene
denkt" (146). This exegetical helplessness before the passage is confirmed
by I. T. Beckwith in 1919 (653) and repeated by R. H. Mounce in 1977:
"Verses 1–5 are often referred to as in some respects the most enigmatic
in the book" (266). Such an exegetical conundrum is surprising because
the passage has a clearly marked composition and structure: It consists of:

1. *vision:* 14:1 describes the 144,000 with the Lamb on Mount Sion,
2. *audition:* 14:2–3 announce the voice from heaven and choral song
   before the throne of God which none could learn except the
   144,000 and
3. *explanation:* 14:4–5 identify the 144,000 with a four-fold charac-
   terization: they are virgins, followers of the Lamb, a firstfruit, and
   blameless.

The literary context of this segment is also clear: The 144,000 around the
Lamb on Mount Sion are the anti-image of the beast and its followers
which were depicted in the preceding chapter 13. The tableau is followed
by three angelic proclamations to the whole world; the first angel proclaims the gospel of God's judgment and justice to all the world. These
"glad tidings" consist especially in the "fall of Babylon," as the second
angel underlines (14:8). The third angel threatens those who worship the
beast with eternal punishment (14: 9–11). The whole section of proclamation is concluded with two sayings addressed to Christians: 14:12 is a
comment of the seer with respect to the *hypomonē* or consistent resistance of the saints while the *makarismos* in 14:13 is pronounced by a voice
from heaven. It refers to those who "die in the Lord," a traditional
Christian expression.

While one might quibble over the translation of certain expressions
in the angelic warnings or in the description of the two beasts and their
charagma, the overall interpretation of the context is not contested. The
zeitgeschichtlich interpretation of the beast and its cult-agent as referring
to Rome is now widely accepted, although exegetes might differ on
whether the "beast" refers to Nero or Domitian. Although today we have
widespread agreement on the 144,000 as the anti-image to the followers
of the beast, commentators do not come to the same conclusions as to
their identity. Some of the following identifications are suggested. The
144,000 are understood as Jewish-Christians, elect and "saved" Christians, Christian ascetic males, the eschatologically saved and protected
"holy rest" of Israel, the "perfect" victims and sacrifice, the highpriestly
followers of the Lamb, the military army of the Lamb gathering on Sion
for the messianic battle, those who have followed the Lamb into death, or
those who follow the Lamb in heaven (Boecher: 56–63).

For each of these interpretations (and others could probably be
added) some contextual or tradition-historical argument can be adduced.

The possibility of interpretational variance would increase even more if we would hold a church-or world-historical rather than eschatological *zeitgeschichtlich* interpretation, or if we would see the visions of the book as predictions of events in our times and as promises to readers of today rather than to those in the first century. Finally, a "timeless" interpretation would add a different kind of variance insofar as it sees in the 144,000 symbols of "timeless truth" about discipleship, victory or sacrifice; structuralist charting of opposites or types in turn could endow such a synchronic interpretation with apparent scientific exactitude. No wonder many exegetes and Christians throughout the centuries have relinquished an understanding of the book in despair while others have found it to be a source not only of spiritual but also artistic inspiration.

Rather than add one more "definite" interpretation of the 144,000 followers of the Lamb on Mount Sion, I would like to explore some of the conditions and possibilities for interpreting the language of Rev in general and of this passage in particular. I will do so in order to complement my analysis of Rev's composition, form, and macro-structure (Fiorenza, 1968 and 1977a), as well as its prophetic-apocalyptic setting (Fiorenza, 1980), with an analysis of its rhetorical language and symbolic universe. I have selected this text as an example to show how the rhetorical language of a text must be explored so that its symbolic-poetic images make "sense" within its overall context and it has "meaning" and the power of "persuasion" in its own particular historical-social situation.

I will therefore argue that Rev must be understood as a poetic-rhetorical construction of an alternative symbolic universe that "fits" its historical-rhetorical situation. An adequate interpretation of the text, therefore, must: first, explore the poetic-evocative character of Rev's language and symbols, second, assess its rhetorical dynamics in a "proportional" reading of its symbols to elucidate their particular interrelations and the author's persuasive goals; and third, show why the construction of Rev's symbolic universe is a "fitting" response to its historical-rhetorical situation. It has become clear by now that I understand symbolic not to be just linguistic-semantic but also always social communicative. They need to be analyzed as *text* as well as *subtext* in terms of their historical-social "world": as *subtext* insofar as history is not accessible to us except in textual reconstructions although history itself is not a text. In other words, we are never able to read a text without explicitly or implicitly reconstructing its historical subtext within the process of our reading (Jameson: 68–91).

1. The Mytho-Poetic Language of Rev.

In his 1972 presidential address Norman Perrin insisted that literary ciriticism "has to include consideration of the ways in which literary types and forms of language function, and a consideration of the response they evoke from the reader" (1974: 10). He argues that Jesus' preaching of the *basileia tou theou* has been misunderstood as apocalyptic conception because its symbolic language character has been overlooked. In his understanding of symbol Perrin follows Wheelwright's distinction between steno-and tensive-symbol (1975; Perrin, 1976: 21ff). Whereas a steno-symbol always bears only a one-to-one relationship and is mostly used in scientific discourse, the tensive symbol can evoke a whole range of meanings and can never be exhausted or adequately expressed by one referent.

According to Perrin, Jewish as well as early Christian apocalyptic symbols are generally steno-symbols whereby each symbol has a one to one meaning relationship with the persons and events depicted or predicted. This is also the case when authors no longer refer to persons or events of the past but express their hope and vision for the future. Apocalyptic language is a secret code or sign-system depicting events that can be equated with historical persons or theological themes. Insofar as Perrin classifies apocalyptic symbols as steno-symbols or "signs" which must be decoded into a one-to-one meaning, he perpetuates the dichotomy between apocalyptic language and eschatological content or essence that has plagued scholarship in the past 200 years.

The notion that the "essence" of theological meaning can be distilled from apocalyptic language reflects two rather prevalent but nevertheless inadequate assumptions in biblical interpretation: on the one hand the assumption that we are able to separate linguistic form and theological content and on the other hand the claim that imaginative-symbolic language can be reduced to abstract-philosophical language and conceptuality (Fiorenza: 1983). Already in 1779 J. G. Herder had poked fun at such an attempt:

> It (Rev) carries, like everything else, its destiny along with itself. . . . The book consists of symbols; and philosophers cannot endure symbols. The truth must exhibit itself pure, naked, abstract, in a philosophical way. . . . No question is asked whether the symbols are pregnant with meaning, true, clear, efficient, intelligible, or whether there is in the whole book nothing but symbols. It is enough that there are symbols. We can make nothing out of symbols. At the best they are mere descriptions of the truth and we wish for demonstrations. Deductions, theorems, syllogisms we love. . . . Nature herself attempers different minds in various ways. She gives to one more of the power of abstraction, to another more of the power of synthesis; seldom are both found in company. In our academic education, there are unspeakably more teachers of that than of this. One is formed more for abstraction than for inspection; more for analysis that for pure comprehension, experience, and action. . . . Full of his systems

of learning, or prejudices, and polemic hypotheses, let him indeed read anything in it, but let him not venture to condemn. . . . To the dumb one does not speak. The painter does not
perform his work for the blind (Stuart: Vol. II, 502–503).

The American scholar Moses Stuart, who in 1845 published an
excerpt from Herder's book *Maran Atha* as an appendix to his two
volume commentary on the Apocalypse, also underlined the aesthetic
character of the work. He develops the following three hermeneutical
principles: 1. The Apocalypse is a book of poetry; 2. it has to be understood in terms of *Oriental* poetry and therefore requires the same principles of interpretation as the *parables* of Jesus; and 3. *generic* and not
specific and individual representations are to be sought in the book
before us. Therefore in discussing 14:1–5 he points to the "episode"
character of this passage but insists that "all which is intended by the
symbols there exhibited, is merely to indicate the certainty of victory. . . ." (Vol. I, 202).

This tendency to reduce the particular historical symbolic universe
and literary expression of Rev to the "generic" has prevailed among
scholars who have advocated a literary analysis of Rev in the most recent
past. Paul Minear has most consistently pursued a literary-critical analysis of Rev's mythopoieic language and symbols. He objects to an understanding of Rev as a system of signs in need of decoding, of symbols as
equations with historical events and persons, and of images forecasting
definite incidents and happenings.

He argues for instance, against an interpretation of Rev 17–18 that
understands these chapters as anti-Roman polemics. To "equate Babylon
with Rome would be literalism and historicism of the worst sort. The
figure Babylon can convey the prophetic message and mentality without
such an explicit association. We do not first require an exact knowledge of
his immediate circumstances to grasp his message" (246). According to
Minear the symbol Babylon as well as "the prophetic master-image of
warfare between the rival kings points to realities of a primordial and
eschatological order" (233); it points to the archetypal conflict of the
demonic and the divine. "The invisible struggle among transcendent
powers is for the prophet himself a fully contemporaneous reality, yet the
struggle itself could not be compressed within the bounds of specific
circumstances" (246).

In a similar fashion Jacques Ellul asserts that those exegetes who
understand Babylon as the symbol of Rome and the "seven kings" as
Roman emperors confuse the symbolic language of Rev with a secret
code. According to him "Babylon is not the symbol of Rome, it is Rome, a
historical reality which is transformed into a more polymorphous reality
of which Babylon traditionally has been the expression. Rome is an

actualized symbol, the historical presence of a permanent complex and multiple phenomenon . . . it is the historical actualization of the Power" (189). According to him Rome is not just the historical representation of ultimate Power but also of "the City" as the construction of all human culture and all civilization. It stands for all cities, those of the past and of the present. Lohmeyer and Schlier (1958, 1964) had already argued in a similar fashion.

While Minear stresses that the historical references to Rome enhance our understanding of the underlying mythological, archtypal reality Babylon, Ellul maintains that the historical reality Rome is the representation of *the* ultimate Power and City. It seems that for both scholars the concrete historical reality and conditions of Roman power and rule and its oppressive consequences for Christians in Asia Minor have become the symbolic manifestations of ultimate, transhistorical realities and archetypes. However this interpretation overlooks the fact that not Rome but the image of Babylon is the symbolic representation in Rev. To understand the symbolic representation not in historical but in archetypal or philosophical terms does not avoid its interpretation as "representation" of something which the interpreter is able to name. Archetypal, ontological interpretation *reduces* symbolic language to essential substance but does not explore its evocative powers in a given historical situation.

Rather than explore and highlight "the disposition of the work for openness," essentialist interpreters assume it is like "an apricot with a hard and definite meaning at its core" (Barthes: 50 and Rosenthal: 133). To understand Rev as a poetic work and its symbolic universe and language as an asset rather than as a "scholarly confusion" it becomes necessary for interpreters to acknowledge the ambiguity, openness, and indeterminancy of all literature. Nevertheless, an intellectually rigorous and historically careful reading of Rev can show that

> this indeterminacy of meaning has nothing in common with the conception that poetic language has no *particular* meaning, but is valuable only as a stimulus of feeling. Indeterminacy sees the language of poetry and fiction as at least as precise as ordinary language, but as having a different function—that of opening up rather than limiting meanings. The indeterminacy is not on the surface; we know exactly what (the writer) did and even why he (sic) did it. What is open are the full implications, the values, and the various incidents. The "confusion" . . . is at "the deep level where it is required" . . . because a literary experience is by nature open (Heyman: 352; emphasis and parentheses added).

In order to explore the whole range of the symbols in Rev 14:1–5—take, e.g., the symbol of Mount Sion, which in Perrin's terms is a symbol of ancestral vitality—it would be necessary to develop a lexicon of Rev's imagery with respect to its sources and its idioms together with a history of its traditions and interpretations as well as their influence or effective history. Although G. Herder had already demanded such a lexicon it is still a *desideratum* of scholarship today. The range, for instance, of the symbol of "Mount Sion" becomes obvious in the commentaries ad loc. Reference is made to the historical Mount Sion, its uses as a short form for Jerusalem, to the heavenly Jerusalem, to eschatological expectations that the Messiah will appear on Mount Sion for eschatological warfare, as well as that the "holy rest" of the people of God will be gathered and protected there. However attempts to show that the author means the heavenly and not the historical or the eschatological and not the heavenly temple-berg are not conclusive.[1] Moreover, attempts to show that the seer is here influenced by a definite prophetic (cf. 2 Kgs 19:20–34; Is 11:9–12; 24; 23; 25:7–10; Zeph. 3:13; Micha 4:6–8; or Joel 2:32) or apocalyptic text and expectation (cf. e.g. 4 Ezra 13:15–50; *Apoc Bar* 40:1–2 or 4 Ezra 2:42–47) are also not conclusive. Yet this indeterminacy could become a plus if we would understand apocalyptic language as poetic language i.e. as opening up rather than limiting, as evoking rather than defining meanings. Only then would we be able to perceive the strength of the image with all its possible overtones of meanings for the writer as well as for the audience.

II. The Rhetorical Strategy of Rev

However if Rev is not to be likened to an "apricot with a hard core" but more to an "onion" consisting of layers and layers of meaning, then the question arises how are we able to say that it is an "onion" and not a heap of apple peels. In other words, how can we delineate the "particular" meaning of Rev without ending up in total confusion and without accepting any abstruse interpretation that is proposed for the book's often bizarre symbols? Is the book "open" to any interpretation or does its "particularity" require that a proposed "meaning" must make "sense" with regard to the overall structure of the book as well as with respect to its "function" within a particular historical situation?

These questions can be further explored if we consider Rev not just as a symbolic-poetic work but also as a work of visionary rhetoric. While the poetic work seeks to create or organize imaginative experience, the rhetorical seeks to "persuade" or "motivate" the people "to act right"

---

[1] The "indeterminacy" of meaning is given in the text: On the one hand Mount Sion is clearly distinguished from "heaven" for while the voice comes "from heaven" the 144,000 stand on Mount Sion. Nevertheless the issue is not clear cut since the 144,000 are also characterized as "following the Lamb" who stands before the throne of God in "heaven" (cf. ch. 5) or shares God's throne in the New Jerusalem.

(Burke, 1956 and 1962; also Rueckert and Duncan, 1962). Poetry works by representation and is fulfilled in creation while rhetoric seeks to teach and instigate; poetry invites imaginative participation, rhetoric instigates change of attitudes and motivations. Or in the words of Amos Wilder: "Our visions, stories, and utopias are not only aesthetic: they engage us" (79).[2]

Since participation and persuasion, imagination and change are not exclusive of each other, poetic and rhetorical elements can be successfully intertwined in a single work. Speaker, audience, subject matter and "rhetorical situation" are constitutive for any rhetorical utterance. In these terms Rev is a poetic-rhetorical work. It seeks to persuade and motivate by constructing a "symbolic universe" that invites imaginative participation. The strength of Rev's persuasion for action lies not in its theological reasoning or historical argument but in the "evocative" power of its symbols as well as in its hortatory, imaginative, emotional language and dramatic movement, which engages the hearer (reader) by eliciting reactions, emotions, convictions and identifications. In writing down "the words of prophecy" to be read in the worship assembly of the community, John seeks to motivate and encourage Christians in Asia Minor who have experienced harrassment and persecution. He does not do so simply by writing a letter of exhortation but by creating a new "plausibility structure" and "symbolic universe" within the framework of a prophetic-pastoral letter. Apocalyptic vision and explicit parenesis have the same function. They provide the vision of an "alternative world" in order to encourage Christians and to enhance their staying power in the face of persecution and possible execution.

Rather than "essentialize" the individual image, therefore, we must trace its position within the overall form-content *gestalt* of Rev and see its relationships to other images and within the "strategic" positions of the composition. Images are not simply patterns or ornaments but they are "about something." Only a "proportional" analysis of Rev's images can determine what they are about within the structure of the work by determining the phase of actions in which they are invoked. Such an analysis of symbolic relations must highlight the hortatory or persuasive functions of the multivalent images and symbols in producing cooperative or non-cooperative attitudes and actions. Whereas the poetic image can employ a full range of meanings and often contains a complete bundle of meanings which can be contradictory if they are reduced to their ideational equivalents, rhetorical symbols are related to each other within the structure of a work in terms of the ideas, values, or goals of the

[2]I presented this paper in a much shorter and less developed form at the SBL annual meeting in 1980, and I would like to thank Professor Wilder for his very helpful response to the earlier form.

author, which at least partially must be shared with the audience (Duncan, 1953: 109–10). In interpreting Rev as a rhetorical work we must therefore look *first* for the strategic positions and textual relations of the symbols and images within the overall dramatic movement of the book. *Second*, we must pay attention to the explicit rhetorical "markers" that seek to "channel" the audience's understandings, emotions, and identifications in such a way that it is persuaded and moved to the desired actions.

First, since I have elsewhere analyzed the overall compositional movement of Rev, I will presuppose this analysis here in order to indicate how Rev 14:1–5 makes "sense" within the overall dramatic action. According to my interpretation, this segment belongs to the central section of Rev 10:1–15:5, which, in ever new episodal images interprets the present situation of the community on earth in its confrontation with Rome's power and cult (1981, 107–50; for a different understanding, see Lambrecht, 77–104). An "episode" is thereby understood as a "brief unit of action" that is integral but distinguishable from the continuous narrative. If we assume that the "narrative" line of Rev is indicated by the 4 seven series, then this segment is similar in function to the first seven series of the messages and it is the center around which the seven plagues series are grouped.

The vision of the 144,000 with the divine name on their foreheads is clearly an antithetical vision to those of the dragon and the two beasts. It continues the motif of the measuring of the temple, the two witnesses, the woman with the child and anticipates the vision of the victors who sing the song of Moses and the Lamb (15:2–4). It is also interlinked with other heavenly-earthly-eschatological visions of redemption and salvation: on the one hand it recalls the exaltation and enthronement of the Lamb in ch. 5, the "sealing of the 144,000 elect of the tribes of Israel as well as the eschatological great multitudinous company of the Lamb in ch. 7 and on the other hand it points forwards to the victory of the Lamb and those with him in 17:14, to the vision and audition of the "sacred marriage of the Lamb" in 19:10; the messianic millenial reign in 20:4–6 and to the "liturgical" service of those with the divine name on their heads in the New Jerusalem (22:3–5). It also alludes to the promise to the victor in 3:12 and the New "Sion"/Jerusalem in 21:1–22:5.

At the same time the vision of the 144,000 followers of the Lamb is the anti-vision of the "Lamb-like" beast and its followers who have taken the beast's name on their right hand and foreheads (ch. 13) as well as the antipode to the gathering of the anti-divine forces at Har Magedon (16:17). It is a "warning" to those who are in the process of losing their share in the new Jerusalem. Similarly the audition refers the audience back to the heavenly liturgies of 5:11–12; 7:11–12; 11:15–19; 12:10–12 and points forward to the song of the eschatological victors in 15:2–4 and 19:1–

5. Its antidote are the worship of the dragon and the blasphemies of the beast from the sea (13:4–6; 16:11, 21) as well as to the lament of the kings, merchants, and seafarers over Babylon (18:9–20).

These auditions have the same function of commenting on the dramatic actions and of guiding the perception of the audience which the choir had in the classical drama. By juxtaposing visions and auditions of salvation with those of the anti-divine powers the seer seeks to persuade and motivate his audience to make their decision for salvation and for the world of God in the face of the destructive divine power represented by the beasts and Babylon as the symbols of Rome. This function is underlined by the explanatory remark that closes the vision and audition in 14:3: It underlines this eschatological tension of decision by stressing that only the 144,000 are able to "learn" the "new song" which the heavenly choir sings. They are those who are bought free, or "separated out," or liberated from the earth. (apo implies their separation from the earth).[3]

Second: The strategic function of the vision and audition of 14:1–3 is underlined by its explicit interpretation in 14:4–5, by the following section with three angelic proclamations to all of humanity in 14:6–11, and by the special words of blessing to the Christians in 14:12–13. They function as rhetorical markers that appeal to the active decision of the audience and make sure that the multivalent images and symbols are understood in a certain way. They must be understood in the context of the explanatory remarks of ch. 13 and the proclamation of 14:6–13.

The interpretation of 14:1–5 understands those who are bought free from the earth as *parthenoi*, as followers of the Lamb, and as spotless firstfruits. The present status of the eschatologically redeemed is a consequence and outcome of their behavior in the past. The first and last part of the interpretation stress the cultic purity of the 144,000 who are characterized in this vision as highpriests, because they have the name of God and the Lamb on their foreheads. The middle section of the interpretation elaborates their "being with the Lamb" as following the Lamb. This interpretation is grammatically difficult because the text leaves open whether they were or are followers of the Lamb. If the statement is parallel to the other two in structure then "*ēsan*" should be inserted. However this makes the grammatical reading of the sentence difficult. As the sentence stands now the reader can add the past and the present simultaneously: They have been and still are followers of the Lamb (Guthrie). Whereas the beast from the abyss will "go" (*hypagei*) to destruction (17:18), the Lamb leads to eschatological salvation (cf. 7:17). Yet we are also reminded of the oracular pronouncement in 13:10: "If

---

[3] Rev 5:9 which speaks about the redemption of Christians uses *agorazein* with *ek*. See Fiorenza, 1974.

anyone is to be taken captive, into captivity s/he goes *(hypagei)*." Following the Lamb in the past included going to captivity, while it now on the eschatological Sion means salvation and fullness of life.

Whereas the statement that the 144,000 are firstfruits and spotless because in their mouth was found no lie, is clear in the context of the book, the explanation that they are *parthenoi* for they have not soiled or defiled themselves with women is most difficult. However, part of the difficulty results from the mistaken assumption of exegetes that they must take this statement literally (Lindijer),[4] whereas they usually do not take either *agorazein*, Mount Sion, *hypagein, aparchē or amōmoi* in a literalist sense but interpret them within the language context of the book. To assume that either the heavenly or the eschatological followers of the Lamb are a class of exclusively male ascetics[5] seems unfounded in the overall context of the book. The expression *parthenoi* probably points within the present scene to the cultic purity of the Lamb's followers as well as to their representation of the "bride of the Lamb," the New Jerusalem which is qualified as "holy" in 21:9–11. The anti- image to the holiness of the bride arrayed in white linen is that of Babylon who corrupts the nations with oppressive power.[6] The meaning of "women" could also allude to the prophetess in Thyatira called Jezebel, who in John's view "seduces" Christians to idolatry and accommodation to pagan society. This possibility is enhanced but not proven if we consider that the expression "in their mouth was found no lie" not only refers to the list of vices which exclude from the New Jerusalem (21:7; 22:15) but also to those people who claim to be Jews but lie (3:9) and to the second beast, the false prophet (16:13; 19:20; 20:10).

Thus, the interpretation of the vision and audition is not given in less symbolic language and cannot be reduced to a one to one meaning. Its function is to underline the agency of the 144,000. While the vision and audition highlight the election of those who are with the Lamb on Mount Sion, its interpretation stresses that their action and life is the precondition for such eschatological salvation. It thus has the same rhetorical function as the angelic proclamation, which calls all of humanity—of which the 144,000 are the firstfruits—to the worship of God, announces the fall of Babylon in whose abominations the 144,000 *parthenoi* did not share, and threatens with eternal punishment the worshipers of the beast

[4] For a review of interpretations given to this difficult passage see Lindijer: 124–42.

[5] A. Yarbro Collins (1979: 100) suggests that Rev's approval of celibacy might have been inspired by the Israelite traditions of holy war and priesthood. John's exclusively male terminology is therefore explainable since only men were warriors and priests in Israel.

[6] Rather than see *parthenoi* in the context of Rev's symbolic action Lindijer seeks to connect the word with all the other passages in the NT, contemporary Jewish, and Early Christian writings which speak about virgins/virginity/celibacy.

who take its sign, while those who have the name of God on their
foreheads are promised participation in the liturgy of heaven in the
future.

Here, at this opposition between the worship of God and that of the
beast, the *hypomonē*, i.e., the consistent resistance or staying power, of
the saints, who keep the word of God and the faith of Jesus, comes to the
fore. The macarism at the end of this section sums up its overall rhetorical
message and thus forms a transition to the judgment visions in 14:14–20.
"Blessed [*makarismos*] are the dead," according to a word of the Spirit,
who have died "in the Lord," i.e., as Christians. Like the souls under the
heavenly altar in 6:9–11 they can rest from their labors because their
deeds or what they have become in their actions follow them.

In conclusion: The vision and audition of Rev 14:1–3 function within
the context of the book to highlight the election as well as the eschatological salvation of the 144,000, while the attached interpretation
(14:4–5) underlines that their life-practice is the condition for eschatological salvation. The tableau functions at the same time as *anti-
image* to that of the beast and its followers as well as to the glory of
Babylon. Thus the whole section 14:1–5 in its wider context underlines
the fundamental decision that the audience faces: either to worship the
anti-divine powers embodied by Rome and to become "followers" of the
beast (cf. 13:2–4) or to worship God and to become "companions" of the
Lamb on Mount Sion. This decision jeopardizes either their life and
fortunes here and now or their future life and share in the New Jerusalem, Mount Sion.

The images of eschatological salvation and the heavenly world of God
seek to mobilize the reader's emotions, to attract and persuade them to
make the right decision here and now and to live accordingly in this life.
At the same time they seek to alienate their allegiances and affects from
the present symbols of Roman power by ascribing to it images of degrada-
tion, ugliness and ultimate failure and defeat. With ever new images and
symbols of redemption and salvation the visionary rhetoric of Rev 10:1–
15:4 seeks to persuade the audience to decide for the worship of God and
against that of the beast, which is shown doomed to failure and destruction. Rev does not only seek to convince Christians that this is the right
decision but also seeks to provoke them to stake their lives on it.

III. The Rhetorical Situation of Rev

My elaboration of the rhetorical strategy of Rev has already indicated
the kind of rhetorical situation which has generated it. It now remains to
elaborate why Rev's particular rhetorical response to the social-political
and religious situation of the churches of Asia Minor is a "fitting" response. In other words, the social-historical-policital parameters which

are the ultimate horizon of Rev as of any other cultural artifact must be so (re)constructed

> as to constitute not merely a scene or background, not an inert context alone but rather a structured and determinate situation, such that the text can be grasped as an active response to it. . . . The text's meaning then, in the larger sense of *Bedeutung* will be the meaningfulness to a gesture that we read back from the situation to which it is precisely a response (Jameson, 83).

What is the rhetorical situation to which Rev's particular world of vision can be perceived as an active response? In addressing this question it must be kept in mind that it is the rhetorical situation that calls forth a particular rhetorical response and not vice versa.

A rhetorical situation is characterized by exigency and urgency. An exigency which cannot be modified through the rhetorical act is not rhetorical. Thus the controlling exigency of the situation specifies the mode of discourse to be chosen and the change to be effected. In other words, any rhetorical discourse obtains its rhetorical character from the exigency and urgency of the situation that generates it. However the rhetorical situation is not only marked by urgency but also constituted by two types of constraints: those which affect the audience's decision or action on the one hand and those which are limitations imposed on the author (Blitzer).

The exigency of Rev's rhetorical situation is best characterized by the letter of Pliny to the emperor Trajan:

> In the meanwhile the method I have observed towards those who have been denounced to me as Christians is this: I interrogated them whether they were Christians: if they confessed it I repeated the question twice again adding the threat of capital punishment; if they still persevered, I ordered them to be executed. . . . Those who denied they were, or had ever been Christians, who repeated after me an invocation to the Gods, and offered adoration with wine and frankincense to your image, which I had ordered to be brought for that purpose, together with those of the Gods, and who finally cursed Christ—none of which acts it is said, those who are really Christians can be forced into performing, these I thought it proper to discharge. Others who were named by that informer, at first confessed themselves Christians and then denied it. . . . They all worshipped your statue and the images of the Gods and cursed Christ.[7]

---

[7] Letters X:96; transl by W. M. L. Hutchinson, *Pliny: Letters*, II (The Loeb Classical Library: Cambridge: Harvard University Press, 1969) 401–2.

Pliny states here in plain words what Rev tells us in images and symbols, especially in ch. 13. Yet Rev adds another aspect, when it stresses that those who do not have the mark of the beast are not able to buy or to sell (Collins, 1977:252–54). Not only threat to life, imprisonment, and execution but also economic deprivation and destitution are to be suffered by those who refuse to take the mark of the beast, i.e., to be identified as its followers. Although exegetes are not quite able to explain the mark of the beast and its number (Boecher: 84–87; Reicke: 189–91; Baines: 195f), its economic significance is plain. In other words the beast not only threatens the followers of the Lammb with death, but also makes it impossible for them to have enough to live.

Under the Flavians, especially Domitian, the imperial cult was strongly promoted in the Roman provinces. Domitian demanded that the populace acclaim him as "Lord and God" and participate in his worship. The majority of the cities (Ramsay; Yamauchi; Hemer) to which the prophetic messages of Rev are addressed were dedicated to the promotion of the Emperor cult. Ephesus was the seat of the proconsul and competed with Pergamum for primacy. Like Smyrna it was a center of the emperor cult, had a great theater and was famous for its gladiatorial games. Pergamum was the official center of the imperial cult. Already in 29 BCE the city had received permission to build a temple to the "divine Augustus and the goddess Roma" which is probably referred to in Rev 3:13 by the expression "the throne of Satan." In Thyatira the emperor was worshipped as Apollo incarnate and as the son of Zeus. In 26 CE Sardis competed with ten other Asian cities for the right of building a temple in honor of the emperor but lost out to Smyrna. Laodicea was the wealthiest city of Phrygia and had especially prospered under the Flavians.

The Asiarchs, the highpriests of the Asian Koinon (assembly), presided over the imperial cult. One high priest was probably elected annually from one of the Asian cities to the most prestigious office a wealthy citizen could aspire to. "These priests wore unusually ornate crowns adorned with miniature busts of the imperial family" (Yamauchi: 110). In such an environment Christians were bound to experience increasing conflicts with the imperial cult, especially since they claimed Jesus Christ and not the Roman emperor as "their Lord and God." Rev knows of harassment and persecutions of individual Christians in various localities. It anticipates an increase of persecutions and sufferings for the near future, not least because of the increasing totalitarianism of the reign of Domitian.

This experience of harassment, persecution, and hostility challenged Christians' faith in Christ as Lord. Their experience of hunger, deprivation, pestilence and war undermined their belief in God's good creation and providence. Christians experienced painfully that their situation in no way substantiated their faith conviction that they already participated in Christ's kingship and power (Fiorenza, 1972). This tension between theological conviction and experienced reality must have provoked difficult theological questions that seemed to have been addressed differently by leading prophets in the churches of Asia Minor. Rev implicitly informs us of such a theological dilemma by arguing against rival Christian apostles and prophets and by indicting the Jewish community as a "synagogue of Satan." In a situation where the leader does not control the production of symbols or where there are competing voices, s/he must defend their message over and against heresies and extend its range of consensual validations.[8] These are the rhetorical constraints on the audience that intensify the exigency of the political situation of Rev.

First: the political situation was aggravated and the necessity to make a decision more pressing because Jewish Christians like John could less and less claim Jewish political privileges for themselves. Jews had the privilege of practicing their religion in any part of the empire and were exempted from military service and the imperial cult. However, under the Flavians their situation had become more precarious. Vespasian ordered that all Jews and proselytes had to pay a special tax to the Romans in place of the tax formerly paid to the Jerusalem temple. Domitian (Smallwood; Keresztes) enforced the tax and singled out for payment especially the proselytes and God-fearers who were not Jews by birth. Moreover, Judaism was regarded with suspicion because of its strange customs and refusal to participate in the civil religion of its political environment. After the destruction of Jerusalem and the temple the self-interest of Jewish communities of Asia Minor demanded that they get rid of any potential political "trouble makers" and "messianic elements" in their midst, and Christians seemed to be certainly among them (Hengel).[9]

The message to the churches of Smyrna and Philadelphia reflect this conflict. John's identification of the synagogue as a congregation of Satan should not be misread as anti-Judaism since he has great appreciation for the faith and the symbols of "true Judaism." But true Judaism for him apparently is messianic apocalypticism. As a Jewish Christian John is well aware that the established Jewish communities of Asia Minor could not tolerate the deviance of Christians who seem also to have been poor and powerless in Smyrna and Philadelphia and to have experienced slander from their Jewish communities.[10]

---

[8] Duncan (1953: 87) stresses the "persuasive functions of symbols in the production of cooperative and non-cooperative attitudes."

[9] For the "muted and fragmentary form" of apocalyptic elements in rabbinic literature, cf. Saldarini.

[10] It is debated whether the author has Jewish or Jewish Christian communities in mind. H. Kraft (61) thinks of a Jewish-Christian group which seeks to avoid persecution by calling themselves "Jews." However this is not stated in the text.

Second: Not only among Jews but also among Christians was advocated a tendency to adaptation and acquiescence to the political powers. John bitterly polemicizes against rival Christian prophets in Ephesus, Pergamum and Thyatira. Ephesus is praised for rejecting "the false apostles" and for its hatred of the works of the Nicolaitans, whereas Pergamum is severely criticized for tolerating those who hold the teaching of Balaam. The community in Thyatira in turn is censured for accepting the influence and teaching of a woman prophet and her school.[11] It is likely that all three code names "Nicolaitans, Balaam, and Jezebel" characterize the same group of Christian prophets who allowed eating food sacrificed to idols and accepted compromise with the emperor cult. This theological stance had great political, economic, and professional advantages for Christians in Asia Minor, for the meat sacrificed to idols was served at meetings of trade guilds and business associations as well as private receptions (Mounce: 102–4).

This alternative prophetic position thus proposed a theological compromise that allowed Christian citizens to participate actively in the commercial, political, and social life of their cities. They probably justified their stance with reference to Paul (Rom 13:1–7). Like Timothy they might have urged their congregations "to make supplications, prayers and intercessions for kings and those in high places" in order to be able to lead a "quiet and peaceable" life "respectful in every way" (I Tim 2:2–3). Like I Peter[12] they could have admonished: "Fear God. Honor the emperor" (2:17). Since "honoring the image of the emperor" did not demand creedal adherence but was a civil-political gesture, some might have argued it was possible to do so without compromising one's faith.

Moreover, to oppose the imperial cult and to refuse participation in societal-religious affairs would mean to take the religious claims of the imperial religion at face value. The religious claims of the emperor and state on the one hand, and the claims of God and Christ on the other hand, are not in conflict because both claims belong to a radically different order as is maintained e.g. in Jn 18:36–38. Jesus Christ's claim to kingship and power is not of a political nature but pertains to the spiritual-religious life of the church, since the Christians are taken out of this world and by virtue of their baptism already share in the kingly power of their Lord. No one, not even Satan, can harm the elect for they have insight into the very depth and mystery of the demonic and divine (Fiorenza, 1973: 568–70).

---

[11] For a discussion of Jezebel and the Nicolaitans see Fiorenza, 1973. However, I would be more hesitant today to characterize this group as "gnostizising."

[12] However, N. Brox (116–17) argues that 2:7 is traditional and not formulated by the author of I Peter. Yet the statement fits well in the overall context of the Haustafel admonitions as D. Balch has elaborated.

In responding to this theological challenge John, like Paul before him, stresses that behind idols stands the demonic power of Satan, the ultimate adversary. No compromise with the imperial cult is possible because God and Christ are the true rulers of the world. This different theological response of John is rooted in a different social-political experience. He himself seems to have experienced suffering and exile,[13] while the two communities (Smyrna and Philadelphia) that deserve Christ's praise and receive no censure are obviously poor and without power. Those communities that receive censure are rich, complacent, and do not experience any harassment.

It seems, therefore, that John advocates an uncompromising theological stance toward the imperial religion because, for him and his followers, the dehumanizing powers of Rome and its vassals have become so destructive and oppressive that a compromise with them would mean an affirmation of "those who destroy the earth" (11:18). Therefore Rev stresses "Christ is alive, although he was killed." Those who will resist the powers of death determining their life will share in the power and glory of Christ. To those who are poor, harassed and persecuted the promises to the "victor" are seen as the essentials of life for the eschatological future: food, clothing, home, citizenship, security, honor, power, glory (Georgi).

However to achieve acceptance for his alternative prophetic stance, John did not claim exceptional personal status and authority. He consistently calls himself *ho doulos* rather than *prophētēs* and places himself emphatically on the same level with the audience (1:9). He also does not write a pseudonymous book appropriating the authority of one of the great prophets or apostles of the past for his message. He also does not appeal to any church leaders or offices known in the communities of Asia Minor (Fiorenza, 1980: 116–21; Aune). He does rely on legitimization, but it derives not from human authority but from Christ himself. Like the prophets of old he proclaims: "Thus says the Lord." Like the apocalyptic seers he creates a symbolic universe that is mythological insofar as it represents a conception of reality that points to the ongoing determination of the world by sacred forces.

A strategic legitimating function of symbolic universe for individual as well as communal life according to Berger-Luckmann is the "location" of death. It enables individuals to go on living and to anticipate their own death with the terror of death sufficiently mitigated. "Symbolic universe shelters the individual from ultimate terror" (102). The same is true for its social significance: it is a sheltering canopy over institutions and legiti-

---

[13] For such an understanding see Ramsay (82–92). H. Kraft (40–41) argues, however, that John went to Patmos in order to have a revelatory experience. However, his argument is not convincing.

mates the political order by reference to a cosmic order of justice and power. With respect to the future it establishes a "common frame of reference" bestowing meaning on the suffering of the community and on individual death. The empirical community is transported to a cosmic plane and made majestically independent of the vicissitudes of individual existence.

Such world-construction in myth is primariy occasioned by conflicting definitions of reality which are aggravated if only one party has the power to enforce its own interpretation of reality. This was the case as we have seen in the rhetorical situation of Rev. In constructing a symbolic universe John attempts to maintain the superiority of his prophetic view of reality and of God as well as to help individual Christians face the terror of death. Since the exigency of the situation is defined not just in terms of Roman power but represents political power in cultic terms, Rev's symbolic universe needed to appeal to common traditional cultic symbols in order to be competitive. Yet such an appeal was not possible, since Christians had no cult, no temples, no priests, no sacrifices (Fiorenza, 1976). Since John rejects all pagan cultic activity as idolatry and seeks to alienate his audience from the magnificent symbols and cultic drama of the Emperor cult, he could not, as Ignatius did, appeal to the symbols of the mystery cults. "You are all taking part in a religious procession carrying along with you your God, shrine, Christ, and your holy objects, and decked out from tip to toes in the commandments of Jesus Christ" (Ign. Eph. 9:2).

Although Rev's own open and multivalent images have many overtones derived from Greco-Roman society and religion, the dominant tenor of its symbolic language is the cult of Israel. The symbols of temple, priest, sacrifice, garments, headdress, hymns, altar, incense and cultic purity are all derived from Jewish religion. In taking over these traditional Jewish symbols John makes a plea to Jews and Jewish Christians who "own" the tradition to accept him and his vision. At the same time it must be observed that Rev never uses cultic symbolic language to describe Christian worship and communities. The cultic-religious symbolic language of Israel serves as a "language" to construct the heavenly world and the future, where no cultic mediation is necessary any more (Fiorenza, 1972: 397–416). By employing traditional Jewish cultic symbols John seeks not only to alienate the audience from pagan mysteries and emperor cult, but also to project essential stability, collective coherence, and eternal bliss, in order to overcome their experienced alienation.[14]

---

[14] For the stabilizing effect of ritual and cult see M. Douglas and the review of her work by B. Isenberg and D. E. Owen.

I have argued that the symbolic universe and action of Rev is a "fitting" response to its rhetorical situation. It remains to show how the dramatic action of the overall composition fulfills this rhetorical function. According to K. Burke (1951; Rueckert: 208–26) the mythic or ritual structure which follows the form of a cathartic journey moves the audience from alienation through purification to redemption. The first part, which is considered a *viaticum*, is "the way in." It states the primary conditions in terms of which the journey is to be localized or specified in time. This function is fulfilled by the first section, the seven messages of Rev (1:9–3:21).

The next part within the journey metaphor is the definite "pushing off from shore" and the certainty "of being underway." On a particular journey one can be underway for varying lengths of time. Chs. 4–9 culminating in the seventh trumpet take the audience "on the way" of the journey which opened up with the death, resurrection and exaltation of Christ.

Eventually according to Burke, one has to arrive at the "withinness of withinness." Here one arrives at knowledge and perception of the tensions (pollution, psychosis, civic disorder, class conflicts), i.e., at the exigency of the rhetorical situation that is symbolized and explored. Chs. 10–14; 15:2–4 represent structurally this "withinness of withinness" of Rev's symbolic drama.

From this point on "we are returning" and shall go back to the starting point, but with a "difference" which is constituted by an emotional or intellectual "splitting," a "separating out" which happens in Rev in chs. 15:1–19:10. The last part of the dramatic action completes the journey and the separating out process. The journey is complete "when the passion (persecution and suffering) has been transformed into an assertion." Rev closes with such a "final separating out" and an assertion in 19:11–22:5. Language cannot remove or correct "the brute realities" of the social-political exigency and of religious "tensions" but it can help us to control their destructive effects. In taking his audience on the dramatic-cathartic journey of Rev, John seeks to "move" them to control their fear and sustain their vision.

Finally, a theological interpretation of the NT has to assess the impact of John's world of vision and dramatic symbolic action on the contemporary reader and audience. W. C. Booth has argued for a revived ethical and political criticism that would "appraise the quality of the response invited by the whole work. What will it do with or to us if we surrender our imaginations to its path?" (59). Critics of Rev have pointed out that the book preaches vengeance and revenge but not the love of the Sermon on the Mount (Collins, 1980: 204). It is therefore sub-christian, the Judas of the NT. I myself in turn have argued that the book is written "with a jail-house" perspective, asking for the realization of God's justice and power. It therefore can only be understood by those "who hunger and thirst for justice" (1981).

This dispute can be clarified through the concept of "rhetorical situation" that I have tried to develop here. If the "rhetorical situation" generates a "fitting" response then Rev cannot be understood when its "rhetorical situation" no longer "persists." Wherever it persists, however, the book will continue to evoke the same response sought by its author. In other words, wherever a social-political-religious "tension" generated by oppression and persecution persists or re-occurs, the dramatic action of Rev will have the same cathartic effects it had in its original situation.[15]

Wherever a totally different "rhetorical situation" exists, however, the book no longer elicits a "fitting" response. What I am arguing here is that we cannot reduce "the reader" to a timeless, ideal reader if we do not want to essentialize and dehistoricize the book. Rather than pose an abstract reader we must detect and articulate our own presuppositions, emotions and reactions to the work in an explicit way, as well as sort out what kind of quality of response becomes dominant in our own reading.

What will Rev do to us if we surrender our imagination to its dramatic action? For example, the symbols of Rev for both the oppressive and eschatologically redemptive communities are female because cities were personified as women. Moreover Rev symbolizes idolatry in the prophetic and cultic language of Israel as "whoring" or as "defilement with women." In our present rhetorical situation where we have become conscious of androcentric language and its socializing function we can detect a quite different rhetorical function and impact of these symbols. They no longer seek to persuade all Christians to persistent resistance and loyal faithfulness unto death but they appeal to quite different emotions. Rev engages the imagination of the contemporary reader to perceive women in terms of good or evil, pure or impure, heavenly or destructive, helpless or powerful, bride or temptress, wife or whore. Rather than instill "hunger and thirst for justice," the symbolic action of Rev therefore can perpetuate prejudice and injustice if it is not "translated" into a contemporary "rhetorical situation" to which it can be a "fitting" rhetorical response.

---

[15] This explains why the political left as well as the political right can appeal to the book. It is therefore important in preaching and teaching to elaborate the original "rhetorical situation" of the book. Since it does not address a democratic and highly technological society, the book would be misunderstood if it were seen e.g. as advocating political quietism and resignation in the face of the possible nuclear devastation of the world.

LIST OF WORKS CONSULTED

Aune, David E.
    1981   "The Social Matrix of the Apocalypse of John." *Biblical Research*
                36: 16–32.

Baines, W. G.
    1975   "The Number of the Beast in Revelation 13:18." *HeyJ* 16: 195–96.

Balch, D.
    1981   *Let Wives Be Submissive: The Domestic Code in 1 Peter.* SBLMS
                26. Chico: Scholars Press.

Barthes, R.
    1966   *Critique et Verité.* Paris: Editions de Seuil.

Beckwith, I. T.
    1967   *The Apocalypse of John.* Grand Rapids: Baker Book House,
                reprint

Berger, P. L. and Th. Luckmann
    1967   *The Social Construction of Reality. A Treatise in the Sociology of
                Knowledge.* Garden City: Doubleday Anchor Books.

Blitzer, L. F.
    1974   "The Rhetorical Situation." Pp. 247–60 in *Rhetoric: A Tradition
                in Transition.* Lansing: Michigan State University Press.

Boecher, O.
    1975   *Die Johannesapokalypse.* Erträge der Forschung 41; Darmstadt:
                Wissenschaftliche Buchgesellschaft.

Booth, W. C.
    1982   "Freedom of Interpretation: Baktin and the Challenge of Femi-
                nist Criticism." *Critical Inquiry* 9:45–76.

Bousset, W.
    1906   *Die Offenbarung Johannis.* Meyer, 6th ed. Göttingen: Van-
                denhoeck & Ruprecht.

Brox, N.
    1979   *Der erste Petrusbrief.* EKK XXI. Benzinger-Neukirchener Ver-
                lag.

Burke, K.
    1951   "Othello: An Essay to Illustrate a Method." *Hudson Review.* 4:
                165–203.
    1956   *The Philosophy of Literary Form. Studies in Symbolic Action.*
                New York: Vintage Books.
    1962   *A Grammar of Motives and a Rhetoric of Motives.* Cleveland:
                World Publication Company.

Collins, A. Yarbro
    1977   "The Political Perspective of the Revelation to John." *JBL* 96:
                241–56.

1979   *The Apocalypse*. NTM 22. Wilmington: Michael Glazier.

1980   "Rev. 18: Taunt-Song or Dirge?" Pp. 185–204 in *L'Apocalypse johannique et l'Apocalyptique dans le Nouveau Testament*. Ed. J. Lambrecht. BETL 53; Louvain: University Press.

Douglas, Mary
1973   *Natural Symbols*. New York: Vintage Books.

Duncan, H. D.
1953   *Language and Literature in Society*. Chicago: University of Chicago Press.

1962   *Communication and Social Order*. New York: The Bedminster Press.

Ellul, J.
1977   *Apocalypse. The Book of Revelation*. New York: Seabury Press.

Fiorenza, Elisabeth Schüssler
1968   "The Eschatology and Composition of the Apocalypse." *CBQ* 30: 537–69.

1972   *Priester für Gott. Studien zum Herrschafts- und Priestermotiv in der Apokalypse*. NTA 7. Munster: Aschendorff.

1973   "Apocalyptic and Gnosis in the Book of Revelation and Paul." *JBL* 92: 565–81.

1974   "Redemption as Liberation. Apoc. 1:5f and 5:9f." *CBQ* 36: 220–32.

1976   "Cultic Language in Qumran and in the New Testament. *CBQ* 38: 159–77.

1977a   "Composition and Structure of the Revelation of John." *CBQ* 39: 344–66.

1977b   "The Quest for the Johannine School." *NTS* 23: 402–27.

1980   "Apokalypsis and Propheteia: The Book of Revelation in the Context of Early Christian Prophecy." Pp. 105–28 in *L'Apocalypse johannique et l'Apocalyptique dans le Nouveau Testament*. Ed. J. Lambrecht. BETL 53; Louvain: University Press.

1981   *Invitation to the Book of Revelation*. Garden City: Doubleday.

1983   "The Phenomenon of Early Christian Apocalyptic: Some Reflections on Method." Pp. 295–316 in *Apocalypticism in the Mediterranean World and the Near East* Ed. David Hellholm. Tubingen: J. C. B. Mohr

Georgi, D.
1980   "Die Visionen vom himmlischen Jerusalem." Pp. 351–72 in *Kirche. Festschrift für G. Bornkamm zum 75. Geburtstag*. Eds. D. Lührmann and G. Strecker. Tübingen: J. C. B. Mohr.

Guthrie, Donald
1981   "The Lamb in the Structure of the Book of Revelation." *Vox Evangelica* 12: 64–71.

Hemer, C. J.
1975   "Unto the Angels of the Churches." *BH* 11: 4–27, 58–87, 110–35, 164–90.

Hengel, M.
1983   "Messianische Hoffnung und politischer 'Radikalismus' in der jüdisch-hellenistischen Diaspora." Pp. 655–86 in *Apocalypticism in the Mediterranean World and the Near East.* Ed. David Hellholm. Tubingen: J. C. B. Mohr.

Heyman, L. W.
1976   "Indeterminacy in Literary Criticism." *Soundings* 59: 345–56.

Isenberg, B. and D. E. Owen
1977   "Bodies Natural and Contrived: The Work of Mary Douglas." *RSR* 3: 1–16.

Jameson, F. R.
1982   "The Symbolic Inference; on Kenneth Burke and Ideological Analysis." Pp. 68–91 in *Representing Kenneth Burke.* Eds. Hayden White and M. Brose. Baltimore: The Johns Hopkins University Press.

Keresztes, P.
1973   "The Jews, the Christians, and Emperor Domitian." *VigChr* 27: 1–28.

Kraft, H.
1974   *Die Offenbarung des Johannes.* HNT 16a. Tubingen: J. C. B. Mohr.

Lambrecht, J.
1980   "A Structuration of Revelation 4, 1–22, 5." Pp. 77–104 in *L'Apocalypse johannique et l'Apocalyptique dans le Nouveau Testament.* Ed. J. Lambrecht. BETL 53; Louvain: University Press.

Lindijer, C. H.
1970   "Die Jungfrauen in der Offenbarung des Johannes XIV 4." Pp. 124–42 in *Studies in John. Festschrift J. N. Sevenster.* Suppl. Nov. T. 24. Leiden: Brill.

Lohmeyer, E.
1953   *Die Offenbarung des Johannes.* 2nd ed. Tübingen: J. C. B. Mohr.

Minear, Paul S.
1968   *I Saw a New Earth. A Complete New Study and Translation of the Book of Revelation.* Washington: Corpus Publications.

Mounce, R. H.
1977   *The Book of Revelation.* Grand Rapids: William B. Eerdmans.

Perrin, Norman

1974   "Eschatology and Hermeneutics." *JBL* 93: 1–15.

1976   *Jesus and the Language of the Kingdom*. Philadelphia: Fortress
            Press.

Ramsay, W. M.
1904   *The Letters to the Seven Churches of Asia*. New York: A. C.
            Armstrong & Son.

Reicke, Bo
1972   "Die jüdische Apocalyptik und die johanneische Tiervision."
            RechSR 60: 173–92.

Rosenthal, Peggy
1975   "Deciphering S/Z." *College English* 37: 125–44.

Rueckert, W. H.
1982   *Kenneth Burke and the Drama of Human Relations*. Berkeley:
            University of California Press.

Saldarini, A. J.
1977   "The Uses of Apocalyptic in the Mishna and Tosepta." *CBQ* 39:
            396–409.

Schlier, H.
1958   "Zum Verstandnis der Geschichte nach der Offenbarung des
            Johannes." Pp. 265–74 in *Diet Zeit der Kirche*. Freiburg:
            Herder.

1964   "Jesus Christus und die Geschichte nach der Offenbarung des
            Johannes." Pp. 358–75 in *Besinnung auf das Neue Testament*.
            Freiburg: Herder.

Smallwood, E. M.
1956   "Domitian's Attitude Towards Jews and Judaism." *Classical Phi-
            lology*. 51:1–13.

Stuart, M.
1845   *Commentary on the Apocalypse*. 2 Vol. New York: Van Nostrand
            & Terrett.

Wheelwright, P.
1975   *Metaphor and Reality*. 6th ed. Bloomington: University of In-
            diana Press.

Wilder, A.
1976   *Theopoetic. Theology and Religious Imagination*. Philadelphia:
            Fortress Press, 1976.

Yamauchi, E.
1980   *The Archaeology of New Testament Cities in Western Asia
            Minor*. Grand Rapids: Baker Book House.

A SOCIOLOGICAL ANALYSIS OF TRIBULATION IN THE APOCALYPSE OF JOHN

Leonard Thompson
Lawrence University

ABSTRACT

Tribulation, oppression, and distress enter into the discussion of the Apocalypse of John as both literary motifs and elements in the sociopolitical situation of Christians in the Roman province of Asia. Sociological analysis offers ways of relating the two, but only in conjunction with considering each separately. The following essay thus proceeds along these lines: (1) an examination of some aspects of the literary theme of tribulation in the Apocalypse, (2) an assessment of the sociopolitical situation of Asian Christians under Domitian, and (3) a schematic proposal for relating the literary and sociopolitical aspects of tribulation.

1 Aspects of the Literary Theme

The Apocalypse is rich as a literary document. Through poetic and imagistic language the seer creates a world which cannot be interpreted as simply an allegory of the sociohistorical times. Undoubtedly, the seer makes commentary upon life both inside and outside the church in his references to Jews in the "synagogue of Satan," to fellow Christians as followers of "Jezebel, Balaamites, and Nicolaitans," to Rome as "Babylon, the Great Whore" or to the emperors as the "heads" of the demonic beast. Such language, however, does not simply describe in code universally observable social realities of Jews, fellow Christians, and the Roman Empire; the language creates a symbolic universe which transforms and re-presents social *realia* in terms of its own order. For that reason the structure of John's literary world is to be found in the interconnectedness of his language, not in correspondences to some external order of reality.

1.1 Visions of Tribulation

The theme of tribulation dominates many of John's visions (4:1–22:5).

At the opening of the fifth seal, the seer "saw under the altar the souls of those who had been slain for the word of God and for the witness they had borne; they cried out with a loud voice, 'O Sovereign Lord, holy and true, how long before thou wilt judge and avenge our blood on those who dwell upon the earth?' Then they were each given a white robe and told to rest a little longer, until the number of their brethren should be complete, who were to be killed as they themselves had been" (RSV: 6:9–11). In the second vision of Chapter 7 an innumerable crowd of a variety of people wearing white garments (cf. those under the altar, 6:11) with palm branches in their hands appear before the throne and the Lamb whom they acclaim in the form of a doxology (7:9–10). The crowd is identified as those "who have come out of the great tribulation; they have washed their robes and made them white in the blood of the Lamb" (7:14). Several visions portray tribulation in connection with conflicting or warring situations. In various guises demonic forces distress those who follow the true God: the beast and the two witnesses (11:1–13); the dragon and the woman with her offspring (12:1–17); the beasts from the sea or earth and the saints (13:1–14:12); or Babylon the harlot and the witnesses of Jesus (17:1–19:5).

The symbolic universe of the seer contains its own spatiotemporal frame. Thus, those "under the altar" were slain prior to the "time" of the "altar vision," but no information is given about how that "time" relates to the social, historical situation of the churches in Asia Minor.[1] So also the time of the "great tribulation" is past only relative to the vision in Chapter 7. The seer's descriptions of warfare and conflict contain sufficient references and allusions to Rome and the imperial cult to conclude that the seer expected tribulation and oppression from political and economic institutions in Asia, but those descriptions do not report past hostilities between Christians and various agencies in the Roman and provincial governments. Even the "great tribulation" of Chapter 7 need not indicate massive oppression in either past, present, or future. In the only other occurrence of the phrase in the Apocalypse, the errant prophetess Jezebel and those committing fornication with her are threatened with "great tribulation" unless they repent (2:22). Elsewhere in the New Testament the phrase can refer to eschatological suffering (e.g., Matt. 24:21), but it need not (cf. Acts 7:11). Thus, tribulation is a significant theme in the seer's visions, but that theme must be explored in the context of the seer's linguistic universe rather than in the time and space of the first-century Asia.

1.2   Tribulation in the Churches and John's Life

The theme of tribulation is also prominent in the messages to the

---

[1] Cf., for example, 6:17 where the great day of the wrath of God and the Lamb is referred to in the aorist tense.

seven churches (Rev. 2:1–3:22). For the most part, distress is created because of matters internal to the church (e.g., false apostles, false teachings) or because of eschatological threats ("I will come to you . . ."). There are, however, a few references to crises stemming from relationships outside the community. At Pergamum, alongside eschatological threats and internal disorders, there is clear reference to the martyrdom of Antipas: "Antipas my witness, my faithful one, who was killed among you, where Satan dwells" (RSV: Rev. 2:13). Those at Pergamum are urged to "hold fast my name" and "not deny my faith" even though one has been killed in their midst.[2] Lohmeyer comments: "The special highlighting of the name indicates how uncommon and impressive was death 'for the sake of the faith'" (25).

In the message to those at Smyrna (2:10–11), reference is made to tribulation (2:10–11) which the seer may well expect in the near future from the sociopolitical situation, but he does not refer to present social distress.

Conflict with the Jewish synagogue is also a potential source of distress. To the church at Smyrna Jesus says: "I know your tribulation and your poverty (but you are rich) and the slander of those who say that they are Jews and are not, but are a synagogue of Satan" (RSV: 2:9). "Slander" (*blasphemian*) is strong language to use against Jews, for elsewhere in the Apocalypse the term is reserved for activity of the Beast (cf. 13:1, 5, 6; 17:3).[3] In the letter to the Philadelphians the conflict is set forth in a reversal of the present power structure: "Behold, I will make those of the synagogue of Satan who say that they are Jews and are not, but lie— behold, I will make them come and bow down (*proskynēsousin*) before your feet, and learn that I have loved you" (RSV: 3:9). Elsewhere in the Apocalypse "bow down" is done only before superhuman figures such as God, the beast, or the dragon. Even an angel commands John not to "bow down" before him (19:10; 22:8–9). Here, however, the one dictating says that he will cause those false Jews to come and worship at the feet of the Philadelphians.[4] Conflict with the synagogue probably arises for John because, on the one hand, Christians had lost their "Jewish shelter" in dealing with the Romans, and on the other hand, Asian Jews participated fully in the social and policital structures of Roman life (cf. 2.3 below).

The most significant passage in the Apocalypse regarding tribulation

[2] The grammar and text of *kai en tais hēmerais Antipas* are problematic. "Holding fast the name [or "faith" or "word"]" and "not denying the faith" are general exhortations. Nowhere in the Apocalypse do these phrases occur as technical terms for response to political persecution. Cf. the parallel phrases in 2:3, 3:8, 14:12 and the references in 3:10 and 16:15.

[3] In Chapter 16 the verbal form of the root is used to describe "men" blaspheming God, 16:9, 11, 21.

[4] The seer may here be playing on the post-exilic tradition that gentiles are expected to come and bow down before the Jews, cf. Isa. 49:23 and Zech. 8:20–23.

involves a statement about John himself: "I John, your brother, who share with you in Jesus the tribulation and the kingdom and the patient endurance, was on the island called Patmos on account of the word of God and the testimony of Jesus" (RSV: Rev. 1:9). For our purposes, two phrases in this verse are crucial. (1) *sygkoinōnos en tę̄ thlipsei kai basileią kai hypomonę̄ en Iēsou.* Since the definite artlcle occurs only once in the Greek text, all three nouns are linked to "in Jesus" so as to describe what John and fellow Christians share with Christ, i.e., the terms describe Christian existence as a participation in aspects of the life of Jesus (cf. Moulton: 181). The terms *thlipsis* and *hypomonē* could refer to social, political realities as well as faithful participation in Christ, but the coordination of those terms with *basileia* favors the interpretation that all three terms refer to life in Christ. Social, political realities may contribute to that description of Christian existence, but they cannot be seen as the cause or occasion for the seer's statement. (2) *egenomēn en tę̄ nēsǫ tę̄ kaloumenę̄ Patmǫ dia ton logon tou theou kai tēn martyrian Iēsou.* John here uses very neutral, general language. The finite verb, which simply indicates his presence on the island, is repeated in the next sentence to indicate that he "was" in the spirit on the Lord's Day. That repetition draws Patmos into a sacral, spatial homologue with the sacral time of the Lord's Day and the sacral state of being "in the Spirit." The preposition *dia* is also a general term, signifying cause, occasion, or purpose. Here, as in the Apocalypse generally, it signifies either a contributory or necessary cause, in this case, of John's being on Patmos. The prepositional phrase as a whole refers to the content, not the preaching of the Christian message. The genitive *Iēsou* is subjective, referring to the witness made by Jesus which John and the others also proclaim (cf. Rev. 1:2). Thus the language of 1:9–10 does not give a hint of a suggestion that John was banished, deported, relegated, or imprisoned on Patmos; nor is there any evidence from Roman sources that Patmos was a prison settlement.[5] Nor was it a deserted, barren isle, as is sometimes suggested; it had sufficient population to support a gynmasium two centuries before the Common Era, and around the time of John an inscription refers to the presence of the cult of Artemis (Saffrey: 393–407).

1.3   The Proclamation and Imitation of Jesus

The reference in Rev. 1:9 to "participation in Jesus" introduces an important aspect of the theme of tribulation in the symbolic universe of the seer. For John "suffering" is probably the most essential ingredient in the Christian proclamation. He introduces his message in 1:2 as "the word of God and the testimony [*martyria*] of Jesus Christ" (Rev. 1:9).

---

[5] In a list of islands in the southern Aegean, Pliny the Elder refers to it as "Patmus circuitu xxx" (*N.H.* 4.12.69). For a list of islands of deportation mentioned by ancient authors, see Saffrey: 398.

Later, in one of the visions an angel identifies himself as a "fellow servant" with the "brethren who hold the testimony of Jesus" (Rev. 19:10), In 3:10 Jesus identifies the gospel as "the word of my patient endurance [*hypomonē*]." In each of those instances the gospel message is linked to Jesus' suffering and crucifixion, just as the eschatological Lord is portrayed throughout the Apocalypse as the slain Lamb or the faithful martyr. Images of suffering, death, and sacrifice carry through the introductory vision of Jesus to his final victory.

That "message" becomes embodied in Christians when they "imitate Christ." In different ways the seer parallels the situations of Christ and Christians. To those conquering at Laodicea, the promise is given to sit with the Son of Man upon his throne, just as he conquered and sat with his father upon his throne (3:21, cf. 2:26–28). Moreover, both Christ and faithful Christians conquer by being slain; at 12:10–12, for example, they imitate Christ, conquering the dragon "by the blood of the Lamb" and "by the word of their testimony, for they loved not their lives even unto death." At 6:9 victorious ones in white "had been slain," just as had the worthy Lamb (5:9). And at 7:14 those from the great tribulation wore robes made white through the blood of the lamb.[6] As martyrs they imitate Jesus Christ, the prototype of all faithful martyrs to come (1:5).[7] Christians witness to the message by both holding to and reenacting the testimony made by Jesus. Polycarp offers adequate commentary: "Let us then be imitators of his endurance, and if we suffer for his name's sake let us glorify him. For this is the example which he gave us in himself, and this is what we have believed" (Pol. *Phil*. 8.2).[8]

Imitative witness combines in the seer's verbal symbolics with another aspect of tribulation relevant to a sociology of the Apocalypse. According to the seer's formulation of the Christian message, victory and kingship are disclosed through suffering and crucifixion. The seer actually uses irony in several different contexts.[9] In connection with word plays he describes the poor Smyrnians as rich, and the rich Laodiceans as wretched and poor. Structural irony appears in the dirges over Babylon in Chapter 18, especially the dirge by the angel (18:2–3) who rejoices through that form.[10] Most germane to the present study, however, is

---

[6]Thus, "conquering," "worthy," "white," and sacrificial imagery form a cluster of images, cf. also 14:4; 5:10 and 1:6; 21:7 and 2:18; 2:17 and 19:12.

[7]Cf. 2:13; 11:3; 17:6 and Lohmeyer: 8.

[8]Cf. Pol. *Phil*. 9.1; Ign. *Rom*. 10.3; *Mart. Pol*. 3.1; 19.2.

[9]By irony I mean any kind of dissembling, disguising, or concealing that reverses meaning. Perhaps in a sense all language is ironic (Cf. Kermode). Sometimes, however, the "concealing is called attention to in an explicit manner and invites the reader/hearer to join in collusion with the author. Irony thus contributes to the sense of community which John shares with his readers/hearers, (cf. Booth: 28,42.)

[10]Note especially 18:3 where the motivation for the fall is given; the language is not that of lament. Cf. also Yarbro Collins, 1980:138.

what may be called kerygmatic irony, that is, irony involved essentially in
the formulation, proclamation, and embodiment of the Christian message.[11] In the greeting of 1:4–5 Jesus Christ is given epithets drawn from
the royal ideology of Israel which in their original context express and
enhance the kingly power and royal authority promised to the Davidic
line (cf. LXX Ps. 88:38; Is. 55:4). In the verbal symbolics of the Apocalypse, however, those epithets of power and authority are transformed
through irony. The witness is faithful through crucifixion; and the "firstborn" is numbered among the dead. In short, the seer celebrates the
enthronement of the king who reigns in blood, crucified on the cross. In
the continuing liturgical piece of 1:7, John even identifies the eschatological Lord—who comes on the clouds in the sight of all—as the
"pierced one" whom all will mourn.[12] That theme of the king who reigns
in blood is carried through the entire Apocalypse by such combined
images as the Lion/Lamb (5:5–6), the slain Lamb, and the Word of God
clothed in blood (19:13).

Christian existence shares in the same ironic structures of royalty and
kingship (1:6). Those at Smyrna are exhorted: "be faithful unto death, and
I will give you the crown of life" (2:10). Life comes through death for the
Christian, just as it did for Jesus. As life appears ironically in the guise of
death, so power appears as powerlessness. To the Philadelphians a message is given: "I have placed before you an open door which no one has
the power to close because you have little power and you kept my word
and you did not deny my name" (3:8).[13] Here the Philadelphians' "little
power" is celebrated as a partial reason why no one has power to close the
door. So also the Laodiceans who think that they are rich but are really
poor are urged to buy from the one who bought them by his slain blood
(3:18, cf. 5:9). Color of clothing becomes one means of expressing irony
here, for the "white clothing" which they are urged to buy is of course
made white in the blood of the Lamb (7:14). In the message to the
Ephesians the "tree of life" carries a similar ironic message: those who
conquer are promised to eat from the tree of life (2:7), which in the verbal
symbolics of the Apocalypse is linked to the "healing of the nations" and
"no more accursedness," and thereby to the cross (22:2–3).[14] Kerygmatic
irony also offers the clue to the compatibility of *thlipsis, basileia,* and
hypomonē in 1:9: these three terms characterize both Christ and Chris-

[11] For a general discussion of irony in the New Testament, Cf. Thompson, 1978:221–231, 299.

[12] The preposition *epi* indicates that the mourning is directed at the one who has been pierced
(cf. John 19:37).

[13] To interpret the sentence so that the *hoti* clause goes with *oida* and the *kai* after *dynamin* is
adversative complicates the syntax unnecessarily.

[14] The link to the cross is made through the Greek *xylon* which refers to the cross as well as to
the tree of life (cf. Gal. 3:13; Acts 5:30; 10:39; Pol. *Phil.* 8. Barnabas also plays on the irony of the
"tree": "the kingdom of Jesus is on the cross [*xylou*]" (8.5).

tian existence, for tribulation in itself reveals victory, conquest, and kingship.[15] If the oxymoric foolishness of this overt irony—Paul calls it the folly of the cross—is blunted by temporalizing (present cruelty, future glory) or by compartmentalizing (bodily cruelty, spiritual glory), the seer's radical statement about eschatological existence will be lost.

The seer can, of course, connect tribulation and oppression with other themes; for example, he relishes vengeance, retribution, and coming judgment upon those who oppose Christ and the faithful. Christian tribulation cannot, however, be understood apart from John's emphasis upon imitating the crucified king. Moreover, irony distinguishes his understanding of eschatological existence from Jewish and gnostic apocalypses. In Jewish apocalyptic, suffering and martyrdom are instrumental for the coming of the kingdom, but they are never ironically a manifestation of that kingdom. In the gnostic *Apocalypse of Peter*, irony is unacceptable as a mode of language, for something can produce only "that which is like itself" (75.11). Language is univocal; ironic transformations of weakness into power or crucifixion into kingship cannot occur; and few gnostics were martyred (cf. Pagels: 82–98).

2 Aspects of the Sociopolitical Situation

In what follows I arbitrarily presuppose that the Apocalypse was written in the latter part of Domitian's reign. Most scholars assume that John wrote during the reign of either Domitian or Nero. At the end of the nineteenth century the Neronian date was supported by a consensus which included such outstanding British scholars as Bishop Lightfoot, B. F. Westcott, and F. J. A. Hort. Recently John A. T. Robinson has revived that view. More recent scholarship, however, supports the Domitianic dating. Irenaeus, who came from Asia Minor and knew Polycarp, states that the visions of the Apocalypse were seen "not long ago," but "close to our generation, towards the end of the reign of Domitian" (Iren. *Her.* 5.30.3-Eus. *Hist. Eccl.* 3.18.1). The identification of Babylon with Rome within the Apocalypse and the assumption in Rev. 21:14 that the apostles are figures of the past also favor the Domitianic over the Neronian dating.[16]

2.1 Reassessment of Domitian's Reign

Few students of the Apocalypse today accept Eusebius of Caesarea's comments about widespread persecution under Domitian (*Hist. Eccl.* 3.17–20, 39; 4.18; 5.8, 18; 6.25; 7.25). After reviewing the evidence of both Christian and non-Christian sources, Leon Hardy Canfield concludes that no great persecution occurred under Domitian and if the Apocalypse "does refer to conditions in Asia Minor under Domitian it is

---

[15] Cf. Tert. *ad Scapulam*, 5: "your cruelty is our glory."
[16] For a recent discussion of the dating issue, cf. Yarbro Collins, 1984: 54–83.

the only source for such a persecution" (74–76, 162). Recent commentators on the Apocalypse support Canfield's conclusions (Sweet: 26; Yarbro Collins, 1981:33).

Although most commentators do not assume widespread, state-initiated persecution under Domitian, they do assume that Domitian's tyrannical, oppressive reign and his demands to be acknowledged as "Lord and God," created a social, political situation of tribulation for early Christians. W. H. C. Frend, for example, notes that Domitian's increased demands to be worshipped resulted in "intensified apocalyptic fervour among the Christians in the province [of Asia]" (194), and Yarbro Collins writes that the Apocalypse was probably "written to awaken and intensify Christian exclusiveness, particularly vis-à-vis the imperial cult. . . . Domitian's heightened claims to divinity and his encouragement of the worship of his person was probably the occasion for the author of Revelation to view the Roman emperor as the adversary of God on the model of Antiochus Epiphanes" (Yarbro Collins, 1981:41).[17]

Roman sources provide evidence for such a view of Domitian's reign. Pliny the Younger and Tacitus condemn Domitian's evil claims to divinity and tyranny, and Pliny's younger friend Suetonius makes now famous statements about Domitian's inordinate claims to titles such as *dominus et deus noster.*" Dio Cassius, writing about a century later, repeats and enhances descriptions of Domitian's evil character. Since Roman historians characterize especially the latter part of Domitian's reign as a reign of terror by a tyrant and megalomaniac who claimed and demanded imperial worship from his subjects, their standard portrait of Domitian has been used as evidence for a sociopolitical situation of distress, oppression, and tribulation for Christians in Asia Minor.[18]

Only an uncritical reading of the standard Roman sources allows for an identification of their portrait with actual sociopolitical conditions during Domitian's reign. Footnoting references to Pliny, Suetonius, or Dio Cassius lead to historiographic issues regarding those sources, and not to immediate social, historical realities. W. H. C. Frend writes that the historian of this period works on two levels: "that of prophecy and eschatology when he is concerned with Christian writings, and that of human activity and events when he turns to the Classical authors" (183–184). Such an understanding of the Classical authors cannot be sustained. One must ask, for example, of the standard sources for Domitian: to what extent do they reflect social historical realities from the time of Domitian and to what extent are they shaped by situations and concerns from the life and times of the writers?

[17] More recently Yarbro Collins has modified her position (1984:71–72).

[18] Such evidence is used, even by those who recognize that Roman authors are for the most part concerned with Rome and not the province of Asia.

The standard portrait of Domitian is clearly not drawn by neutral observers. At every opportunity the writers defame Domitian by emphasizing his evil actions, by attributing malicious motivation to good deeds, or by omitting favorable aspects of his reign. They present private information and psychological motivation about Domitian to which they could not possibly have access. Moreover, their maligning of Domitian is contradicted in almost every instance by epigraphic and numismatic evidence as well as by studies in biographies and public careers of senators during Domitian's reign. The standard sources distort virtually every area of Domitian's public and state activity during the time of his emperorship. For example, in contrast to the distortion in those sources, his military campaigns were planned prudently and his triumphs were received modestly (Henderson: 28; Syme, 1936:162–64; Mart. 8.15.78; Stat. *Silv.* 3.3.171; 4.1.34–39; 4.3.159). Under Domitian the empire prospered, for his fiscal policies were on the whole sound (Viscusi; Magie: 566–592). And although his policy to promote qualified provincials and equestrians may well have rankled some senators, his relation to the senate was on the whole amicable throughout his career (Jones). The standard sources also exaggerate Domitian's use of *delatores* (informers) and his supposedly indiscriminate use of *maiestas* (treason) to incriminate men and women (*Pan.* 42.1; McDermott and Orentzel; Waters, 1964:72; Rogers). Finally, with regards to the "reign of terror" in the latter years of Domitian's reign, a study of public careers shows no policy shift in appointments after 89 to suggest greater conflict with the senate or a suspicious, fearful attitude on the part of the emperor (Jones: 35; Waters, 1964:66). Waters concludes: "like the legend of Domitian's extreme sensuality and that of his repression by his father and brother, [the reign of terror] arises from the . . . senatorial group and their desire to cast as bad a light as possible on an emperor who failed to gratify their self-importance" (1964:76).

In sum, the standard portrait of Domitian as a megalomaniacal tyrant who was totally incompetent and destructive to the empire does not accurately describe either Domitian or his reign. That description from post-Domitian sources such as Pliny the Younger, Tacitus, Suetonius, and Dio Cassius reflects certain tendencies and motivations stemming from the Roman writers themselves and their social, historical situation.[19]

2.2   Domitian as Dominus et Deus Noster

As we have seen, most students of the Apocalypse assume that Domitian's aggressive policy to establish his divinity stimulates the crisis

---

[19]Cf. Wilken's comment on Tacitus as a source of Nero's times: "Tacitus's account tells us more about Roman attitudes in his own time . . . than it does about the misfortunes of Christians during Nero's reign" (49).

(or is a significant component in it) to which the Apocalypse is response. His claim to *dominus et deus noster* is even reflected in the Apocalypse in the liturgical response of the twenty-four elders who address God in the Greek equivalent of "our Lord and God" (Rev. 4:11). In light of writings from Domitian's reign, it is difficult to accept these assumptions.

The evidence for Domitian's demands to be called *dominus et deus noster* lies in the standard Roman sources. For example, Suetonius says that Domitian delighted "to hear the people in the amphitheatre shout on his feast day: 'Good Fortune attend our Lord and Mistress [*dominus et domina*]'" (*Dom.* 13:1; cf. *Pan.* 33.4; 52.6). Suetonius also states that Domitian had his procurators send out letters in the name of "our Master and our God [*dominus et deus noster*]" and that "the custom arose of henceforth addressing him in no other way even in writing or in conversation" (*Dom.* 13.2, cf. Dio 67.4.7; 67.13.4). Several writers mention the inordinate number of statues of himself that Domitian had erected: ". . . every approach and step, every inch of the precinct was gleaming with silver and gold" (*Pan.* 52.3). Dio, who writes the story a century later, speaks with greater hyperbole: ". . . almost the whole world . . . was filled with his images and statues constructed of both silver and gold" (Dio 67.8.1).

If the statements of these authors writing after Domitian's reign reflect accurately the situation at the time of Domitian, then we should expect to find the *dominus et deus noster* title in writings from his time. Fortunately, we have from Domitian's last years works of both Statius and Quintilian which were commissioned or requested by Domitian himself. If Domitian demanded that he be called "our lord and god," as Suetonius and others say, then these works should reflect that requirement.

They do not. In a poem celebrating Domitian's seventeenth consulship in 95 C.E.,—one year before his death—Statius refers to the emperor as *Caesar, Germanicus, parens, Augustus,* and *dux,* but never as either *dominus* or *deus* (*Silv.* 4.1). In the same year Statius writes a poem for the opening of the Domitian Road by celebrating Domitian with similar titles—*Caesar, dux, maximus arbiter,* and *parens.*[20] At the beginning of the *Achilleid,* published in 95–96 C.E., Statius addresses Domitian simply as *vates* and *dux* (*Achil.* 1.14–19).[21] In the Preface to Book 4 of the *Institutio Oratoria,* Quintilian acknowledges the honor of tutor which is conferred upon him "by such divine appreciation [*iudiciorum caelestium*]," by "the most righteous of censors," and by the "prince [*princeps*]" (*Inst.* 4. Preface. 2–3). Some form of *dominus* or *deus* would have been natural here, if the climate of times had demanded it.

---

[20] Cf. Dio 67.14.1. Towards the end of Statius's poem, the Sybil does give a lofty title to Domitian: *"hic est deus, hunc iubet beatis pro se Iuppiter imperare terris."*

[21] Dilke notes that A. W. Verrall used the absence of divine epithets as evidence "to try to show why Dante thought Statius a convert to Christianity: (81).

Quintilian does then continue by calling upon the aid of "all the gods and himself [Domitian] before them all [*omnes . . . deos ipsumque in primis*] . . . for there is no deity [*numen*] that looks with such favour upon learning" (*Inst.* 4. Preface. 5). Such lofty language is, however, much the same as Pliny urges Caninius Rufus to use with Trajan: "*Proinde iure vatum invocatis dis, et inter deos ipso, cuius res opera consilia dicturus es, . . .*" (Pliny *Ep.* 8.4.5). Thus neither Statius nor Quintilian, each of whom was writing as an official close to the throne at the end of Domitian's reign, uses those titles which we would expect, given the statements of Pliny and other standard sources of Domitian's reign. Moreover, among the many inscriptions, coins, and medallions from the Domitianic era, there are no references to Domitian as *dominus et deus* (Viscusi: 94).[22] Finally, we must note the counter-evidence from Statius who writes that when Domitian was acclaimed *dominus* at one of his Saturnalia, ". . . this liberty alone did Caesar forbid them" (*Silvae* 1.6.81–84).

In order to reconcile this conflicting evidence, Kenneth Scott proposes a temporal explanation: the longer Domitian reigned the more tyrannical he became. Early in his reign, for example at the time of the banquet mentioned by Statius, "Domitian wished to be considered a *princeps*, a constitutional ruler" (103). Later in his reign, however, he claimed the powers of a *dominate* (tyranny) and became a megalomaniac, demanding the honors of a god (109).[23] For evidence, Scott can turn only to the poet and epigrammatist, Martial, for as we have seen, neither Statius nor Quintilian, writers close to the throne, hint at any shift to a dominate or to Domitianic demands for divine address. In Martial's earliest work he refers to *dominus* as a term of reproach, but in his Fifth Book of epigrams (c. 89 C.E.) he uses both *dominus* and *deus* as titles for Domitian (Scott:107,109; Mart. *Liber Spectaculorum*; Mart. 5.5,8; 7.2,5,34; 8.2,82; 9.28,66). Then later, in the second edition of Book 10, published in the early reign of Trajan, Martial disavows those flatteries that caused him to speak shamelessly of Domitian as lord and god (*dominus deusque*). He goes on to contrast Domitian the *dominus* with Trajan the *imperator* and senator (Mart. 10.72). Scott interprets Martial's repudiation of earlier usage of *dominus et deus* as an indication that here "Martial . . . revealed his true sentiments" about Domitian's dominate (110). Implicit in Scott's remarks is the assumption that Martial uses the

[22] The meaning of DNImperator in *CIL* 2.4722 is uncertain. The *dominus et deus* formula does occur later in reference to Antoninus Pius in an inscription from Tauric Chersonesus (Crimea) (Latyschev: no. 71).

[23] Others have tried to locate a time towards the end of Domitain's reign when he shifted to a dominate. Brian Jones, however, points out problems in locating such a shift (1979:34). Waters observes that both terms, along with the related words, *princeps* and *dominus*, were in use as early as the reign of Tiberius and as late as Constantine. There was no "sudden retroversion from the Dominate of Domitian to the Principate of Trajan" (Waters, 1969:399; Suet. *Galba* 9.2). (Waters is quoting from Beranger.)

dominate terminology in the latter years of Domitian's reign because of
official pressure from the crown, a point difficult to maintain in the face of
the evidence cited above from Statius and Quintilian.[24]

An alternative explanation better accounts for the use of *dominus* and
deus in Martial. As Keith Hopkins has pointed out, "[p]ower is a two-way
process; the motive force for the attachment between the king and the
gods does not come from the ruler alone" (198). Martial, a poet who
sought but never gained entrance into Domitian's inner court, approaches power from below. As a potential beneficiary, Martial probably
uses extravagant titles to show his devotion to Domitian, just as he later
uses extravagant language of repudiation to show his devotion to Trajan
(10.72). Other potential beneficieries approaching power from below also
probably used titles such as *dominus* and *deus* and were eager to display
their zeal for Domitian. So, for example, in *Epigram* 7.34 where Martial
is praising the builder of Nero's baths, he himself is concerned with a
possible response by the malicious crowd who may say: "What do you set
above the many structures erected by [Domitian] our Master and God
[*dominus deusque*]." Martial here concerns himself not with Domitian,
but with the crowd who are also the ones calling Domitian *dominus
deusque*. They—perhaps including lower echelon procurators—were the
ones who used such titles during Domitian's reign. The danger lies not
with imperial policy but with popular opportunism among those seeking
benefits from Domitian (Thompson, 1984:472–473). From a climate of
quick accusations made by people approaching power from below, we
cannot assume imperial repression and tyrannical madness.[25]

A critical examination of the claims made by the standard post-
Domitian sources on Domitian's demand to be called *dominus et deus
noster* in light of evidence from Domitian's reign suggests that the post-
Domitian sources do not reflect accurately political realities from the
time of Domitian. Domitian did not encourage divine titles such as
dominus et deus noster, nor is there evidence that Domitian had become
a mad tyrant seeking divinisation. The presence of the imperial cult,
especially in Asia Minor, is not here being questioned; it had been a
significant force in the social life of the Asian province from the time of
Augustus.[26] There is no indication, however, that Domitian modified the

---

[24] Statius's comment on Domitian's reticence to being called *dominus* is probably an accurate
reflection of Domitian's view throughout his reign (Thompson, 1984:469–475).

[25] Hanna Szelest discusses in some detail Martial's relation to Domitian (1974). Szelest points
out that Martial also twits issues supposedly sensitive to Domitian, e.g., the Lex Julia (cf. Mart.
6.7; 2.60; 6.2, 22, 45, 91) and baldness (Mart. 5.49; 6.57; 12.45; 10.83, cf. Suet. *Dom*. 18.2).
Martial also refers favorably to people like Paetus Thrasea (cf. Mart. 1.8; 4.54; 1.13). Those
elements in Martial's writings witness to the freedom in Domitian's reign to laud the opposition
and to evaluate critically Domitian and his social program.

[26] For Augustus, cf. *OGTS*, no. 458; For Domitian, *IGRR* 4.847.

imperial cult by demanding greater divine honors than either his prede-
cessors or successors (Waters, 1964:74; Prigent: 455–483).

2.3   Domitian and Provincial Life

The province of Asia—prosperous, rich in natural resources, agri-
culture, and industry with harbors and roads of major trade routes
eastward—had been a part of the Roman world well before Caesar
Augustus. By the end of the first century of the Common Era the cities of
the seven churches had assimilated Roman and indigenous social and
cultural forms with little difficulty.[27] The imperial cult meshed well with
both traditional honors given political leaders and with local shrines and
religious practices (McCrum and Woodhead: no. 142, 121, 148; IG 3.1091).
Roman administration of political, economic, and judicial policies was
well integrated into various urban, district, and provincial administrative
units. Social position, rank, and status were spelled out fairly clearly for
all.[28] In short, the seer wrote in a period of time when imperial Rome
offered Asians a coherent, ordered structure of reality which unified
religious, social, economic, political, and aesthetic aspects of the world.
In the language of Peter Berger, cosmic, social, political, and personal
symbolisms were so integrated that urban Asians shared "knowledge"
which allowed them "to move with a measure of confidence through
everyday life" (6).

Under Domitian, more broadly under the Flavians (including Titus
and Vespasian before him), provincial life flourished (Broughton: 666;
Magie: 576–582). Even Suetonius, who does not paint an attractive
picture of Domitian, says "that at no time were they [provincial gover-
nors] more honest or just, whereas after his [Domitian's] time we have
seen many of them charged with all manner of offences" (Dom. 8.2).[29]
Domitian, like his brother and father before him, built and maintained
roads in the provinces, established cities in the interior of the provinces,
and created new offices to oversee their administration (Syme, 1958, 1:68;
Broughton: 744–745; Oliver: 974).[30]

Two inscriptions from the reign of Domitian give us some idea of his
provincial administration. At Hama, Syria, an inscription was discovered
that contained a letter written by Domitian to his procurator, Claudius
Athenodorus. In this letter Domitian, appealing to the authority of his
father, demands that travelling dignitaries not abuse their power of

---

[27] Urbanization and Romanization went together.

[28] There was some ambiguous status, cf. Meeks, 1983:72–73.

[29] Cf. also Front. Strateg. 2.11.7; Silius, Pun. 14.686–688; and McDermott and Drentzel: 30–
31.

[30] On the office of iuridicus, cf. ILS 1015; on curator civitatis, ILS 1017. Domitian apparently
even checked the use of endowment funds for purposes other than those stated by the donor
(Pleket:306–307).

requisitioning beasts of burden, lodging, and guides at the expense of the province. They have no right to request such benefits unless the emperor has given a permit. "It is just," writes Domitian, "to aid the weak provinces which scarcely have enough for necessities" (Mouterde and Mondesert: 278–279; Lewis: 135–142).[31] There are the typical stock phrases in this letter, but Domitian's defense of the province, especially of the weak who have no protection against the traveling dignitary, is unambiguous. In an inscription from Pisidian Antioch, a legate of Domitian who obviously reflects Domitian's policies orders emergency measures to deal with a famine around Antioch in 92–93 C.E. Because of the famine, the price of grain had increased extravagantly. The imperial legate orders every one to make available his grain (deducting for seed and family needs). A sale date is fixed, and a maximum price is allowed up to double the past average. A general principle is also enunciated: "it is most unjust that hunger of one's own fellow-citizens should be the basis for profit to anyone" (D. Robinson: 5–20; Ramsay: 179–184). Domitian's concern for the total provincial population is once again reflected here, as he prevents the wealthy landowners from profiting exorbitantly from the poor, but at the same time allowing them a profit.[32]

These and other inscriptions indicate that not only was Domitian sensitive to the needs of provincials, but also that he strongly opposed the rich and influential taking advantage of the weak and the poor. Inscriptions suggest that Domitian sought justice for *all* classes of provincials—a policy which hindered governors and upperclass provincials from jointly exploiting those below them. As Pleket suggests, that policy may have been an important reason for tension between Domitian and some senators "who still regarded the provinces as a personal domain from which they could acquire personal wealth" (Pleket: 310; Jones: 60–61). Provincial life in Asia undoubtedly embraced certain tensions between the wealthy and the poor as well as between Rome and the East, but during the reign of Domitian the emperor sought to minimize these tensions.

In the province of Asia Jews played a significant role in the social, political life of the people and apparently participated fully in the prosperity of the cities throughout the first and second centuries of the Common Era even when Jews elsewhere were in revolt against Rome.[33] Jews had settled in those cities as early as the third century before the

[31] Domitian is in part concerned with agricultural productivity, for he says that if beasts of burden are used illegally, "the lands will remain untilled."

[32] Pleket observes: "If the emperor really had been a greedy monster, why did he not try to sell the corn grown on his own imperial estates in and around Pisidia at high prices? This argument carries extra weight, because L. Antistius Rusticus is known to have been legatus from 91 until the end of 93 A.D.: it was precisely in that period that, according to Suetonius, Domitian became *inopia rapax*" (308).

[33] In Judea, in 69–70 and again in 132; in Cyrene and Cyprus in 116.

common era, somewhat as peace-keeping forces (Josephus, *AJ* 12.148–53; Kraabel: 5–6). Within the seven cities mentioned in the Apocalypse, the rights of Jews to observe Sabbath and other religious obligations were confirmed and recognized (Kraabel: 6, 52, 136); they built synagogues— at Sardis, by the end of the second century, the synagogue was part of a larger building which served as a social center for the city including a gymnasium, shops, and palestra complex (Kraabel: 180; Hanfmann, 1972, 1975); they contributed financially to the cost of building public buildings (*IGRR* 4.1431);[34] they were members of the guilds and trade unions (*CII* 777; Kraabel: 134–135; Yamauchi: 152); they were citizens of the cities and of Rome; sometimes they served as city councilors, provincial administrators of the Roman government, and even as procurator (Kraabel: 219– 221). Honored members of the synagogue were apparently untroubled by the "religious observances connected with citizenship and office-holding."[35] As Kraabel summarizes: In Asia Minor one kind of diaspora Judaism emerges, "a picture of a number of Ionians, Phrygians and Lydians, each of whom participates in the life of his own city, speaking its language, fitting into its commercial and social life and its government, honoring its traditions, and all the while remaining within the race and the faith of the Jews" (13).

So far as one can tell, Domitian did not try to change in any way the position and contribution of the Jews in Asia. Suetonius says, in a context describing Domitian's supposed financial straits and his use of informers and false accusations to gain wealth, that Domitian extended the "head tax" (the old temple tax) to include not only "those who kept their Jewish origins a secret in order to avoid the tax", but also "those who lived as Jews without professing Judaism" (Suet. *Dom.* 12.2). He goes on to mention a case where a ninety year old man was examined before the procurator and a crowded court, to see if he was circumcised. Nerva, who followed Domitian, may have been more lenient towards the Jews; the reverse side of a coin from his reign reads: "*fisci Iudaici calumnia sublata* [any false charge regarding the Jewish tax is abolished]" (Smallwood, 1966: no. 28). But the exact social context for this legend is not known; it may not be related at all to a change of policy between Domitian and Nerva. In another connection, Dio says that Domitian charged Flavius Clemens and his wife Flavia Domitilla with atheism, "a charge on which many others who drifted into Jewish ways were condemned" (67.14.2). Dio is apparently contrasting Domitian here to Nerva (68.1.2).[36] It is difficult to assess the standard sources in light of their obvious bias

34 Cf. Kraabel's comments (30–31). His translation of the puzzling phrase *hoi pote Ioudaioi* as "those once Judaeans" is convincing.

35 Kraabel, 221. The reference is to Jews at Sardis. Evidence for the place of the Jews in these cities ranges from ii B.C.E. to iv C.E.

36 On the evidence that one or the other of those was Christian, cf. Smallwood, 1956:7–8; Keresztes:7–15.

against Domitian and their attempt to portray him as evil and unjust. If Domitian did attempt to apply the Jewish tax more broadly to all those related in some way to Judaism, it would probably fit his general administrative principles of rationality and consistency. To a great extent, however, the discussion of Jews in these sources has been shaped by the larger context of Domitian's supposed misuse of the treasury and of informers.[37] During this period Josephus is writing his books on Judaism through the support of Domitian; even after Domitian's death, Josephus speaks highly of him (*Vita*, 76). Also, in what Geffcken refers to as a "provincial tradition" about Rome and the emperors (183–189), a third-century Jew speaks (long after Domitian's reign) as "a great kingdom whom all mortals will love throughout the ends of the earth and then there will be rest from war throughout the whole cosmos . . . from east to west, all will be subject willingly and . . . upon him heavenly Sabaoth, the imperishable God dwelling in heaven, will bring much glory" (*Sibylline Oracle* 12.125–132; Pleket: 303). There seems to be a very favorable, provincial tradition about Domitian which differs radically from the standard, Roman literary sources of his reign.[38]

Christian urban dwellers in Asia could apparently also enjoy those relatively peaceful and prosperous times under Domitian. Within that group were probably numbered some or all of the opponents which John rebukes in his seven letters. John's conflict with "Jezebel" and the Nicolaitans, specifically over fornication and eating meat sacrificed to idols, was more broadly over how much Christians should or could accommodate to the larger society (Aune: 28). Could social practices enmeshed with religious, political, and aesthetic aspects of the Roman order be assimilated into the Christian order? Or, in Berger's language, could Christians share with their pagan neighbors the "knowledge" which made it possible for them to move with confidence through everyday life? Those issues impinged upon the social behavior of Christians: to what extent they participated in trade guilds, dinner parties, legal transactions, political rallies, sporting events, legal tender, and theatrical presentations. Whether that participation was unreflective or self-conscious, viewed as irrelevant to or compatible with the faith, it had profound impact on the nature, stability and viability of the church (cf. 1 Cor. 6:1–8,12–20; 8:1–13; 10:23–30). It is obvious from the Apocalypse that different Christian groups had different opinions on the nature and extent of assimilation compatible with the faith, but there is no indication that a social, political climate of persecution and oppression determined Christian opinion.

[37] There is no particular warrant to link *calumnia* on the coin with *maiestas* and neglect of the imperial cult, or the Jewish way of life and *maiestas* in Dio's statement, as does Smallwood (1981:378–385). Both Dio and Martial link Judaism with gladiators (67.14.3; Mart. 7.82), but no intrinsic link should be made between the two.

[38] Cf. Jones:61; Eus. 3.20.5; Tert. *Apol.* 5.

3   Toward a Sociological Theory of Tribulation

Sociological theories of crisis and deprivation have unnecessarily controlled both literary and social, historical analyses of tribulation in the Apocalypse of John. In the previous two sections I have sketched out alternative literary and historical analyses. In what follows, I shall try to make explicit some elements in a revised sociological theory while critiquing crisis and deprivation theories.

3.1   Sociohistorical Causality

In a pioneering collection of essays on sociological analysis of early Christianity, John Gager states an assumption of the crisis theory: "Whatever its date and location, the writing [Apocalypse of John] inescapably presupposes a situation in which believers had experienced suffering and death at the hands of Rome. This is the crisis in which John offers his unique message of consolation . . ." (50). J. A. T. Robinson states the case even more forcefully when he asserts that if there was no crisis in the social sphere, then the Apocalypse would have to be "the product of a perfervid and psychotic imagination" (231, cf. Feuillet: 76–77). With similar assumptions, Schuessler Fiorenza locates the tribulation of Christians specifically in the reign of Domitian, as a result of his demands to be called "Lord and God" and his increasing totalitarianism (Schuessler Fiorenza, 1985:193–194; in this volume: 136).

Crisis theorists make a sharp distinction between social, institutional entities, on the one hand, and symbolic, literary entities, on the other; moreover, they favor social, institutional forces. That is, a social, historical situation is given, independent of apocalyptic interpretation, and that situation "causes" or "occasions" religious and literary expressions.[39] Causality is seen as flowing uni-directionally.[40] The symbolic is malleable to the more "real" social, political situation; while social experience—a social relationship, a political policy, and economic exchange—exists as an impenetrable entity, unaffected essentially by religious, mythic, and literary symbols. As a result, these forces are mapped so that the social, political is positioned squarely in the middle of everyday life, while religious, literary symbolics are on the periphery. Thus, tribulation as a literary motif is seen as a reflection of the more real, sociopolitical situation of oppression and distress.

A sociology of the Apocalypse considers causal connections between the literary and the social, but there is always the need to make clear in any specific situation what kind of causal connection is being made, how approximate it is, and how limited is the situation in which it operates.

[39] So Schuessler Fiorenza: ". . . . it must be kept in mind that it is the rhetorical situation that calls forth a particular rhetorical response and not vice versa" (1985:192; in this volume: 000).

[40] Such a distinction runs deep and wide in the practicing crafts of the academy, even though we "know better" when the question is raised on an abstract level.

Sociopolitical causality is probably more limited than we recognize. Kenelm Burridge makes the astute remark: "the notion that apocalyptic messages may be natural to human groups, culturally prescribed, or an intrinsic part of the evolutionary process is not, at the moment, generally accepted. But it bears thinking about" (100). Secondly, there is a question about the direction of causality: can it ever be uni-directional? When action occurs, both the subject and object are affected. Causal forces can best be understood as feedback loops, so that everything affects everything. Such a formulation is not very tidy, but it reflects more accurately causal situations. Thirdly, there is the question about the externality of causation: are the objects involved affected intrinsically or do they affect each other as one billiard ball strikes another?

The term "transformation" better describes the interaction of forces, granting that everything is in some way connected to everything, that causal forces form feedback loops, and that the objects involved are intrinsically changed when they encounter each other. Transformations occur, for example a caterpillar into a butterfly, within a larger system or structure. If the interaction of the social and the literary is seen as a transformation, then each becomes part of a larger field of forces on the analogy of whorls and eddies in a stream. No sharp distinctions will then be made between social, institutional elements, on the one hand, and symbolic, literary entities, on the other. For as is commonly recognized, social-political relationships have at least a low level of symbolic content, just as literary symbols, ritual gestures, and theological claims express at least minimal social-political relations.

3.2   A Crisis of Faith

According to crisis theories, the social situation of tribulation and oppression created in the communities of Asia Minor a crisis of faith: Christians were the chosen people, protected by God, but they experienced suffering, deprivation, and death (Gager: 51). Schuessler Fiorenza states succinctly this tension between faith and social reality: the "everyday experience of harassment, persecution, and hostility from their Jewish as well as their pagan neighbors challenged the Christians' faith in Christ as the Lord and King of the world" (1981:64).

Recent interpreters who accept this notion of tension between faith and social experience differ somewhat in their understanding of how John handles the tension, but they all assume that his resolution involves rhetorical elements of exhortation and comfort through the construction of an alternative, symbolic world.[41] For Schuessler Fiorenza, John's symbolic universe, created from mythic and cultic images predominately

---

[41] Influences can be seen here from both the sociology of knowledge and structural studies of myth.

from Israelite religion, overcomes present, historical alienation by projecting a future, trans-historical reality that legitimates and gives meaning to suffering and death while it underscores the importance of Christian opposition to pagan, Roman society (1985:192–197; in this volume: 140). By imaginatively participating in this "symbolic universe," Christians are motivated and persuaded to withstand social oppression by faithful obedience (1985:187; in this volume: 130). Gager, applying a structuralist notion that myths overcome unwelcome contradictions between *(inter alia)* hope and reality, argues that the Apocalypse functions to suppress time so as to allow future realities into present experience (1975:50–56). Listening to the Apocalypse read aloud in worship provided "a fleeting experience of the millennium" and "energy needed to withstand the wrath of the beast," but the "real world, in the form of persecution, reasserted itself with dogged persistence for Christian communities" (1975:56).[42] Here one also sees the placement of the symbolic, alternative world on the periphery, and the social, political at the center.

Yarbro Collins has recently presented a more subtle sociological analysis of the Apocalypse (1984). She explicitly introduces into her causative model elements other than social, political phenomena: "factors of background, temperament, and, to some degree, choice of theological perspective are . . . at least as important as aspects of the sociohistorical situation in producing an apocalyptic mentality" (1984:105). As a result, she argues that the book of Revelation is a product of the interaction between a kind of pre-understanding and the sociohistorical situation (1984:106). She retains, however, the notion of a crisis of faith: the seer wrote in response to "the conflict between the Christian faith itself, as John understood it, and the social situation as he perceived it" (1984:106). Therefore, the task of the seer is to overcome the unbearable tension perceived by the author between hope and reality (1984:141). He does this by constructing a symbolic universe with therapeutic value: hearing the work read provides a catharsis of fear and resentment and an internalization of demands to keep apart from the social order and to practice sexual abstinence, poverty, and martyrdom (1984:153–157). That psychosocial function keeps the Apocalypse tied closely to the everyday life of Christians living in Asia Minor.

Any literary critic recognizes that John creates a symbolic universe in the Apocalypse. The critical issue becomes how that symbolic universe relates to social relations. Crisis theorists tend to see John's symbolic construction as an alternative to the social world of everyday life; John

---

[42] Schuessler Fiorenza (1985:8, 167–168 criticizes Gager's symbolic world as too much a psychological construction; it seems to me, however, that both Gager and Schuessler Fiorenza, as well as Yarbro Collins discussed below, give a political, social function to their alternative worlds. Barr is also critical of Gager and Yarbro Collins for not allowing sufficient reality to the alternative symbolic world.

and his readers/hearers participate in it so as to experience momentarily the reality of their hopes, to gain strength and courage to face social oppression, and to resolve tensions experienced between their faith and their social experience. Those theorists assume that there is an ordered, cer⁺ral reality to the social world, and separate from that is another ordered world created by John. Each forms a separate circle. As an alternative to that model, I propose that John's symbolic world is both comprehensive and coherent. It is comprehensive in that John offers his symbolic structure as an all-inclusive world embracing the whole of Christian existence including social, political exchanges in everyday life. His symbolics are misinterpreted if they are seen as an alternative order situated at the periphery of the "real social world." John's symbolic universe is coherent in that, if appropriated, it integrates human experience and makes Christian existence whole. Rather than imagining John's symbolics as a separate circle, they are better understood as a grid or an overlay that orders all experience.

Conflict arises for John, not between elements of Christian existence, but between his comprehensive and coherent world and the comprehensive, coherent universe embodied in the Roman Empire. Rome offered in the public realm a coherent order that united religious, social, economic, political, and aesthetic realities (cf. 2.1 above). In Berger's terms, Rome offered "knowledge" by means of which urban Asians could "move with a measure of confidence through everyday life" (6). The seer judges that public "knowledge" to be false, and he offers to Christians through the Apocalypse true, esoteric knowledge for integrating and ordering Christian existence. The seer opposed any Christian assimilation to the peace, prosperity, and wholeness of public Roman life, because he quite correctly conceived of his all embracing world as incompatible with the all embracing vision implicated in public Roman life. He sought in every way possible to sharpen differences and distinctions between his and Rome's visions of the world so that his esoteric, true knowledge could in no way become confused with or diluted by the false knowledge offered by public Rome. Tribulation as a hyperbolic theme in John's literary world functions not as reflection on tensions between faith and sociopolitical realities but as an expression of the conflict which he perceived between the two "worlds."[43] Their opposition is expressed mythically in John's symbolics by homologizing Rome with evil, demonic forces opposed to the faithful followers of God.[44]

[43] In his Panegeric to Trajan, Pliny's description of the danger, persecution, and oppression under Domitian functions similarly to sharpen the differences between Domitian's old dynasty and Trajan's new era (cf. Thompson, 1984:472–473).

[44] Thus I am convinced by Schuessler Fiorenza's emphasis on rhetoric, but the range of possible rhetorical situations is greater than she considers.

3.3   Assumed Deprivation

Most scholars writing about the Apocalypse still work with a modified version of deprivation theory, i.e., the seer's form of religious expression is a dependent variable upon deprivation experienced or felt in relation to status, role, or position in the social order.[45] Themes of hope, salvation, and vindication in the seer's symbolic universe then function as compensations for Christians who feel deprived in their social situation. In order to make the schema work, however, deprivation has to be defined broadly. John Gager quotes with approval the following definition by Glock: "any and all of the ways that an individual or group may be, or feel disadvantaged in comparison either to other individuals or groups or to an internalized set of standards" (109; Glock:210). By broadening the definition, as Gager points out, one may use it without "reducing the explanation of new religious movements to a single factor, such as economics or politics" and without assuming that early Christians were "nothing but a collection of country yokels and impoverished slaves" (95). On the other hand, such a broadening reduces the explanatory power of "deprivation," for given Glock's definition, any person or group at any time can be seen as deprived, that is, little or no meaningful qualification occurs when a group is said to be deprived. Further, that definition opens the term "deprivation" to characterize not only social relationships but also an individual or group's relations to aesthetic, religious, and ethical standards. So Yarbro Collins uses the phrase "relative deprivation" to describe unfulfilled expectations that arose as a result of faith in Jesus (1984:106). Thus a correlation that originated as a way of explaining certain cultural expressions through patterns of social organization runs the danger of losing its explanatory power entirely.[46] Nonetheless, the correlation of social deprivation and religious compensation serves the crisis theory well, because it supports the notion of a tension between faith and society. The so-called dualist structure of the Apocalypse of John can then be seen as the literary expression of, alternatively, the social experience of deprivation and the religious experience of compensation (cf. Yarbro Collins, 1984:105–107;141–144).

R. L. Gordon's term "reiteration" illumines more fully relationships among elements in John's symbolic world (95).[47] The seer's true knowl-

[45] Two influential works in the broader study of the sociology of religion have been Lewis and Cohn.

[46] Perhaps it never had a great deal; cf. Douglas's comment: "[F]or a sociologist to seek the origins of a class of religious movement in terms of maladjustment and readjustment is to abdicate his role. Either he must use the proposition to prove its own premise, or he must admit it is valueless for explaining negative instances" (1973:24).

[47] Gordon finds in the organization of Mithraism a reiteration or confirmation of ordinary social experience. Cf. also Meeks's essay on John (1972:44–72).

edge integrates, and does not bifurcate, Christian experience. Structures in the seer's literary, religious symbolics and his description of social relations between Christians and the larger world reiterate each other.

Reiteration occurs in all dimensions of Christian existence not because the religious replicates the more fundamental dimension of social structures, but because both reiterate a structure or order implicated in every dimension. Levi-Strauss gives a clue to this process: "Although there is undoubtedly a dialectical relation between the social structure and systems of categories [i.e., symbolic thought], the latter are not an effect or result of the former; each, at the cost of laborious mutual adjustments, translates certain historical and local modalities of the relations between man and the world, which form their common substratum" (214).[48] The "laborious mutual adjustments" do not consist of balancing "impenetrable social deprivation" with "discrete religious compensation"; they rather involve the mutual penetration and transformation of symbolic expressions and social relations as they interact with each other. At bottom, both reflect common structures ("historical and local modalities") which arise out of the process of specific humans adapting in specific ways to their specific environment.

3.4 Proportions and Homologues

As we have seen, most crisis theories assume that the Apocalypse and life experience reflected in it are filled with conflicting oppositions. Most of them also, implicitly or explicitly, draw upon structuralist analyses of myth which assume that a writing such as the Apocalypse mediates binary oppositions or contradictions in human experience. As an alternative sociological approach, I suggest that elements in our thinking and living more often relate as homologues, analogies, and proportions than as binary oppositions. With regard to the Apocalypse of John, proportions and homologues in his literary production disclose the structured processes which guide John's unfolding of Christian existence. For example, tracing references through the book to proper sexual expression yields such proportions as fornication:non-fornication::outside New Jerusalem:inside Jersualem::outside the Church:inside the Church::social accommodation:social isolation.[49] Every dimension, every moment, and every object that can be encountered in life gains meaning by taking its place as a proportion in the seer's world.

Proportions and homologues yield quite a different view of the world from binary oppositions. In terms of the latter, separate forces operate along different lines which create conflict between natural impulses and cultural demands, social disappointments and religious promises, bodily

---

[48] Mary Douglas (1975:161) calls attention to this passage.
[49] Cf. the suggestive comments by Schuessler Fiorenza (1985:183; in this volume: 125).

mortality and spiritual hopes of immortality. These conflicts are seen at the most fundamental level of experiencing and understanding life. None of the clever ruses, such as the Apocalypse of John, can long mediate or blur those fundamental conflicts. In contrast, proportions and homologues underscore the unity and integrity of Christian, and more broadly human existence. Such an emphasis affirms that at their most fundamental level, both the world and our experience of it disclose coherence, integrity, and wholeness. The seer of the Apocalypse fundamentally sees the world along those lines.

4   Tribulation in the Seer's World

In light of these reflections, tribulation becomes an element in the seer's world with several possible dimensions and causes. More is involved than considerations of social oppression and religious persecution. Tribulation correlates in John's world with true knowledge, authentic self expression, and service to the true God. Further, as we have seen, it becomes a means of sharpening the boundary between the seer's world, on the one hand, and Rome's world, on the other.

Within the world of the seer, tribulation and suffering are elements in the gospel testimony of Jesus. Just as Jesus' faithful witness unto death is the central ingredient in the Christian proclamation in the Apocalypse, so imitative witness is central to Christian existence. Both express something more than momentary events in history. The "slain lamb" appears not only on earth but also in heaven, close to the throne (5:6). Further, the Lamb is slain from the foundation of the world and reigns in that form (13:8, cf. 1 Peter 1:19).[50] The crucifixion lies in the deep structure of reality which enfolds all historical disclosures. It is, in turn, unfolded in Christ's rule and Christian existence. A life of tribulation and social oppression express *how* Christians reign with their crucified king and *how* they participate in the power and glory of God. Disclosure of that reality constitutes a central ingredient in true knowledge.

Social, political relations with non-Christians also undoubtedly enter into the seer's world. Whatever the official basis for interrogation and sentencing Christians (the legal grounds for this activity are still debated), it is clear that the government had popular support for prosecuting Christians (cf. Wardman: 127–134). From the viewpoint of the Roman world, Christians had "lost their shelter of tradition" with Judaism, were recognized as atheists who did not worship the communal gods, were non-conformists adhering to a recently formed religion from the East, and possibly participated in sexual orgies and cannibalism. Indeed, if

---

[50] A similar transformation from history to world structure occurs with respect to the resurrection, when the "firstborn from the dead and the *archōn* of the kings of the earth" (1:5) becomes "the *archē* of God's creation" (3:14).

Pliny's correspondence is typical, the populus was more adamant than Roman officials in bringing Christians to trial (Pliny *Ep*.10.96). Trajan (probably following guidelines from the time of Domitian) directs Pliny not to listen to anonymous accusations and not to initiate prosecution by seeking Christians out. At the same time Christianity is viewed clearly as a social ill to be dealt with, if Christians are brought before a tribunal; for in that case they would probably be killed if, after due opportunity was given to them, they did not confess the religious dimension of the common, public Roman life.

In sum, the point is that a myriad of qualities, behavioral traits, religious commitments, psycho-social understandings, and social, political interactions coalesce into a term like "tribulation." Put differently, "tribulation" functions to organize a myriad of elements which interact in a variety of ways.[51] Terms like "oppression," "tribulation," or "persecution" can be used to identify social situations that actually contain quite different ingredients or similar ingredients in different proportions with different levels of causative power. Within the seer's world some of the fundamental elements contributing to the reality of tribulation and oppression were the Christian gospel of the crucified King, faithful behavior as imitation of Christ, social-political relations in the cities of Asia, and the affirmation of Christian separatism from the Roman world. Those elements formed a feed-back loop which created a snowball effect: religious identification with the crucified king shaped psychosocial identity which led to patterns of behavior that supported social-political prosecution which looped back to create a more intense religious identification with the crucified king.[52] In the process, however, John believes that Christians gain true knowledge which replicates itself in all dimensions of their lives to create a comprehensive, whole world.

WORKS CONSULTED

Aune, David E.
      1981   "The Social Matrix of the Apocalypse of John." *BR* 26: 16–32.
Barr, David.
      1984   "The Apocalypse as a Symbolic Transformation of the World: A
                   Literary Analysis." *Int* 38: 39–50.
Berger, Peter.
      1970   *A Rumor of Angels*. Garden City: Anchor Books.

---

[51] Cf. Hinde's discussion of how the term "thirst" can organize and simplify a number of traits observed in animals (48–50).

[52] The loop may be broken into at any point.

Booth, Wayne.
    1974   *A Rhetoric of Irony*. Chicago: University of Chicago Press.
Broughton, T. R. S.
    1938   "Roman Asia Minor." In *An Economic Survey of Ancient Rome*.
                Ed. Tenney Frank. Baltimore: Johns Hopkins Press.
Burridge, Kenelm.
    1982   "Reflections on Prophecy and Prophetic Groups." *Semeia* 21:
                99–102.
Canfield, Leon Hardy.
    1913   *The Early Persecutions of the Christians*. New York: Columbia
                University Press.
Cohn, Norman.
    1970   *The Pursuit of the Millennium*. New York: Oxford University
                Press.
Dilke, O. A. W.
    1954   *Statius: Achilleid*. Cambridge: University Press.
Douglas, Mary.
    1973   *Natural Symbols*. New York: Vintage Books.
    1975   *Implicit Meanings*. London: Routledge & Kegan Paul.
Feuillet, A.
    1965   *The Apocalypse*. Staten Island: Alba House.
Frend, W. H. C.
    1981   *Martyrdom and Persecution in the Early Church*. Grand
                Rapids: Baker Book House.
Gager, John.
    1975   *Kingdom and Community*. Englewood Cliffs: Prentice-Hall, Inc.
Geffcken, Johannes.
    1902   "Roemische Kaiser im Volksmunde der Provinz." Pp. 183–95 in
                *Nachrichten von der Koenigl. Gesellschaft der Wissenschaften
                zu Goettingen, Philologisch-historische Klasse aus dem Jahre
                1901*.
Glock, C. Y.
    1973   "On the Origin and Evolution of Religious Groups." In *Religion
                in Sociological Perspective*. Belmont, CA: Wadsworth Publish-
                ing Co.
Gordon, R. L.
    1972   "Mithraism and Roman Society." *Religion* 2: 92–121.
Hanfmann, G. M. A.
    1972   *Letters from Sardis*. Cambridge: Harvard University Press.
    1975   *From Croesus to Constantine*. Ann Arbor: University of Michi-
                gan Press.

Henderson, Bernard.
　　1927　　*Five Roman Emperors*. Cambridge: University Press.
Hinde, Robert.
　　1982　　*Ethology*. Oxford: University Press.
Hopkins, Keith.
　　1978　　*Conquerors and Slaves*. Cambridge: University Press.
Jones, Brian.
　　1979　　*Domitian and the Senatorial Order*. Philadelphia: The American
　　　　　　Philosophical Society.
Keresztes, Paul.
　　1973　　"The Jews, the Christians, and Emperor Domitian." *VC* 27: 1–
　　　　　　28.
Kermode, Frank.
　　1979　　*The Genesis of Secrecy*. Cambridge: Harvard University Press.
Kraabel, A. T.
　　1968　　"Judaism in Western Asia Minor under the Roman Empire with
　　　　　　a Preliminary Study of the Jewish Community at Sardis." Ph.D.
　　　　　　diss.: Harvard University.
Latyschev, Basilius.
　　1965　　*Inscriptiones Antiquae Orae Septentrionalis Ponti Euxini
　　　　　　Graecae et Latinae Per Annos 1885–1900 Reertae*. Hildesheim:
　　　　　　Georg Olms.
Levi-Strauss, Claude.
　　1966　　*The Savage Mind*. Chicago: University Press.
Lewis, I. M.
　　1971　　*Ecstatic Religion*. Middlesex: Penguin Books.
Lewis, N.
　　1968　　"Domitian's Order on Requisitioned Transport and Lodgings."
　　　　　　Revue Internationale des Droits de l'Antiquité 15: 135–42.
Lohmeyer, Ernst.
　　1953　　*Die Offenbarung des Johannes*. Tübingen: J. C. B. Mohr (Paul
　　　　　　Siebeck).
McCrum, M. and Woodhead, A. G.
　　1961　　*Select Documents of the Principates of the Flavian Emperors*.
　　　　　　Cambridge: University Press.
McDermott, W. C. and Orentzel A.
　　1977　　"Silius Italicus and Domitian." *AJP* 98: 23–34.
Magie, David.
　　1950　　*Roman Rule in Asia Minor*. Princeton: University Press.
Meeks, Wayne.

1972   "The Man from Heaven in Johannine Sectarianism." *JBL* 91: 44–72.

1983   *The First Urban Christians*. New Haven: Yale University Press.

Moulton, James.

1963   *A Grammar of New Testament Greek*. Vol. 3 by Nigel Turner. Edinburgh: T. & T. Clark.

Mouterde, Rene, and Mondesert, Claude.

1957   "Deux Inscriptions Grecques de Hama." *Syria* 34: 278–87.

Oliver, James.

1953   "The Ruling Power." *TAPS* 43: 869–1003.

Pagels, Elaine.

1979   *The Gnostic Gospels*. New York: Random House.

Pleket, Henri.

1961   "Domitian, The Senate and the Provinces." *Mnemosyne* 7: 296–315.

Prigent, P.

1974   "Au Temps de l'Apocalypse, I: Domitien." *Revue d'Histoire et de Philosophie Religieuse*. 54: 455–83.

Ramsay, W. M.

1924–25   "Studies in the Roman Province Galatia." *Journal of Roman Studies* 14–15: 179–84.

Robinson, David M.

1924   "A New Latin Economic Edict from Pisidian Antioch." *TAPA* 55: 5–20.

Robinson, James.

1977   *The Nag Hammadi Library in English*. New York: Harper & Row.

Robinson, J. A. T.

1976   *Redating the New Testament*. Philadelphia: The Westminster Press.

Rogers, Robert.

1960   "A Group of Domitianic Treason Trials." *CP* 55: 19–23.

Saffrey, H. D.

1975   "Relire L'Apocalypse à Patmos." *RB* 82: 385–417.

Schuessler, Fiorenza, Elisabeth.

1981   *Invitation to the Book of Revelation*. Garden City: Image Books.

1985   *The Book of Revelation: Justice and Judgment*. Philadelphia: Fortress.

Scott, Kenneth.

1975   *The Imperical Cult Under the Flavians*. New York: Arno Press.

Smallwood, E. M.
   1956   "Domitian's Attitude toward the Jews and Judaism." *CP* 51: 1–
               13.
   1966   *Documents Illustrating the Principates of Nerva Trajan and
               Hadrian.* Cambridge: University Press.
   1981   *The Jews Under Roman Rule.* Leiden: E. J. Brill.

Sweet, J. P. M.
   1979   *Revelation.* Philadelphia: Westminster Press.

Syme, Ronald.
   1936   *CAH*, Vol. 11.
   1958   *Tacitus.* Oxford: Clarendon Press.

Szelest, Hanna.
   1974   "Domitian and Martial." *Eos* 62: 105–14.

Thompson, Leonard.
   1978   *Introducing Biblical Literature.* Englewood Cliffs: Prentice-
               Hall, Inc.
   1984   "Domitianus Dominus: A Gloss on Statius *Silvae* 1.6.84." *AJP*
               105: 469–75.

Viscusi, Peter.
   1973   "Studies on Domitian." Ann Arbor: University Microfilms.

Wardman, Alan.
   1982   *Religion and Statecraft Among the Romans.* Baltimore: Johns
               Hopkins University Press.

Waters, Kenneth.
   1964   "The Character of Domitian." *Phoenix* 18: 49–77.
   1969   "Traianus Domitiani Continuator." *AJP* 90: 385–405.

Wilken, Robert.
   1984   *The Christians As the Romans Saw Them.* New Haven: Yale
               University Press.

Yamauchi, Edwin.
   1980   *The Archaeology of the New Testament Cities in Western Asia
               Minor.* Grand Rapids: Baker Book House.

Yarbro Collins, Adela.
   1980   "Revelation 18: Taunt-Song or Dirge?" Pp. 185–204 in *L'Apoc-
               alypse johannique et l'apocalyptique dans le Nouveau
               Testament.* Ed. J. Lambrecht. Gembloux: J. Duculot.
   1981   "Dating the Apocalypse of John." *BR* 26: 33–45.
   1984   *Crisis and Catharsis: The Power of the Apocalypse.* Phila-
               delphia: Westminster Press.

SCHOLARS PRESS

A TRADITION OF COMMITMENT TO SCHOLARSHIP

Sense and Absence
J. Lee Magness
Attempts a fresh literary analysis of the suspended ending to the second gospel. In the course of his study, Magness describes how open endings have been interpreted by modern literary theory and, secondly, how such endings have been used in ancient literary and Biblical texts. A close re-reading of Mark concludes the study; in that re-reading, Magness offers the intriguing thesis that Mark's "sense of absence" encourages his readers to make sense of that absence for themselves in a positive and powerful way.

Code: 06 06 15

Cloth $14.95 (10.95)
Paper $10.95 (7.95)

Semeia 14
Apocalypse: The Morphology of a Genre
John J. Collins, editor
Volume 14 of Semeia presents the results of a comprehensive survey of all apocalyptic texts from the period 250 B.C. to 250 C.E. Jewish, Early Christian, Gnostic, Greek and Latin, Rabbinic, and Persian apocalypses are examined to determine the constitutive elements of the genre and to identify the different types within it. This work represents the efforts of five members of the Apocalypse Group of the SBL Forms and Genres project.

Code: 06 20 14

Paper $10.95 (7.95)

The Chreia in Ancient Rhetoric.
Volume I: *The Progymnasmata*
Ronald F. Hock, Edward N. O'Neil
The chreia, a literary and rhetorical genre of antiquity, was of great influence in ancient literature. This volume includes the main texts of the Progymnasmata, rhetorical works dealing with the chreia. Each is presented with the Greek or Latin text, an English translation, introductory notes, and commentary. An important work for scholars of ancient literature, rhetoric, history of philosophy, and education.

Code: 06 02 27

Cloth: $25.25 (16.75)
Paper: $16.75 (11.25)

---

*( ) denotes price available to members of sponsoring societies and subscribers to Scholars Press journals. Write for information. Prepayment (check M/C or Visa) required GA residents add 4% sales tax. Postage/handling: first item $1.00, $.50 for each thereafter, $4.00 maximum. Outside US $2.00 surcharge.

SCHOLARS PRESS CUSTOMER SERVICES
P.O. Box 4869, Hampden Station, Baltimore, MD 21211
(301) 338-6946